Phillip K. Trocki

Modern Curriculum Press
Parsippany

EXECUTIVE EDITOR   Wendy Whitnah

PROJECT EDITOR   Diane Dzamtovski

EDITORIAL DEVELOPMENT
DESIGN AND PRODUCTION   The Hampton-Brown Company

ILLUSTRATORS   Anthony Accardo, Harry Briggs, Roberta Collier-Morales, Cathy Diefendorf, Mark Farina, Sandra Forrest, Ron Grauer, Shana Gregor, Meryl Henderson, Masami Miyamoto, Rik Olson, Doug Roy, John Sandford, Rosalind Solomon, Katherine Tillotson.

PHOTO CREDITS   5, Gordon L. Kallio/Image Bank; 7, Andy Caulfield/Image Bank; 9, David Bownell/Image Bank; 11, Bill Ross/Westlight; 13, Uniphoto/Pictor; 21, Grant Huntington; 23, Dr. Nigel Smith/Animals Animals; 29, Myrleen Ferguson/Photo Edit; 33, Ted Levin/Animals Animals; 37, Okapia/Photo Researchers; 41, Santi Visalli/Image Bank; 44, Giraudon/Art Resource; 53, A. Hubrich/Image Bank; 57, Jeff Lepore/Photo Researchers; 61, AP/Wide World Photos; 64, Neil Leifer/Sports Illustrated; 65, Uniphoto/Pictor; 69, Courtesy of Ray Sarapillo; 77, Uniphoto/Pictor; 81, Marty Stouffer Prod./Animals Animals; 85, Virginia P. Weinland/Photo Researchers; 89, Barbara Rios/Photo Researchers; 93, Nancy J. Pierce/Photo Researchers; 101, Tony Freeman/Photo Edit; 105, Lia Roosendaal/The Chronicle, Vermont; 109, G.I. Bernard/Animals Animals; 113, Pam Francis; 117, Scott Warner/Courtesy of U.S. Assoc. for Blind Athletes; 125, Grant Huntington; 129, Archive Photos; 133, Chris Bjornberg/Photo Researchers; 137, Harry Engels/Photo Researchers; 140, Tim Davis/Photo Researchers; 141, Photo Researchers; 143, Mary Kate Denny/Photo Edit.

COVER DESIGN   The Hampton-Brown Company
COVER PHOTO   John Kelly/Image Bank

Typefaces for the cursive type in this book were provided by Zaner-Bloser, Inc., Columbus, Ohio, copyright, 1993.

ISBN 0-8136-2819-9

7 8 9 10   97

TABLE OF CONTENTS

Learning to Spell a Word

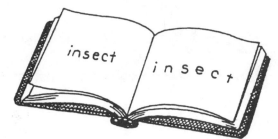

1. Say the word.
   Look at the word and say the letters.

2. Print the word with your finger.

3. Close your eyes and think of the word.

4. Cover the word and print it on paper.

5. Check your spelling.

Making a Spelling Notebook

A Spelling Notebook will help you when you write. Write the words you're having trouble with on a sheet of paper. Add the paper to a notebook or folder. Whenever you need help to spell a word, look in your Spelling Notebook.

Name _____

/k/, /kw/, and /n/

Warm Up

Do you know what to do in case of an earthquake?

Earthquake

The ground trembles. Buildings **shake** and wobble. Dishes are **knocked** off shelves. Take cover **quickly!** It's an **earthquake!**

Most of us have never felt a quake, but nearly half a million happen each year. Only about one thousand of them are felt by people. Quakes can be violent. They can destroy property and lives.

Most earthquakes are caused by movements of the earth's surface. Scientists use a machine called a *seismograph* to measure the force of a quake. Scientists can't tell when a quake will happen, but some think that animals could help predict quakes. Many animals—apparently **knowing** that the earth is about to shake—act nervous just before an earthquake occurs.

 Say each boldfaced word in the selection. Which sounds are not spelled the way they are pronounced?

On Your Mark

Take your Warm Up Test. Then check your spelling with the List Words on the next page.

5

Pep Talk

Sometimes a sound is not spelled the way you would expect. In the word <u>earthquake</u>, the sound for /kw/ is spelled with the letters **qu.** The /n/ sound in <u>knocked</u> is spelled with **kn**. The /k/ sound is not only spelled with **k,** but also with **ch** and **ck.**

LIST WORDS

1. quiet
2. aches
3. shake
4. knocked
5. jacket
6. quarter
7. quickly
8. knowing
9. quarrel
10. speaker
11. questions
12. kneeling
13. earthquake
14. mechanic
15. orchestra
16. knothole
17. inquire
18. sequence
19. require
20. character

Game Plan

Spelling Lineup

Write each List Word under the correct heading. You will use some words more than once.

kn spells /n/

1. _____
2. _____
3. _____
4. _____

k spells /k/

5. _____
6. _____
7. _____

ch spells /k/

8. _____
9. _____
10. _____
11. _____

ck spells /k/

12. _____
13. _____
14. _____

qu spells /kw/

15. _____
16. _____
17. _____
18. _____
19. _____
20. _____
21. _____
22. _____
23. _____

Alphabetical Order

Write each group of List Words in alphabetical order.

earthquake	1. _____		orchestra	9. _____
kneeling	2. _____		sequence	10. _____
character	3. _____		require	11. _____
aches	4. _____		shake	12. _____

knowing	5. _____		quarter	13. _____
jacket	6. _____		quickly	14. _____
knothole	7. _____		quarrel	15. _____
inquire	8. _____		questions	16. _____

Puzzle

Read each clue. Write List Words to fill in the puzzle.

ACROSS
1. what we ask
4. twenty-five cents
8. short coat with sleeves
9. a group of musicians
10. silent
11. pains

DOWN
2. the person who is talking
3. tapped with your knuckles
4. in a fast way
5. a person who uses tools to work with machines
6. violent movement of the earth's surface
7. order of things

Flex Your Spelling Muscles

Writing

Special effects are used to create earthquakes and other disasters in the movies. What <u>earthquake</u> scenes can you imagine? Pretend that you are on a movie set watching those scenes being filmed. Use as many List Words as you can to describe what you see and hear.

Proofreading

The following article has ten mistakes. Use the proofreading marks to fix the mistakes. Then write the misspelled List Words correctly on the lines.

Proofreading Marks
⬯ spelling mistake
∧ add something

   Scientists have been trying foryears to accurately predict earthquakes. Noowing as quikely as possible when an earthqwake will occur could save thousandsof lives. In California in 1989, special sensorsin a science lab picked up a rise in earth noise twelve days before a quake hit San Francisco. The noise, which increased greatly three hours before the earthquake hit, continued until power to the sensors was noacked out. Scientistsstill have quastons about these sensors. They think the sensors rekwire more testing to find out whether they can really help predict earthquakes.

1. _____

2. _____

3. _____

4. _____

5. _____

6. _____

Now proofread your description of an imagined earthquake scene. Fix any mistakes.

Go for the Goal

Take your Final Test. Then fill in your Scoreboard. Send your mistakes to the Word Locker.

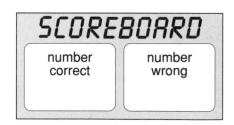

★ ★ ★ ★ ★ ★ ★ ★ ★ ★ All-Star Words ★ ★ ★ ★ ★ ★ ★ ★ ★ ★

qualify   hammock   kindness   knob   leprechaun

Use each All-Star Word in a sentence, but leave a blank for the word.
Trade sentences with a partner. See if you can guess the missing words.

Name _____

Hard and Soft c and g

Warm Up

Do you think dogs would be good students?

Teacher's Pet

Welcome to dog school. Here dogs are trained to sit, lie down, roll over, and heel. That may not sound like much to you, but, to a dog, those are hard subjects.

According to the famous dog trainer Barbara Woodhouse, there are some secrets that dog trainers should know to help their pupils **graduate.**

"Be a leader," she says. Dogs are pack animals, and they love being told what to do. However, don't ask the dog to do anything it cannot do. Make **certain** that you show your pet that you love it and that you are **grateful** for its efforts.

Here's an example of how to train your dog. First, make him or her sit at one end of the room. Wave your hand in front of the dog's face and say, "Stay!" Then walk a short distance away. Wave your hands in a **gesture** that signals the dog to come to you. Say, "Come!" If your pet follows your command be sure to offer lots of praise. Dogs learn by repetition, so if your dog doesn't learn on the first try, try again a **couple** of times a day. Go easy though! Dogs don't like too much learning.

When asked to describe what life at dog school is like, one pup replied, "Ruff!"

Look back at the boldfaced words. Say each word. What do you notice about the sounds that the letters **c** and **g** make?

On Your Mark

Take your Warm Up Test. Then check your spelling with the List Words on the next page.

9

LIST WORDS

1. concert
2. certain
3. circus
4. couple
5. credit
6. celebrate
7. village
8. graduate
9. grateful
10. coupon
11. shortage
12. gesture
13. generous
14. garage
15. license
16. sausage
17. gadget
18. regular
19. dangerous
20. icicles

Game Plan

Spelling Lineup

Write each List Word under the correct heading. You will use some words more than once.

c as in <u>cent</u>

1. _____
2. _____
3. _____
4. _____
5. _____
6. _____

c as in <u>cow</u>

15. _____
16. _____
17. _____
18. _____
19. _____
20. _____

g as in <u>danger</u>

7. _____
8. _____
9. _____
10. _____
11. _____
12. _____
13. _____
14. _____

g as in <u>garden</u>

21. _____
22. _____
23. _____
24. _____
25. _____

Classification

Write the List Word that belongs in each group.

1. snow, sleet, _____

2. barn, shed, _____

3. play, performance, _____

4. town, city, _____

5. hot dog, hamburger, _____

6. clown, ringmaster, _____

7. tool, invention, _____

8. scary, hurtful, _____

9. normal, usual, _____

10. two, pair, _____

11. card, paper, _____

12. need, lack, _____

Alphabetical Order

Write each group of List Words in alphabetical order.

grateful	generous
garage	gesture
graduate	gadget

couple	certain
concert	credit
coupon	celebrate

1. _____

2. _____

3. _____

4. _____

5. _____

6. _____

7. _____

8. _____

9. _____

10. _____

11. _____

12. _____

Flex Your Spelling Muscles

Writing

Many people love to talk about the funny or smart things their pets do. Write a story about something special your pet or a pet you know did. Try to use as many List Words as you can.

Proofreading

The journal entry below contains twelve mistakes. Use the proofreading marks to fix the mistakes. Then write the misspelled List Words correctly on the lines.

Proofreading Marks
◯ spelling mistake
ℯ take out something

Saturday, January 24

My dog did a most amazing thing today. I was taking him for a walk in the vilage when he suddenly stopped by a a garaje. He wouldn't move. I looked along the side and saw a little boy sitting there crying. The day was so cold I was afraid his tears would turn turn to isicles! I was sertin he was lost. My dog went right up to him and licked his face. A cuple of minutes later we found his mom up the the street. She had been looking all over for him and was very gateful to us. She offered me me a gift. I said that was a jenerous gestur, but I was just happy that my dog and I could help.

1. _____

2. _____

3. _____

4. _____

5. _____

6. _____

7. _____

8. _____

Now proofread your story about a pet. Fix any mistakes.

Go for the Goal

Take your Final Test. Then fill in your Scoreboard. Send your mistakes to the Word Locker.

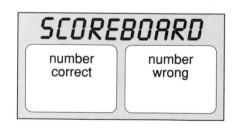

★ ★ ★ ★ ★ ★ ★ ★ ★ **All-Star Words** ★ ★ ★ ★ ★ ★ ★ ★ ★

sincere   gorge   concern   passage   casual

Try to use all five words in a single sentence. Then get together with a partner and compare sentences.

/f/

Warm Up

Can you name a dangerous circus job?

A Purr-fect Job

He cracks his whip, and a lion jumps up onto the backs of two horses. Another crack, and the horses begin to gallop. There is great danger here in the circus ring, but this lion tamer isn't **frightened.** He's more afraid of hurting the animals.

Perhaps the most famous lion tamer of all time, Gunther Gebel-Williams was a star of Ringling Brothers and Barnum and Bailey Circus. He has trained tigers to jump through hoops and stallions to take lions for a ride! Gunther joined the circus when he was twelve years old. His father died during World War II, and a circus family adopted him. He has been "under the big top" ever since. Today he is retired, but his daughter has a circus show with horses, and his son has taken over Gunther's role as lion tamer.

Circus life is **tough** and requires hard work and **effort.** Animal trainers have to keep themselves in top **physical** shape. They rise early and work with animals all day long. There may be more than a hundred of them to care for! Yet, when the trainers and animals perform their shows, the audience's **laughter** and amazement make all the hard work worth it.

Look back at the boldfaced words. Say each word. What do you notice about the way the /f/ sound is spelled?

On Your Mark

Take your Warm Up Test. Then check your spelling with the List Words on the next page.

The /f/ sound can be spelled four ways:
f as in <u>frightened</u>
ff as in <u>suffer</u>
ph as in <u>paragraph</u>
gh as in <u>enough</u>

LIST WORDS

1. frightened
2. suffer
3. paragraph
4. effort
5. autographs
6. telephone
7. dolphins
8. enough
9. laughter
10. symphony
11. physical
12. photography
13. atmosphere
14. flawless
15. geography
16. triumph
17. typhoid
18. hyphen
19. typhoon
20. tough

Game Plan

Spelling Lineup
Write each List Word under the correct heading.

f spells /f/

1. _____
2. _____

ff spells /f/

3. _____
4. _____

gh spells /f/

5. _____
6. _____
7. _____

ph spells /f/

8. _____
9. _____
10. _____
11. _____
12. _____
13. _____
14. _____
15. _____
16. _____
17. _____
18. _____
19. _____
20. _____

500 REALLY FUNNY JOKES

Synonyms

Synonyms are words that have the same or nearly the same meanings.
Write the List Word that is a synonym for each word given.

1. perfect _____

2. strong _____

3. work _____

4. signatures _____

5. plenty _____

6. victory _____

7. scared _____

8. storm _____

9. dash _____

10. disease _____

Vocabulary

Write the List Word that matches each clue.

1. the air around the earth _____

2. of the body, not the mind _____

3. the art of taking pictures _____

4. sound of joy or amusement _____

5. to have pain _____

6. group of related sentences _____

7. musical piece for an orchestra _____

8. the study of the surface of the earth _____

9. instrument that carries speech _____

10. sea mammals _____

Flex Your Spelling Muscles

Writing

Pretend that you are an animal photographer. Write a letter telling a friend about one of the pictures you've taken. What animal does the picture show? Was it difficult to get the shot? Use as many List Words as you can.

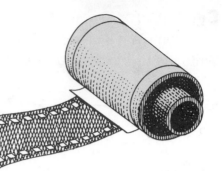

Proofreading

The poster below has eleven mistakes. Use the proofreading marks to fix the mistakes. Then write the misspelled List Words correctly on the lines.

Proofreading Marks
- spelling mistake
- add apostrophe

Come one, come all!
Dont wait!
Afternoon shows at Tyfoon Bay!
See the dolfins perform with flauless grace.
Watch the sailors triumh over the pirates in an exciting, noisy, and touf sea battle.
Join in with everyones laufter and cheers.
Hear the symfony play.
If you love fotography, be sure to bring your camera.
Telefone 555-3244 for more details.

1. _____
2. _____
3. _____
4. _____
5. _____
6. _____
7. _____
8. _____
9. _____

Now proofread your letter. Fix any mistakes.

Go for the Goal

Take your Final Test. Then fill in your Scoreboard. Send your mistakes to the Word Locker.

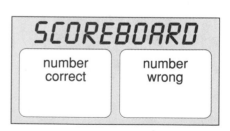

SCOREBOARD

number correct	number wrong

★ ★ ★ ★ ★ ★ ★ ★ **All-Star Words** ★ ★ ★ ★ ★ ★ ★ ★

waffle   festival   cough   telegraph   phonograph

Write a paragraph using all five words, but leave out three or four letters in each word. Then trade paragraphs with a partner. Complete each other's words.

kn, gn, wr, and rr

Warm Up

Why is it a good idea to have signs everyone can read?

Signs of the Times

It seems everywhere you look today, there are signs. Until recently, road signs contained only words. Today, people travel a great deal, so our highway signs have been changed to signs that everyone can read. Even if you're traveling in a **foreign** country, you can now "read" the language on many signs.

International symbols are not only used on highways. Symbols have been **designed** to point out places that are commonly **known** among travelers. A large *H* on a square sign points to a hospital. A picture of a spoon, knife, and fork points out a restaurant.

There are even international symbols that point out local buildings. Now, no matter what country you're in, you can just follow the sign and the **arrow.** You'll arrive at the library. The only problem you might have is not being able to read the language in which the books are **written.**

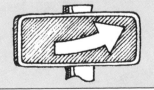 Say each boldfaced word. Listen for the /n/ sound or the /r/ sound. What do you notice about how these sounds are spelled?

On Your Mark

Take your Warm Up Test. Then check your spelling with the List Words on the next page.

The List Words contain either the /n/ sound you hear in <u>now</u> or the /r/ sound you hear in <u>rip</u>. The /n/ sound can be spelled **kn** as in <u>known</u> and **gn** as in <u>assign</u>. The /r/ sound can be spelled **wr** as in <u>written</u> and **rr** as in <u>arrow</u>.

LIST WORDS

1. wreath
2. known
3. typewriters
4. written
5. wrapper
6. arrow
7. correct
8. mirror
9. surround
10. knead
11. knotted
12. resign
13. designed
14. assign
15. wrinkled
16. foreign
17. wrestler
18. campaign
19. cologne
20. knuckles

Game Plan

Spelling Lineup

Write each List Word under the correct heading.

kn spells /n/

1. _____
2. _____
3. _____
4. _____

gn spells /n/

5. _____
6. _____
7. _____
8. _____
9. _____
10. _____

rr spells /r/

11. _____
12. _____
13. _____
14. _____

wr spells /r/

15. _____
16. _____
17. _____
18. _____
19. _____
20. _____

Rhyming

Write the List Word that rhymes with each word given.

1. feed   _____

2. twinkled _____

3. teeth   _____

4. spotted _____

5. cone   _____

6. buckles _____

7. bitten _____

8. trapper _____

Vocabulary

Write the List Word that best completes each sentence.

1. Carlos _____ the scenery for the class play.

2. Aunt Clara will _____ from her job.

3. The first _____ country I visited

   was Denmark.

4. The _____ entered the ring.

5. Robin Hood's _____ hit the center

   of the target.

6. She was wearing some _____ that smelled

   like roses.

7. The city of Boston is _____ as

   "The Cradle of Liberty."

8. Mr. Hall will _____ the topics

   for our reports.

9. Mrs. Blake saw her reflection in the _____ .

10. The senator ran a successful _____ .

11. New _____ were ordered

    for our library.

12. Beautiful mountains _____

    the valley.

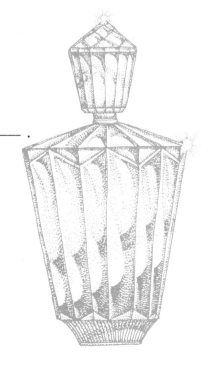

Flex Your Spelling Muscles

Writing

Think of all the different signs that might <u>surround</u> you. Now create your own sign. Design a symbol, such as an <u>arrow</u>, to help show your sign's message. Then write a paragraph about your sign. Use as many List Words as you can.

Proofreading

The following article has ten mistakes. Use the proofreading marks to fix the mistakes. Then write the misspelled List Words correctly on the lines.

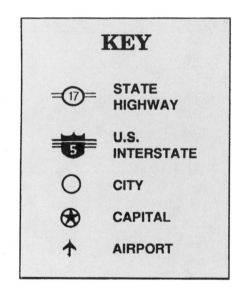

Proofreading Marks

⬭ spelling mistake

⊙ add period

Reading maps can be difficult at first, especially maps that are poorly desined With a little practice, however, you can master the art of map-reading. Open a map carefully and smooth out any rinkled sections with the palm of your hand or with your nuckles Then look for the key, which shows the ritten meanings of the map symbols Once these symbols are nown, you can figure out the corect route to take from your starting point to your destination

1. _____   4. _____

2. _____   5. _____

3. _____   6. _____

Now proofread your paragraph about your sign. Fix any mistakes.

Go for the Goal

Take your Final Test. Then fill in your Scoreboard. Send your mistakes to the Word Locker.

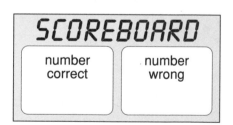

★ ★ ★ ★ ★ ★ ★ ★ ★ **All-Star Words** ★ ★ ★ ★ ★ ★ ★ ★ ★

knowledge   align   ferry   wrath   errand

Work with a partner to write a definition for each All-Star Word. Then look up the words in a dictionary. How many of your definitions are similar to the ones in the dictionary?

/əl/ and /l/

Warm Up

Should we devote an entire week to
honoring pickles?

Pickle Power

We celebrate Mother's Day, Father's Day,
Valentine's Day, and Thanksgiving. We even
remember Groundhog Day, but is there a Pickle
Day? No, there's a Pickle Week! That's right—seven
whole days devoted to honoring the humble **pickle.**

The idea may **tickle** your funny bone or **fuel** your
imagination, but it's a fact. International Pickle Week
was started in 1948 by several pickle packers. They
claimed that celebrating pickles would be a good way
to remind us of our history.

After all, North America was named after the
explorer Amerigo Vespucci. The pickle packers said that
Vespucci was a pickle peddler himself. It is said that he made
sure the spicy, **oval**-shaped food was on board ships headed to
the New World. History books, however, don't mention the
explorer's cucumber connection.

In any case, International Pickle Week is official. It is listed in
Chase's Calendar of Events, which lists a reason to celebrate almost
every day of the year. People really "relish" celebrating this holiday!

Look back at the boldfaced words. How is the last syllable
in each word spelled? Say each word and listen to the
sound made by the last syllable.

On Your Mark

Take your Warm Up Test. Then check your spelling with the List Words
on the next page.

Pep Talk

The /əl/ and /l/ sounds can be spelled in different ways. Listen to the sound made by the syllables spelled **le, el,** and **al** in the List Words. The letters **le, el,** and **al** all spell the same sound in the last syllable of words such as <u>pickle</u>, <u>towels</u>, and <u>final</u>.

LIST WORDS

1. final
2. oval
3. fuel
4. equals
5. pickle
6. tickle
7. double
8. jungle
9. panel
10. towels
11. cancel
12. plural
13. mammal
14. sparkled
15. whistle
16. aisle
17. scramble
18. channel
19. spiral
20. jingle

Game Plan

Spelling Lineup

Write each List Word under the correct heading.

le spells /l/ or /əl/

1. _____
2. _____
3. _____
4. _____
5. _____
6. _____
7. _____
8. _____
9. _____

el spells /l/ or /əl/

10. _____
11. _____
12. _____
13. _____
14. _____

al spells /l/ or /əl/

15. _____
16. _____
17. _____
18. _____
19. _____
20. _____

Classification

Write the List Word that belongs in each group.

1. walkway, path, _____

2. stop, call off, _____

3. same, alike, _____

4. desert, forest, _____

5. last, concluding, _____

6. single, triple, _____

7. number, singular, _____

8. round, square, _____

9. course, passage, _____

10. bird, fish, _____

Definitions

Write a List Word to match each definition clue. Find the answer
to the riddle by reading down the letters in the shaded box.

1. to cover a wall with wood   ___ ___ ___ ___ ___

2. more than one   ___ ___ ___ ___ ___

3. in a circle   ___ ___ ___ ___ ___

4. mix up   ___ ___ ___ ___ ___

5. a way to make someone laugh   ___ ___ ___ ___ ___

6. shaped like an egg   ___ ___ ___ ___

7. used for drying   ___ ___ ___ ___ ___

8. a preserved cucumber   ___ ___ ___ ___ ___ ___

9. used to supply heat or power   ___ ___ ___ ___ ___

10. a noisemaker   ___ ___ ___ ___ ___ ___

11. glittered   ___ ___ ___ ___ ___ ___ ___

Riddle: What do you get when you cross a cat and a pickle?

Answer: ___ _____ _____

Flex Your Spelling Muscles

Writing

Can you think of a reason to have a holiday? It can be a silly reason or a serious one. Write a paragraph that tells about your holiday. Tell why it should be celebrated. Use as many List Words as you can.

Proofreading

The want ad below has eleven mistakes. Use the proofreading marks to fix the mistakes. Write the misspelled List Words correctly on the lines.

Proofreading Marks

⬭ spelling mistake

∧ add something

Are you tired of the workday jungel Do you feel that life is a constant scamble? Do you have ideas that once sparkeld, but are now dull Then you may be the person who fits the job of advertising manager for our pickel products. You will be responsible for writing a new jingel for television commercials. You will also lead a panell to think of new ways to market our products. Does all this tikel your fancy This is our finel offer!

So call 555-1243 to set up an appointment.

1. _____
2. _____
3. _____
4. _____
5. _____
6. _____
7. _____
8. _____

Now proofread your paragraph about a holiday. Fix any mistakes.

Go for the Goal

Take your Final Test. Then fill in your Scoreboard. Send your mistakes to the Word Locker.

SCOREBOARD

number correct	number wrong

★ ★ ★ ★ ★ ★ ★ ★ **All-Star Words** ★ ★ ★ ★ ★ ★ ★ ★

general   dismal   muscle   noble   easel

Write a question using each All-Star Word. Then get together with a partner and ask each other your questions. Try to answer each one.

Instant Replay • Lessons 1–5

Time Out

Take another look at ways to spell the sounds /k/, /kw/, and /n/, at soft and hard sounds for **c** and **g,** and at different ways to spell the sounds /f/, /r/, and /l/ or /əl/.

Check Your Word Locker

Look at the words in your Word Locker. Write your most troublesome words for Lessons 1 through 5.

_____

_____

Practice writing your troublesome words with a partner. Take turns writing each word as the other slowly spells it aloud.

Lesson 1

Listen for the /kw/ sound in <u>quarrel</u>. Notice how the /k/ sound is spelled in <u>speaker</u>, <u>mechanic</u>, <u>jacket</u>, and <u>camp</u>. The /n/ sound can be spelled with **kn**, as in <u>knowing</u>.

List Words
quiet
aches
shake
knocked
jacket
quarter
quickly
kneeling
sequence
character

Write a List Word that belongs in each group.

1. events, order, _____

2. fast, rapidly, _____

3. shiver, rattle, _____

4. silent, calm, _____

5. nickel, dime, _____

6. plot, setting, _____

7. pains, sores, _____

8. coat, sweater, _____

9. standing, sitting, _____

10. rapped, tapped, _____

Lesson 2

The letters **c** and **g** each have a soft sound and a hard sound. Listen for the sounds of **c** in <u>certain</u> and <u>coupon</u>. Listen for the sounds of **g** in <u>gadget</u>.

List Words

concert
circus
couple
celebrate
graduate
gesture
garage
license
dangerous
icicles

Write a List Word that matches each clue.

1. a sign of winter _____

2. a shelter _____

3. complete high school _____

4. have a party _____

5. band performance _____

6. sharp knife _____

7. wave a hand _____

8. a pair _____

9. permits driving a car _____

10. has tents and clowns _____

Lesson 3

The /f/ sound can be spelled four ways: **f, ff, ph,** and **gh,** as in <u>frightened</u>, <u>suffer</u>, <u>typhoon</u>, and <u>laughter</u>.

List Words

frightened
effort
autographs
dolphins
enough
atmosphere
flawless
triumph
hyphen
tough

Write the List Word that is a synonym for the word given.

1. dash _____
2. plenty _____
3. victory _____
4. signatures _____
5. hard _____

6. perfect _____
7. attempt _____
8. scared _____
9. air _____
10. porpoises _____

The /r/ sound can be spelled **wr** as in <u>wreath</u> and **rr** as in <u>mirror</u>. The /n/ sound can be spelled **kn** as in <u>knot</u> and **gn** as in <u>sign</u>.

List Words

wreath
typewriters
wrapper
correct
surround
knead
resign
foreign
campaign
knuckles

Write the List Word next to its dictionary sound-spelling.

1. (kam pān´) _____

2. (tīp´rīt ərz) _____

3. (fôr´in) _____

4. (nēd) _____

5. (rēth) _____

6. (rē zīn´) _____

7. (kə rekt´) _____

8. (sər round´) _____

9. (nuk´əlz) _____

10. (rap´ər) _____

The /l/ or /əl/ sound in the last syllable of a word can be spelled **le, el,** or **al,** as in <u>tickle</u>, <u>fuel</u>, and <u>mammal</u>.

List Words

final
oval
equals
pickle
double
towels
plural
whistle
aisle
channel

Write a List Word to complete each sentence.

1. This _____ has the best TV programs.

2. Hang the wet _____ on the line to dry.

3. The bride and groom marched up the _____ .

4. That loud _____ hurts my ears.

5. This _____ is too sour for my taste.

6. The astronauts began the _____ countdown.

7. Four times four _____ sixteen.

8. Two frisky puppies are _____ trouble.

9. The _____ form of <u>child</u> is <u>children</u>.

10. The picture frame has an _____ shape.

List Words

aches
shake
kneeling
sequence
circus
celebrate
graduate
dangerous
dolphins
enough
wreath
resign
foreign
equals
aisle

Write the List Word that matches each clue.

1. resting on a knee or knees _____

2. one who has finished school _____

3. to honor in a special way _____

4. pains _____

5. matches _____

6. to give up one's position _____

7. a ring of leaves or flowers _____

8. as much as needed _____

9. succession _____

10. unsafe _____

11. water animals _____

12. a show with clowns _____

13. an open way for passing _____

14. outside one's country _____

15. to tremble _____

Go for the Goal

Take your Final Replay Test. Then fill in your Scoreboard.
Send any misspelled words to your Word Locker.

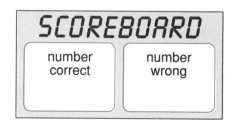

SCOREBOARD	
number correct	number wrong

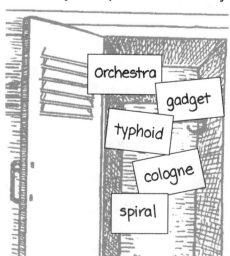

Orchestra
gadget
typhoid
cologne
spiral

Clean Out Your Word Locker

Look in your Word Locker. Cross out each word you spelled correctly on your Final Replay Test. Circle the words you're still having trouble with. Add the words you circled to your Spelling Notebook. What do you notice about the words? Watch for those words as you write.

Vowel Digraphs ai, ay, oa, and ow

LESSON 7

Warm Up

Which country in the world has the most gum chewers?

A Sticky Subject

Parents and teachers always seem to **complain** about it.

"It's bad for your teeth!" they might warn you.

"If anyone **swallows** it, it might become lodged in the throat!" you might hear.

In case you haven't guessed, they're talking about chewing gum. You must admit, the complaints are well-founded. Gum is messy, and many people are careless with it. Instead of wrapping it after chewing, some people end up **throwing** it or dropping it. That makes for sticky shoes and ruined floors. Those who say that gum is bad for your teeth are also correct. We all know that too much sugar helps cause tooth **decay**. If you must chew, make the gum sugarless!

In spite of it all, many people love to chew gum. Americans can **boast** of chewing more gum than any other people in the world. If the gum we chewed in just one year were stuck together, it would weigh 200 million pounds!

Bubble gum offers gum chewers their greatest challenge. Just for the record, the largest bubble ever blown was made by Susan Montgomery Williams of Fresno, California, in 1979. Using three pieces of gum, Susan blew a bubble that measured 22 inches in diameter!

Say the boldfaced words in the selection with the vowel digraphs **ai** and **ay**. How are they alike? Say the boldfaced words with the vowel digraphs **oa** and **ow**. How are they alike?

On Your Mark

Take your Warm Up Test. Then check your spelling with the List Words on the next page.

A vowel digraph is made from two vowels that work together to make one sound. The vowel digraphs **ai** and **ay** spell the /ā/ sound you hear in <u>drains</u> and <u>decay</u>. The vowel digraphs **oa** and **ow** spell the /ō/ sound you hear in <u>coast</u> and <u>borrow</u>.

LIST WORDS

1. complain
2. braid
3. drains
4. coast
5. toasted
6. decay
7. roasting
8. throwing
9. tomorrow
10. borrow
11. boast
12. swallows
13. foamy
14. poach
15. cocoa
16. fainted
17. scarecrow
18. gained
19. hoax
20. painful

Game Plan

Spelling Lineup
Write each List Word under the correct heading.

/ō/

1. _____
2. _____
3. _____
4. _____
5. _____
6. _____
7. _____
8. _____
9. _____
10. _____
11. _____
12. _____
13. _____

/ā/

14. _____
15. _____
16. _____
17. _____
18. _____
19. _____
20. _____

Synonyms

Write the List Word that means the same or almost the same as each word given.

1. sore _____

2. swooned _____

3. cooking _____

4. weave _____

5. warmed _____

6. trick _____

7. increased _____

8. brag _____

9. sudsy _____

10. strawman _____

Definitions

Write a List Word to match each definition clue. Then use the numbered letters to solve the riddle. Copy each numbered letter onto the line below with the same number.

1. tossing __ __ __ __ __ __ __
         3   4   13

2. to rot or break down __ __ __ __ __
               6   1

3. the day after today __ __ __ __ __ __ __ __
          10 5   8   9

4. hot chocolate __ __ __ __ __
          2

5. cook eggs in liquid __ __ __ __ __
          12   7

6. to take for a time __ __ __ __ __ __
         11

7. pipes for carrying off water __ __ __ __ __ __
                  14

Riddle: Where is the best place for having a gum-chewing contest?

Answer: __ __ __ __ __ __ __ __ __ __ __ __ __ __
     1   2   3   4   5   6   7   8   9   10 11 12 13 14

Flex Your Spelling Muscles

Writing

Some people think that chewing gum is a bad habit. What other bad habits do people complain about? Biting fingernails and popping knuckles are two candidates. Do you have any ideas on how a bad habit might be broken? Write your ideas. Tell what steps to take in breaking the bad habit.

Proofreading

The following article has ten mistakes. Use the proofreading marks to fix each mistake. Write the misspelled List Words correctly on the lines.

Proofreading Marks	
⬭	spelling mistake
≡	capital letter
∧	add something

   Where do you think chewing gum came from It came from the dried sap of a jungle tree called *sapodilla* that was chewed by the aztecs. They called it *chictli.* chewing gum showed up on the east coost of the united States in 1871. Do you know what happened Many people loved the gum, but others began to complayn that chewing drayns moisture from the salivary glands and if a person swalloes it, the stomach will be upset. It was not until the mid-1900s that people began to worry about tooth decai.

1. _____   3. _____   5. _____

2. _____   4. _____

Now proofread what you wrote about bad habits. Fix any mistakes.

Go for the Goal

Take your Final Test. Then fill in your Scoreboard. Send your mistakes to the Word Locker.

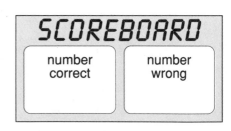

SCOREBOARD

number correct	number wrong

★ ★ ★ ★ ★ ★ ★ ★ ★ **All-Star Words** ★ ★ ★ ★ ★ ★ ★ ★ ★

sorrow   stain   betray   toadstool   sparrow

Write a story with the All-Star Words. Then erase the All-Star Words. Trade papers with your partner. Try to fill in the missing words to finish each other's story.

Vowel Digraphs ee and ea

Warm Up

Why are feathers a bird's treasure?

On the Wing

It is said that birds of a **feather** flock together. Birds may not be in **agreement** with that statement. That's because no two feathers are exactly the same. Feathers come in a variety of shapes, colors, and sizes. One large bird alone can have as many as 25,000 feathers from head to tail.

Feathers are indeed beautiful, but they also serve a purpose. Feathers help a bird fly. Smaller feathers help streamline the **creature** so that it will not resist air. The larger wing and tail feathers help lift it into the sky. Feathers help birds stay **healthy** by serving as a **sweater** to keep them warm and dry. Each quill has thousands of tiny shafts that lock together, **keeping** the bird dry **underneath**. Water simply rolls off the bird's back. In warmer weather, the feathers act to cool the bird.

From the great condor to the tiny hummingbird, feathers are a bird's **treasure**.

Say the boldfaced words in the selection. Which vowel digraph makes an /ē/ sound? Which vowel digraph makes an /ē/ sound and an /e/ sound?

On Your Mark

Take your Warm Up Test. Then check your spelling with the List Words on the next page.

Pep Talk

Words with the vowel digraph **ee** have the /ē/ sound you hear in the word <u>speech</u>. The vowel digraph **ea** also spells the /ē/ sound, as in the word <u>underneath</u>. Sometimes the vowel digraph **ea** spells the /e/ sound, as in the word <u>steady</u>.

LIST WORDS

1. feather
2. sweater
3. underneath
4. agreement
5. meadows
6. speech
7. needles
8. keeping
9. treasure
10. northeast
11. steady
12. creature
13. breathe
14. pleasure
15. succeed
16. sweeter
17. healthy
18. preacher
19. leather
20. wealth

Game Plan

Spelling Lineup
Write each List Word under the correct heading.

ee spells /ē/

1. _____
2. _____
3. _____
4. _____
5. _____
6. _____

ea spells /ē/

7. _____
8. _____
9. _____
10. _____
11. _____

ea spells /e/

12. _____
13. _____
14. _____
15. _____
16. _____
17. _____
18. _____
19. _____
20. _____

Vocabulary

Complete each sentence with a List Word that contains the vowel digraph that is underlined.

1. The movie was a double f<u>ea</u>ture.

   It starred a monster and a furry _____.

2. The pirate's map said, "Six feet down, m<u>ea</u>sure.

   There you will find my buried _____."

3. What has fuzzy skin outside and is juicy _____?

   Is it an apple, a plum, or a p<u>ea</u>ch?

4. The sailboat captains began to get the sails r<u>ea</u>dy,

   now that the wind was strong and _____.

Dictionary

Write the List Words that would be found on a dictionary page with each pair of guide words given. Be sure to write them in alphabetical order.

In a dictionary, guide words at the top of a page show the first and last entries on that page.

hour/jewel

age/northwest

1. _____

2. _____

3. _____

4. _____

5. _____

6. _____

7. _____

8. _____

9. _____

10. _____

please/wear

11. _____

12. _____

13. _____

14. _____

15. _____

16. _____

17. _____

18. _____

19. _____

20. _____

Flex Your Spelling Muscles

Writing

There are numerous kinds of birds people can see if they watch for them. What is your favorite bird? Write a description and explain why you like this bird. Try to use as many List Words as you can.

Proofreading

The following story summary has fourteen mistakes. Use the proofreading marks to fix each mistake. Write the misspelled List Words correctly on the lines.

Proofreading Marks
⬭ spelling mistake
⊙ add period
ℛ take out something

The Greek myth of Daedalus and Icarus tells of a father and son who are held prisoner by a king of great wealt After the the father sees a bird's fiether, he builds two pairs of wings made of feathers and wax In a a speich to his son, Daedalus says they will suced in escaping if they stay steadee and do not fly too close to the sun. At first, they fly over meadoews, keping low Excited by what he sees, Icarus forgets what his father told him. He flies too high over the sea His wings melt and and he falls into the ocean.

1. _____   5. _____

2. _____   6. _____

3. _____   7. _____

4. _____

Now proofread what you wrote about your favorite bird. Fix any mistakes.

Go for the Goal

Take your Final Test. Then fill in your Scoreboard. Send your mistakes to the Word Locker.

SCOREBOARD

number correct	number wrong

★ ★ ★ ★ ★ ★ ★ ★ **All-Star Words** ★ ★ ★ ★ ★ ★ ★ ★

measure   heal   peasant   degree   seek

Look up the definitions of the words in a dictionary. Select and write one definition of each word. Trade papers with a partner. See if you can write the All-Star Word next to the appropriate definition.

Vowel Digraphs <u>au</u> and <u>aw</u>

Warm Up

Where is the Garlic Capital of the World?

The Stinky Rose

Each summer, the town of Gilroy, California, has a festival that draws thousands of visitors. They don't come for fruit as ordinary as **strawberries**; they come for garlic. You may think that people would **squawk** over such a fuss made over something called "the stinky rose," but the truth is that it is one of the world's favorite flavorings.

Gilroy is known as the "Garlic Capital of the World." Indeed, more garlic is grown here than in any other place in North America. Each year hundreds of pounds of garlic are **hauled** to the festival to make the various types of food. Although visitors participate in such events as the Garlic Golf Tournament, the Great Garlic Gallop (a 10-kilometer race), they mostly come here to eat—garlic bread, garlic sauce, garlic anything! Participants have been known to throw **caution** to the wind and not worry about the strong smell. In fact, people may even be seen **gnawing** on cloves of garlic! By the time the festival is over, about a ton of garlic has been eaten.

One thing is certain. If you're heading to Gilroy's festival, you won't have to ask for directions. Just follow your nose. Some people think that garlic produces an **awfully** strong smell. To the people of Gilroy, however, it's the sweet smell of success.

Say the boldfaced words in the selection. What do you notice about the vowel sounds made by the vowel digraphs **au** and **aw**?

On Your Mark

Take your Warm Up Test. Then check your spelling with the List Words on the next page.

The vowel digraphs **au** and **aw** sound alike. They spell the /ô/ sound in <u>hawk</u> and <u>pause</u>.

LIST WORDS

1. hawk
2. faucet
3. author
4. pause
5. daughter
6. withdraw
7. hauled
8. awfully
9. unlawful
10. lawyer
11. strawberries
12. squawk
13. saucers
14. drawer
15. caution
16. vault
17. naughty
18. gnawing
19. awkward
20. exhaust

Game Plan

Spelling Lineup
Write each List Word under the correct heading.

au spells /ô/

1. _____
2. _____
3. _____
4. _____
5. _____
6. _____
7. _____
8. _____
9. _____
10. _____

aw spells /ô/

11. _____
12. _____
13. _____
14. _____
15. _____
16. _____
17. _____
18. _____
19. _____
20. _____

Classification

Write the List Word that belongs in each group.

1. artist, painter, _____

2. soot, smoke, _____

3. wait, rest, _____

4. terribly, horribly, _____

5. wall safe, piggy bank, _____

6. warning, advice, _____

7. judge, juror, _____

8. carried, dragged, _____

9. screech, scream, _____

10. cups, plates, _____

11. illegal, wrong, _____

12. child, son, _____

13. remove oneself, back out, _____

14. robin, crow, _____

15. closet, cupboard, _____

16. drain, sink, _____

Puzzle

Write List Words to fill in the puzzle.

ACROSS
2. chewing
3. terribly
4. warning
7. one who practices law

DOWN
1. safe storeroom
3. a published writer
5. not graceful
6. not behaving properly

Flex Your Spelling Muscles

Writing

Do you like garlic? What about <u>strawberries</u>? Write your opinion for or against garlic or strawberries. Try to convince your audience to think as you do. Use as many List Words as you can.

Proofreading

This book review has thirteen mistakes. Use the proofreading marks to fix the mistakes. Write the misspelled List Words correctly on the lines.

Proofreading Marks
⬭ spelling mistake
∧ add something

The awthor of *Strauberries* has some funny ideas about what makes a goodmystery. His language is awkword ashe tells about the unlauful theft of prize fruit froma large volt. The fruit is hawled away by a store owner's daughter to stopits sale to a rival store in the next town. Clues are found on a fauset and in sawsers. Thisstory does not have a real ending either. It just stops.

1. _____
2. _____
3. _____
4. _____
5. _____
6. _____
7. _____
8. _____

Now proofread your opinion about garlic or strawberries. Fix any mistakes.

Go for the Goal

Take your Final Test. Then fill in your Scoreboard. Send your mistakes to the Word Locker.

SCOREBOARD

number correct	number wrong

★ ★ ★ ★ ★ ★ ★ ★ **All-Star Words** ★ ★ ★ ★ ★ ★ ★ ★

awe   thawed   sprawl   slaughter   audience

Talk with your partner about the meanings of the words. Then take turns orally giving each other clues about one of the words. See if you can guess each other's words.

Vowel Digraphs ie and ei

Warm Up

Do you believe everything you see?

Seeing Isn't Believing

Art is something you hang on the walls, right? Wrong! For some artists, the whole world is a canvas.

You are walking down the street, and you see a doorway. Stepping up to it, you try to turn the doorknob. You discover you can't get your hand around it. The door won't open. Suddenly you realize you've been **deceived**! There is no door. There is no doorknob **either**. It's just a wall painting, or a mural. A mural this life-like proves that you can't always **believe** what you see. The French have a name for this kind of art. They call it *trompe l'oeil* (trawmp-loy). These words mean "deceive the eye."

Many artists around the world are turning blank walls into **pieces** of art. Some have painted window boxes and flowers under real windows, while others have supplied the windows, too. There are artists who have gone so far as to create bridges and tunnels on the sides of buildings. These mural painters also work indoors. A clever artist can turn a boring ceiling into a baseball **infield**.

The next time you see a field of corn growing on an apartment house, take a second look. There may be less there than meets the eye.

Say the boldfaced words in the selection. What vowel sounds do you hear? What do you notice about the vowel digraphs?

On Your Mark

Take your Warm Up Test. Then check your spelling with the List Words on the next page.

The digraph **ie** usually spells /ē/, as in <u>believe</u>. The digraph **ei** can spell /ā/, as in <u>freight</u>, or /ē/, as in <u>deceit</u>. Here's a helpful rule:

> **I** appears before **E**
> except after **C**,
> or when **ei** sounds like **A**,
> as in <u>eighty</u> or <u>vein</u>!

The words <u>either</u> and <u>neither</u> are tricky! Unlike the other List Words, they do not follow this rule.

LIST WORDS

1. deceived
2. received
3. brief
4. believe
5. infield
6. review
7. freight
8. vein
9. shield
10. pieces
11. eighty
12. niece
13. yield
14. either
15. neither
16. deceit
17. grief
18. thief
19. achieve
20. conceive

Game Plan

Spelling Lineup

Write each List Word under the correct heading.

ie

1. _____
2. _____
3. _____
4. _____
5. _____
6. _____
7. _____
8. _____
9. _____
10. _____
11. _____

ei after c

12. _____
13. _____
14. _____
15. _____

ei as in <u>freight</u>

16. _____
17. _____
18. _____

ei in "No Rule" words

19. _____
20. _____

Antonyms

Write the List Word that is an antonym for each word or phrase given.

1. lengthy _____

2. neither _____

3. joy _____

4. truth _____

5. either _____

6. nephew _____

7. told the truth _____

8. sent _____

Rhyming

Write the List Words that rhyme with each word given.
You will write up to three List Words for some items.

1. lane _____

2. relieve _____ _____ _____

3. field _____ _____

4. believed _____ _____

5. weight _____

Classification

Write the List Word that belongs in each group.

1. baggage, cargo, _____

2. study, recheck, _____

3. short, concise, _____

4. parts, bits, _____

5. cheated, lied, _____

6. sister, nephew, _____

7. know, think, _____

8. sadness, worry, _____

9. get, win, _____

10. sixty, seventy, _____

11. badge, armor, _____

12. slow, stop, _____

13. form, develop, _____

14. took, got, _____

15. not, nor, _____

16. heart, blood, _____

17. burglar, robber, _____

18. base, outfield, _____

Flex Your Spelling Muscles

Writing

A realistic painting of a barn on the side of a building can actually make you think there's a barn next to that building. Have you ever thought you saw something that turned out to be something else? Write about your experience or make one up.

Proofreading

This article has thirteen mistakes. Use the proofreading marks to fix the mistakes. Then write the misspelled List Words correctly on the lines.

Proofreading Marks	
⬭	spelling mistake
⌃	add something

One of the greatest mural artists to achieeve fame was Diego Rivera. He was born in Guanajato Mexico on December 8 1886. A reveiw of his work shows that he had great respect for the common people. He also showed the greef he felt at how poorer people were treated by the government. He did not beleeve that people should yeild to those who wanted to rule them unfairly. His murals appeared on walls in schools in government buildings and in palaces. He traveled to Detroit New York City and San Francisco to paint. He recieved many honors while he was alive.

1. _____   4. _____

2. _____   5. _____

3. _____   6. _____

Now proofread your writing about your experience with something that turned out to be something else. Fix any mistakes.

Go for the Goal

Take your Final Test. Then fill in your Scoreboard. Send your mistakes to the Word Locker.

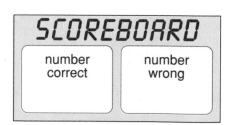

SCOREBOARD

number correct	number wrong

★ ★ ★ ★ ★ ★ ★ ★ **All-Star Words** ★ ★ ★ ★ ★ ★ ★ ★

disbelief   relieved   grieve   eighteen   leisure

Write a sentence for each word, leaving a blank where the word would be written. Trade papers with a partner and try to finish each other's sentences.

Diphthongs <u>ou</u>, <u>ow</u>, <u>oi</u>, and <u>oy</u>

Warm Up

How does the wind make a cold day colder?

The Big Chill

How many times have you **counted** on the thermometer to tell you how warmly to dress, then when you got outside it seemed much much colder? What was different? Was it the **moisture** in the air? Did you wear the wrong clothing? Perhaps, but more often than not, if the wind was blowing, it was the windchill factor.

Does that mean that the wind has **joined** the cold to make things worse? Not really. When the air is still, your body heat forms a type of shield against the cold. But when the wind blows, that shield is broken. As a result, you feel much colder. The change in temperature has more to do with you than the air temperature.

Here is a chart to find out the temperature when there's wind. Check the temperature on a thermometer, then find out the wind speed by watching the weather report. Knowing the effect of the windchill could make your trip to school a little more **enjoyable**. You might also want to stick with **crowded** areas to keep warm and **avoid** windy streets. And, oh, wear that wind breaker!

Windchill Factor Chart

Wind Speed (Miles per hour)	Air Temperature (Fahrenheit)						
	25	20	15	10	5	0	-5
4	25	20	15	10	5	0	-5
5	22	16	11	6	0	-5	-10
10	10	3	-3	-9	-15	-22	-27
15	2	-5	-11	-18	-25	-31	-38
20	-3	-10	-17	-24	-31	-39	-46
25	-7	-15	-22	-29	-36	-44	-51
30	-10	-18	-25	-33	-41	-49	-56

Say the boldfaced words with **ou** and **ow** in the selection. What difference is there in the /ou/ sound in these words? Say the boldfaced words with **oi** and **oy** in the selection. What difference is there in the /oi/ sound in these words?

On Your Mark

Take your Warm Up Test. Then check your spelling with the List Words on the next page.

Pep Talk

The sounds made by combining the two vowels, or diphthongs, **ou** and **ow** spell the /ou/ sound you hear in <u>boundary</u> and <u>crowded</u>. The diphthongs **oi** and **oy** spell the /oi/ sound you hear in <u>poise</u> and <u>loyalty</u>.

Notice that the words <u>choir</u> and <u>courageous</u> and the last syllables in <u>mountainous</u> and <u>poisonous</u> do not have diphthong sounds.

LIST WORDS

1. crowded
2. joined
3. voyage
4. soiled
5. enjoyable
6. counted
7. powder
8. oyster
9. poise
10. boundary
11. loyalty
12. moisture
13. poisonous
14. mountainous
15. courageous
16. choir
17. toiled
18. broiled
19. avoid
20. joint

Game Plan

Spelling Lineup

Write each List Word under the correct heading. You will use some words more than once.

ou and **ow** spell /ou/

1. _____
2. _____
3. _____
4. _____
5. _____

ou spells /u/

6. _____
7. _____
8. _____

oi spells /ī/

9. _____

oi and **oy** spell /oi/

10. _____
11. _____
12. _____
13. _____
14. _____
15. _____
16. _____
17. _____
18. _____
19. _____
20. _____
21. _____
22. _____

Synonyms

Write the List Word that is a synonym for each word or phrase given.

1. worked _____

2. dirty _____

3. journey _____

4. mobbed _____

5. toxic _____

6. edge _____

7. hilly _____

8. dampness _____

9. connected _____

10. brave _____

11. fun _____

12. numbered _____

13. keep away from _____

14. chorus _____

Alphabetical Order

Write each group of List Words in alphabetical order.

crowded	1. _____
counted	2. _____
broiled	3. _____
boundary	4. _____
choir	5. _____
courageous	6. _____
avoid	7. _____
enjoyable	8. _____

powder	9. _____
loyalty	10. _____
oyster	11. _____
poise	12. _____
mountainous	13. _____
joint	14. _____
poisonous	15. _____
moisture	16. _____

Flex Your Spelling Muscles

Writing

Has there ever been a time when you felt really cold? Recall or imagine how you would feel. Then write your thoughts and tell what you did to get warm. Try to use as many List Words as you can.

Proofreading

This science article has eleven mistakes. Use the proofreading marks to fix the mistakes. Then write the misspelled words correctly on the lines.

Proofreading Marks	
⬭	spelling mistake
≡	capital letter
⌄	add apostrophe

   Its true that mowtainous areas can affect the weather far away. they form a boyndary that breaks up clouds and releases moistchure. as a result, one side might have cool, enjoiable rains, while the other side is broyled by the sun. thats why many people live on one side of mountains and avoud the other side.

1. _____   4. _____

2. _____   5. _____

3. _____   6. _____

Now proofread your writing about feeling cold. Fix any mistakes.

Go for the Goal

Take your Final Test. Then fill in your Scoreboard. Send your mistakes to the Word Locker.

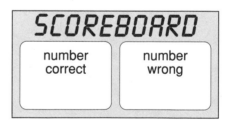

★ ★ ★ ★ ★ ★ ★ ★ ★ ★ **All-Star Words** ★ ★ ★ ★ ★ ★ ★ ★ ★ ★

powerful   outrageous   destroyed   spoiled   snout

Work with a partner to write definitions for each All-Star Word. Compare your definitions to those in your dictionary. How close did you come?

Instant Replay • Lessons 7–11

Time Out

Take another look at all the words that have vowels that work together to make one sound. These vowels are called vowel digraphs and diphthongs. Think about how these sounds are spelled in different ways.

Check Your Word Locker

Look at the words in your Word Locker. Which words for Lessons 7 through 11 did you have the most trouble with? Write them here.

_____

_____

Practice writing your troublesome words with a partner. Take turns saying each word, and then saying the vowel sound made by the digraph or diphthong. Write the words.

Lesson 7

Two vowels that produce one sound are called vowel digraphs. The vowel digraphs **ai** and **ay** both make the vowel sound /ā/, as in <u>fainted</u> and <u>decay</u>. The vowel digraphs **oa** and **ow** both make the vowel sound /ō/, as in <u>cocoa</u> and <u>tomorrow</u>.

List Words
complain
decay
boast
scarecrow
throwing
foamy
gained
coast
hoax
painful

Write a List Word that is a synonym for the word given.

1. strawman _____

2. increased _____

3. sudsy _____

4. aching _____

5. brag _____

6. groan _____

7. pitching _____

8. rot _____

9. trick _____

10. shore _____

The vowel digraphs **ee** and **ea** both make the vowel sound /ē/, as in <u>sweeter</u> and <u>breathe</u>. Sometimes the vowel digraph **ea** makes the vowel sound /e/, as in the word <u>wealth</u>.

List Words

feather
underneath
meadows
speech
needles
northeast
pleasure
healthy
preacher
leather

Study the relationship between the first two underlined words. Then write a List Word that has the same relationship with the third underlined word.

1. <u>Concrete</u> is to <u>sidewalks</u> as <u>grass</u> is to ——————————.

2. <u>Skin</u> is to <u>human</u> as —————————— is to <u>bird</u>.

3. <u>Touch</u> is to <u>hand</u> as —————————— is to <u>voice</u>.

4. <u>Good</u> is to <u>bad</u> as —————————— is to <u>sick</u>.

5. <u>Teacher</u> is to <u>school</u> as —————————— is to <u>church</u>.

6. <u>In</u> is to <u>out</u> as <u>over</u> is to ——————————.

7. <u>Pain</u> is to <u>sadness</u> as —————————— is to <u>joy</u>.

8. <u>Hammers</u> are to <u>carpentry</u> as —————————— are to <u>sewing</u>.

9. <u>Fabric</u> is to <u>dress</u> as —————————— is to <u>belt</u>.

10. <u>New Mexico</u> is to <u>southwest</u> as <u>Maine</u> is to ——————————.

The vowel digraphs **au** and **aw** both make the same vowel sound. Listen for the same vowel sound in <u>vault</u> and <u>unlawful</u>.

List Words

hawk
withdraw
strawberries
squawk
author
awfully
saucers
pause
unlawful
caution

Write the List Words that fit each description.

1. What the people do who leave the burning house:

—————————— with ——————————

2. What small plates of red fruit are: ——————————

of ——————————

3. What an illegal stop is: an —————————— ——————————

4. What a mother bird is when her baby is threatened:

a —————————— that will ——————————

5. What a very clumsy writer is: an ——————————

awkward ——————————

The vowel sound /ē/ is spelled with the vowel digraph **ie**, as in infield. The vowel sounds /ā/ and /ē/ can both be spelled with the vowel digraph **ei**, as in freight and conceive.

List Words

received
brief
believe
freight
vein
pieces
niece
neither
grief
thief

Write five List Words that could be found listed between each set of the dictionary guide words given. Write the words in alphabetical order.

achieve/nephew

1. _____
2. _____
3. _____
4. _____
5. _____

night/yield

6. _____
7. _____
8. _____
9. _____
10. _____

The diphthongs **ow** and **ou** spell the vowel sound /ou/ in the words powder and counted. The diphthongs **oi** and **oy** spell the vowel sound /oi/ in the words broiled and oyster.

List Words

voyage
enjoyable
oyster
boundary
loyalty
mountainous
courageous
choir
toiled
broiled

Write a List Word that belongs in each group.

1. brave, daring, _____

2. boiled, baked, _____

3. fun, pleasant, _____

4. worked, labored, _____

5. shell, pearl, _____

6. border, edge, _____

7. music, conductor, _____

8. devotion, faithfulness, _____

9. journey, trip, _____

10. rocky, hilly, _____

List Words

decay
boast
underneath
speech
hawk
pause
believe
oyster
courageous
toiled

Write a List Word to solve each clue.

1. brag about yourself _____

2. take a break _____

3. to rot _____

4. have faith _____

5. not on top _____

6. not being afraid _____

7. where a pearl hides _____

8. big bird _____

9. worked hard _____

10. way of speaking _____

Go for the Goal

Take your Final Replay Test. Then fill in your Scoreboard.
Send any misspelled words to your Word Locker.

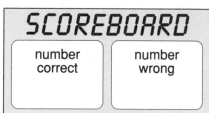

SCOREBOARD

number correct	number wrong

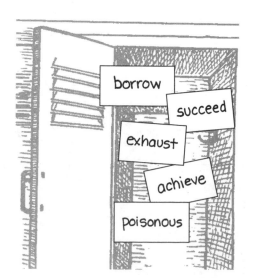

borrow
succeed
exhaust
achieve
poisonous

Clean Out Your Word Locker

Look in your Word Locker. Cross out each word you spelled
correctly on your Final Replay Test. Circle the words you're
still having trouble with. Add the words you circled to your
Spelling Notebook. What do you notice about the words?
Watch for those words as you write.

Prefixes <u>un</u>, <u>in</u>, <u>dis</u>, and <u>trans</u>

Warm Up

What kind of campers spend time in the sky?

Bird People

Many people have discovered the **unusual** sport of hang gliding. In the uncrowded skies human birds glide through the air like eagles. These "birds" are really "hang gliders," a term which also refers to their vehicles.

Hang gliders seek new thrills as part of their exciting sport. Some gliders have combined their lofty sport with the down-to-earth fun of a cookout. They call their new sport "sky camping." How do they do it?

They begin with the **transport** of their gear to the launch site. That's usually the highest cliff they can find. Then they hitch up their harnesses and wings. Hang gliders always **include** a parachute—just in case. When the air currents catch them, they're off! The gliders travel a sky trail between mountain peaks. Some of them fly as high as 20,000 feet above the earth. That's as high as some jet planes travel. They glide at about 25 miles an hour. After flying a **distance** of 30 or 40 miles they find their "nest." Here, they set up camp. Then after a good night's rest, they're off again. Sky camping trips can last for days.

"Sometimes we fly in formation with the eagles and hawks," said one pilot. You might think that this would **disturb** the birds, but the pilot insists that the birds don't mind.

Some sky campers think that they will go on traveling forever. Maybe they can. After all, the sky's the limit.

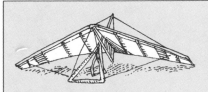

Say the boldfaced words in the selection. These words have word parts called prefixes that are added to the front of the words or word parts to make new words. What prefixes can you find in the boldfaced words?

On Your Mark

Take your Warm Up Test. Then check your spelling with the List Words on the next page.

Pep Talk

A prefix is a word part that is added to the beginning of a root or root word to make a new word. The prefix **trans** means <u>across</u> or <u>over</u>, as in <u>transplant</u>. The prefixes **un** and **dis** mean <u>not</u>, as in <u>unselfish</u> and <u>disgrace</u>. The prefix **dis** can also mean <u>away</u> or <u>opposite of</u>, as in <u>distance</u> and <u>disturb</u>. The prefix **in** can mean <u>not</u> or <u>into</u>. It can also mean <u>to cause</u> <u>to become</u>, as in <u>increase</u>.

LIST WORDS

1. transport
2. transfer
3. increase
4. disgrace
5. uncovered
6. discontinue
7. uncooked
8. discovered
9. include
10. inhale
11. disturb
12. incomplete
13. unjust
14. transplant
15. unusual
16. unselfish
17. insecure
18. distance
19. inspire
20. inexpensive

Game Plan

Spelling Lineup

Write each List Word under the correct heading.

words with the prefix **in**

1. _____
2. _____
3. _____
4. _____
5. _____
6. _____
7. _____

words with the prefix **dis**

8. _____
9. _____
10. _____
11. _____
12. _____

words with the prefix **trans**

13. _____
14. _____
15. _____

words with the prefix **un**

16. _____
17. _____
18. _____
19. _____
20. _____

Antonyms

Write the List Word that is an antonym for each word given.

1. complete _____

2. secure _____

3. usual _____

4. continue _____

5. expensive _____

6. decrease _____

7. just _____

8. selfish _____

Missing Words

Write a List Word to complete each sentence.

1. Try not to _____ him, he's reading.

2. Boil the pasta longer, it's still _____.

3. The plant is too big for the pot, so you'll need to _____ it.

4. Try not to _____ the gas fumes.

5. The lack of affordable housing is a _____ to the city.

6. The influence of that music will _____ me to dance.

Definitions

Write the List Word that matches the meaning given.

1. low-priced _____

2. to cause or influence to do something _____

3. contain _____

4. came upon, found out about _____

5. carry from one place to another _____

6. not right, unfair _____

7. to plant in another place _____

8. to stop doing, using, etc. _____

Flex Your Spelling Muscles

Writing

Because sky camping is a new and unusual sport, many people probably know little about it. Write copy for a poster that advertises a sky camping trip, or choose another sporting event to tell about. Use as many List Words as you can.

Proofreading

The following editorial has twelve mistakes. Use the proofreading marks to fix the mistakes. Write the misspelled List Words correctly on the lines.

Proofreading Marks
⬯ spelling mistake
∧ add something

The way some dune buggy riders treat the land is a dissgrase. Why dothey have to ride such a great destanc through the desert Don't they realize they disturb avery fragile environment? I don't mean to be unjust tothose riders who are careful. However, in the past few weeks, people have diskovered greatareas of wild land torn up by dune buggies, and noted an increese in noise. The reports are incompleete now, but there will soon be enough evidence to take action. Isn't it time to inspyre others to help protect our land

1. _____
2. _____
3. _____
4. _____
5. _____
6. _____

Now proofread the copy for your sports poster. Fix any mistakes.

Go for the Goal

Take your Final Test. Then fill in your Scoreboard. Send your mistakes to the Word Locker.

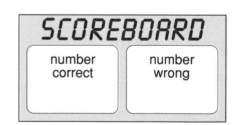

SCOREBOARD	
number correct	number wrong

★ ★ ★ ★ ★ ★ ★ ★ ★ **All-Star Words** ★ ★ ★ ★ ★ ★ ★ ★ ★

transparent   transmit   display   unavailable   invisible

Write a sentence for each word, but mix up the All-Star Words so they are in the wrong sentences. Trade papers with your partner. Correct the sentences by crossing out the wrong word and writing the correct word.

Prefixes en, im, and mis

LESSON 14

Warm Up

How did people obtain food before there were supermarkets?

Wild Meal

Did you know that supermarkets have only been around for about two hundred years? Before that, people "shopped" on the ground!

Would you care for some dandelion salad? Maybe you'd prefer boiled lilies with acorn biscuits. You could also **immerse** pine needles in hot water to make tea. For dessert, there are wild black cherries. All these foods can be "found." They are growing in the woods. Many of the foods found "underfoot" are ready to eat. Of course, some have been cooked to **improve** the taste.

In North America, wild foods were once **impossible** to ignore as an **important** part of people's diets. Native Americans ate acorns, sometimes grinding them into flour for bread. The early settlers often ate dandelion plants, flowers and all. Civil War soldiers ate birch bark!

Today, most of us buy our food in stores, but wild treats can still be found. Be careful, though! Let me **encourage** you to never eat anything that you aren't sure is a food! It's easy to **misjudge** wild plants. You might **mistake** a treat for something that's poisonous. If you do hunt for wild foods, go with an adult who knows about them. You might find some violets. If so, you could make some purple pancake syrup. Now that's really wild!

Say the boldfaced words in the selection. These words are made up of a root or root word and a prefix. What prefixes do you find in the boldfaced words?

On Your Mark

Take your Warm Up Test. Then check your spelling with the List Words on the next page.

The prefix **en** usually means <u>cause to be</u> or <u>make</u>, as in <u>enable</u>.

The prefix **im** usually means <u>not</u>, as in <u>impossible</u>. This prefix can also mean <u>more</u>, as in <u>improve</u>.

The prefix **mis** usually means <u>wrong</u> or <u>wrongly</u>, as in <u>misjudge</u>. This prefix can also mean <u>bad</u> or <u>badly</u> as in <u>misbehave</u>.

LIST WORDS

1. engage
2. encourage
3. impolite
4. improve
5. enable
6. enforce
7. improper
8. misjudge
9. mistrust
10. mistake
11. misplaced
12. endanger
13. impossible
14. misunderstand
15. misbehave
16. endure
17. immerse
18. immobile
19. mistook
20. mispronounce

Game Plan

Spelling Lineup

Write each List Word under the correct heading.

words with the prefix **en**

1. _____
2. _____
3. _____
4. _____
5. _____
6. _____

words with the prefix **im**

7. _____
8. _____
9. _____
10. _____
11. _____
12. _____

words with the prefix **mis**

13. _____
14. _____
15. _____
16. _____
17. _____
18. _____
19. _____
20. _____

Word Parts

Add a prefix from the box to each root word or root to form a List Word. Write the words on the lines.

| en | im | mis |

1. take _____
2. danger _____
3. able _____
4. merse _____
5. force _____
6. prove _____
7. judge _____
8. courage _____
9. took _____
10. gage _____

11. behave _____
12. placed _____
13. trust _____
14. possible _____
15. dure _____
16. polite _____
17. proper _____
18. mobile _____
19. understand _____
20. pronounce _____

$$26 + 27 = 54\ 53$$

Synonyms

Write the List Word that is a synonym for each word given.

1. lost _____
2. dunk _____
3. rude _____
4. bear _____
5. motionless _____

6. doubt _____
7. unsuitable _____
8. unfinished _____
9. unthinkable _____
10. help _____

Four of the List Words have the same or nearly the same meaning: to make or to have made an error. Write the four words on the lines.

11. _____
12. _____
13. _____
14. _____

Flex Your Spelling Muscles

Writing

Would you rather shop in the woods or in a grocery store? Do you think it is fun or boring to go food shopping? Write a paragraph stating your opinion and explain why you think that way.

Proofreading

The following advice article has twelve mistakes. Use the proofreading marks to fix the mistakes. Write the misspelled List Words correctly on the lines.

Proofreading Marks
⬭ spelling mistake
≡ capital letter

   there are many ways to improove your shopping trips. One way is to make a list, and then make sure it is not misplased. read labels on boxes to make sure you don't missunderstand what they contain, and miztrust any wild advertising claims. you don't want to make a mictake. you should go through the entire store so you don't forget anything. shoppers who imerse themselves in the job will indure longer than other people.

1. _____

2. _____

3. _____

4. _____

5. _____

6. _____

7. _____

Now proofread your opinion about food shopping. Fix any mistakes.

Go for the Goal

Take your Final Test. Then fill in your Scoreboard. Send your mistakes to the Word Locker.

```
SCOREBOARD
```
number correct	number wrong

★ ★ ★ ★ ★ ★ ★ ★ ★ **All-Star Words** ★ ★ ★ ★ ★ ★ ★ ★ ★

mislead   enrich   impure   misfortune   impose

Write a sentence for each word, and then erase the prefix. Trade papers with a partner, and add the correct prefix to the words so that they make sense.

Prefixes pre, pro, re, and ex

Warm Up

What athletes do you know that have changed careers?

Artist/Athlete

Many athletes have colorful careers on the field. This athlete has brought color to his new career—as an artist. "I didn't set out to play football. Art was always my first love," explained Ernie Barnes. Barnes, once a **professional** football player, became a successful artist. How exactly did he reflect on his career and **exchange** his shoulder pads for a paintbrush?

Being captain of the Hillside High football team served to **prepare** Barnes for college ball. He was such a good player that 28 different universities offered to provide him with football scholarships. He chose North Carolina Central University in his home state. There, in return for playing ball, he got to study art for free. Again, he proved that he was no average football player. By the time he graduated, he had been drafted by the pros. He played for the San Diego Chargers and later for the Denver Broncos.

Then an injury cut his career short. Rather than give up football altogether, Barnes did something very smart. He asked to be named the official AFL (American Football League) artist. His paintings were presented to New York artists for review. The critics loved his work. The AFL put him back on the payroll—this time as an artist.

Look at the boldfaced words in the selection. How many different prefixes can you find? What do you notice about the meaning of the roots or root words when a prefix is added?

On Your Mark

Take your Warm Up Test. Then check your spelling with the List Words on the next page.

The prefix **pre** usually means <u>before</u>, as in <u>prepare</u>.

The prefix **pro** usually means <u>for</u>, <u>in favor of</u>, or <u>forward</u>, as in <u>propose</u>.

The prefix **re** usually means <u>again</u> or <u>back</u>, as in <u>returning</u>.

The prefix **ex** usually means <u>out of</u> or <u>from</u>, as in <u>export</u>.

LIST WORDS

1. explain
2. exactly
3. reappear
4. pretend
5. reward
6. returning
7. exchange
8. export
9. provide
10. promote
11. protest
12. preserve
13. prepare
14. reflect
15. professional
16. rearrange
17. exist
18. exclaim
19. produce
20. propose

Game Plan

Spelling Lineup

Write each List Word under the correct heading.

words with the prefix ex

1. _____
2. _____
3. _____
4. _____
5. _____
6. _____

words with the prefix pro

7. _____
8. _____
9. _____
10. _____
11. _____
12. _____

words with the prefix pre

13. _____
14. _____
15. _____

words with the prefix re

16. _____
17. _____
18. _____
19. _____
20. _____

REWARD!
Lost German Shepherd
Answers to the name:
"KING"
Please call 555·1234
if found

Word Parts

Add the prefix **pre**, **pro**, **re**, or **ex** to each root word or root to form a List Word.
Then write the List Word. It should match the definition given.

1. _____ plain _____ make understandable

2. _____ port _____ to send goods from one country to sell in another

3. _____ arrange _____ to arrange in a different way

4. _____ actly _____ precisely the same

5. _____ fessional _____ a person in a profession

6. _____ claim _____ to cry out

7. _____ ward _____ something that is given in return for a good deed

8. _____ pare _____ to make or get ready

9. _____ turning _____ bringing back or going back again

10. _____ test _____ to argue against

11. _____ serve _____ to save or protect

12. _____ appear _____ to appear again

Rhyming

Write the List Word that rhymes with each word given.

1. defend _____

2. divide _____

3. shortchange _____

4. insist _____

5. suspect _____

6. compose _____

7. devote _____

8. reduce _____

Flex Your Spelling Muscles

Writing

Think of someone you admire because of what they have accomplished. Write a letter to this person telling why you admire him or her. Try to use as many List Words as you can.

Proofreading

This biographical article has thirteen mistakes. Use the proofreading marks to fix the mistakes. Write the misspelled List Words correctly on the lines.

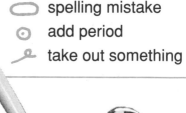

Proofreading Marks
⬯ spelling mistake
⊙ add period
℮ take out something

One of the greatest profesional baseball players of all time was Hank Aaron He played for the Atlanta Braves for 22 years In that time, he worked hard to promote and preeserve equality in in baseball. He also set more than one record that still esists today He might say his his greatest reword was his election to the Baseball Hall of Fame in 1982 There is no need to exsplain Hank Aaron. His career will continue to promoote the best in baseball for a long time to come

1. _____
2. _____
3. _____
4. _____
5. _____
6. _____

Now proofread your letter. Fix any mistakes.

Go for the Goal

Take your Final Test. Then fill in your Scoreboard. Send your mistakes to the Word Locker.

SCOREBOARD

number correct	number wrong

★ ★ ★ ★ ★ ★ ★ ★ ★ **All-Star Words** ★ ★ ★ ★ ★ ★ ★ ★ ★

prevent   proceed   reprint   extend   exceed

With your partner, look up and write definitions for the words in a dictionary. Then label each definition with the wrong All-Star Word. Trade papers with another team and match words and definitions correctly.

Prefixes fore, post, over, co, com, and con

Warm Up

What type of aircraft flies without wings?

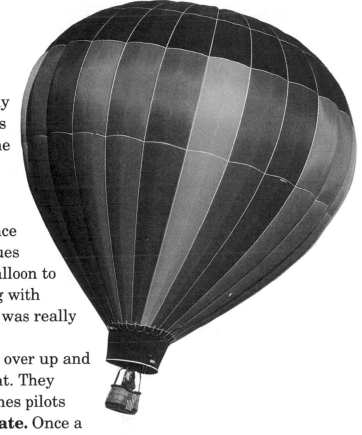

Up, Up, and Away

Hot-air ballooning is a popular sport for many adventurous people. Sport balloonists sometimes **compete** in hot-air balloon championships in the United States and Europe. Under the right **conditions**, balloonists can travel more than 5,000 miles in three and a half days!

Hot-air ballooning has not changed much since 1783. That's when two inventive brothers, Jacques and Joseph Montgolfier, constructed the first balloon to successfully carry a person. After experimenting with smoke-filled paper bags, they discovered that it was really hot air that caused balloons to rise.

Since hot-air balloon pilots only have control over up and down movements, the weather must be just right. They listen to the **forecas**t before taking off. Sometimes pilots have to **postpone** trips until the winds **cooperate.** Once a flight begins, the beauty below helps any frightened passengers **overcome** their fears.

When the balloon finally comes back down to earth, there's work to be done. First, the air must be squeezed out of the envelope. That's another name for the balloon itself. Then the balloon must be folded and put away. It's a big job that requires everyone's help.

Look at the first five boldfaced words. How are their first syllables alike? What do you notice about the word parts in <u>overcome</u>?

On Your Mark

Take your Warm Up Test. Then check your spelling with the List Words on the next page.

Pep Talk

The prefix **fore** means <u>in front of</u> or <u>before</u>, as in <u>forewarn</u>. The prefix **post** means <u>after</u>, as in <u>postwar</u>. The prefix **over** means <u>above</u> or <u>too much</u>, as in <u>overreact</u>. The prefixes **co, com**, and **con** mean <u>with</u> or <u>together</u>, as in <u>cooperate</u>.

LIST WORDS

1. postpone
2. postwar
3. overlooked
4. overboard
5. forecast
6. forearm
7. overreact
8. conserve
9. conditions
10. consoled
11. compete
12. forewarn
13. overcome
14. company
15. cooperate
16. conquer
17. foresee
18. contribute
19. commend
20. committee

Game Plan

Spelling Lineup

For each List Word, find the meaning of its prefix. Write the List Word under the correct heading.

<u>above</u> or <u>too much</u>

1. _____
2. _____
3. _____
4. _____

<u>after</u>

5. _____
6. _____

<u>in front of</u> or <u>before</u>

7. _____
8. _____
9. _____
10. _____

<u>with</u> or <u>together</u>

11. _____
12. _____
13. _____
14. _____
15. _____
16. _____
17. _____
18. _____
19. _____
20. _____

MEETING TODAY!
Postponed until 1:00 3:00

Puzzle

Read each clue. Write List Words to fill in the puzzle.

ACROSS

2. comforted
6. to put off or delay
8. to keep from being wasted
10. to arm beforehand
11. to take part in a contest
12. the ways people or things are
15. from a ship into the water
16. to defeat
17. to see or know beforehand
18. to give together with others

DOWN

1. to predict
3. to respond with more feeling than is necessary
4. to warn ahead of time
5. to win or defeat
6. after the war
7. failed to notice
9. a group of people joined together in some work
12. to work together to get something done
13. to praise
14. a group of people chosen for a task

Flex Your Spelling Muscles

Writing

Imagine that you have just taken your first hot-air balloon flight. Write what you would tell your group about the trip. Were you <u>overcome</u> by the beauty of the land? Did you <u>conquer</u> your fear of being so high up in the air? Tell your group about your trip. Did anyone feel the same way?

Proofreading

The following weather report has ten mistakes. Use the proofreading marks to fix the mistakes. Then write the misspelled List Words correctly on the lines.

Proofreading Marks	
⬯	spelling mistake
≡	capital letter
⊙	add period

The forcast for the weekend does not look promising Extremely windy and wet comditions will exist for the next two days. a cold front moving in from the north will bring lots of moisture. Gale-force winds may contribut to air traffic delays A warning has been issued for sailors and balloonists to pospone their plans for the weekend. people may be concoled, however, by knowing that we foresey a warming trend by the middle of the week.

1. _____   4. _____

2. _____   5. _____

3. _____   6. _____

Now proofread what you wrote about your balloon trip. Fix any mistakes.

Go for the Goal

Take your Final Test. Then fill in your Scoreboard. Send your mistakes to the Word Locker.

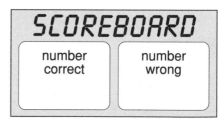

SCOREBOARD

number correct	number wrong

★ ★ ★ ★ ★ ★ ★ ★ ★ **All-Star Words** ★ ★ ★ ★ ★ ★ ★ ★ ★

postgame   connect   foresight   overdue   commence

Work with your partner to write definitions for each All-Star Word. Then match your definitions to those in your dictionary. How closely did your definitions match?

Prefixes sub, mid, bi, and tri

Warm Up

What kind of sport is motocross?

BMX

Most people think that **bicycles** are for traveling on land. To some bikers, though, bikes are for flying.

They call it BMX. The letters stand for Bicycle Motocross. A motocross is a race for motorcycles, but these racers **substitute** bicycles for motorcycles. A BMX race, however, is more than just a bike race. In the **triple**-point race, the action twists and turns through a special course. Riders pedal around steep, banked turns. They crank up and down hills. They jump over "whoop de doos." That's BMX talk for bumps in the track. A good whoop de doo can send a biker right into **midair**!

It sounds dangerous, doesn't it? It can be. That's why BMX riders must wear protective gear. The small, sturdy bikes are specially made for racing, also.

BMX races are always held under the watchful eyes of adults. That's to make sure that no one will overdo the whoop de doo.

Whether it's doing wheelies or midair double turns, BMX means action. It's a sport that takes practice and a lot of nerve!

Look at the boldfaced words in the selection. How many different prefixes can you find? How do the roots or root words change meaning when the prefixes are added?

On Your Mark

Take your Warm Up Test. Then check your spelling with the List Words on the next page.

The prefix **sub** usually means <u>under</u>, <u>below</u>, or <u>not quite</u>, as in <u>subside</u>.

The prefix **mid** means <u>in the middle part</u>, as in <u>midday</u>.

The prefix **bi** usually means <u>two</u>, as in <u>bisect</u>.

The prefix **tri** usually means <u>three</u>, as in <u>tripod</u>.

LIST WORDS

1. trio
2. subject
3. midwinter
4. submit
5. midnight
6. triangle
7. midstream
8. triple
9. middle
10. bicycles
11. bisect
12. subscribe
13. midair
14. substitute
15. subtract
16. biceps
17. tripod
18. midday
19. subdue
20. subside

Game Plan

Spelling Lineup

Write each List Word under the correct heading.

words with the prefix **tri**

1. _____
2. _____
3. _____
4. _____

words with the prefix **mid**

5. _____
6. _____
7. _____
8. _____
9. _____
10. _____

words with the prefix **bi**

11. _____
12. _____
13. _____

words with the prefix **sub**

14. _____
15. _____
16. _____
17. _____
18. _____
19. _____
20. _____

Definitions

Write a List Word to match each definition clue.

1. take away _____

2. three times as much _____

3. three-sided figure _____

4. arm muscles _____

5. 12:00 A.M. _____

6. middle of the winter _____

7. three people who play music _____

8. 12:00 P.M. _____

9. stand, frame on three legs _____

10. to make less strong or harsh _____

Word Parts

Make List Words by circling a prefix to add to each root or root word. Write the words on the lines.

1. mid / bi   sect _____

2. sub / pre   side _____

3. bi / sub   scribe _____

4. bi / mid   cycles _____

5. mis / sub   ject _____

6. sub / tri   stitute _____

7. ex / sub   mit _____

8. tri / mid   dle _____

9. re / mid   stream _____

10. tri / mid   air _____

Flex Your Spelling Muscles

Writing

Riding or racing on a bicycle, roller skates, or roller blades can be a wonderful experience. Recall an experience you have had on a bike or skates, or imagine what it must be like. Then write a poem about the experience and your feelings.

Proofreading

This article has twelve mistakes. Use the proofreading marks to fix the mistakes. Then write the misspelled List Words correctly on the lines.

Proofreading Marks
⬭ spelling mistake
⌄ add apostrophe
∧ add something

In 1896 bicickles filled Americas streets. People were quick to subskribe to the new craze and subbstitue horses with two-wheeled vehicles. Young people enjoyed midaye rides in the country while others rode to work. Orville and Wilbur Wrights bicycle shop was busy. However new ideas would subdoo the craze. The automobile would become the subjek of great interest and the Wright brothers would soon be flying in middair in an airplane.

Now proofread your poem about bicycling, skating, or rollerblading. Fix any mistakes.

1. _____
2. _____
3. _____
4. _____
5. _____
6. _____
7. _____

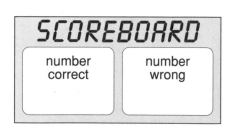

Go for the Goal

Take your Final Test. Then fill in your Scoreboard. Send your mistakes to the Word Locker.

SCOREBOARD

number correct	number wrong

★ ★ ★ ★ ★ ★ ★ ★ **All-Star Words** ★ ★ ★ ★ ★ ★ ★ ★

submarine　midway　bifocals　triplets　submerge

With a partner, write the All-Star Words on slips of paper, put them in an envelope, and take turns pantomiming and guessing the words.

Instant Replay • Lessons 13–17

Time Out

A prefix is added to a root or root word to make a new word.
Look again at the List Words. Think about what the prefixes mean.

Check Your Word Locker

Look at the words in your Word Locker. Write your
troublesome words from Lessons 13 through 17.

_____

_____

With a partner, write each prefix on a slip of paper. Take turns
drawing a prefix, giving its meaning, and writing a word with the prefix.

Lesson 13

Prefixes and Their Meanings

in = <u>not</u>, <u>into</u>, and <u>to cause to be</u>   **un** = <u>not</u>

dis = <u>not</u>, <u>away</u>, and <u>opposite of</u>   **trans** = <u>across</u> or <u>over</u>

List Words
transport
transfer
increase
discontinue
discovered
disturb
incomplete
unjust
unusual
insecure

Write the List Word that completes each sentence.

1. The office building had an _____ design.

2. Flatbed trucks are used to _____ heavy lumber.

3. With only eleven eggs, the dozen was _____.

4. Don't _____ her when she's concentrating.

5. If the medicine causes a rash, _____ its use.

6. Buy these on sale, before they _____ the price.

7. Let's encourage him, he's feeling somewhat _____.

8. Some students feel that certain rules are _____.

9. More ruins have been _____ in Peru.

10. Take bus No. 10 and then _____ to bus No. 20.

Prefixes and Their Meanings

en = <u>cause to be</u> or <u>make</u>, as in <u>encourage</u>   **im** = <u>not</u>, as in <u>impolite</u>; <u>more</u>, as in <u>improve</u>

mis = <u>bad</u> or <u>badly</u>, as in <u>misbehave</u>

List Words

encourage
impolite
improve
enable
improper
mistrust
misplaced
impossible
misbehave
immobile

Write a List Word that is an antonym for each word given.

1. obey _____   6. believe _____

2. ruin _____   7. prevent _____

3. likely _____   8. discourage _____

4. mannerly _____   9. movable _____

5. located _____   10. correct _____

Prefixes and Their Meanings

pre = <u>before</u>, as in <u>prepare</u>   **re** = <u>again</u> or <u>back</u>, as in <u>rearrange</u>

pro = <u>for</u>, <u>in favor of</u>, or <u>forward</u>,   **ex** = <u>out of</u> or <u>from</u>, as in <u>export</u>

as in <u>promote</u>

List Words

explain
returning
protest
exchange
preserve
exist
reappear
pretend
reward
promote

Write a List Word to complete each sentence.

1. If it doesn't fit, _____ it for another.

2. Well done! We will now _____ you to manager.

3. If you want to be seen again, _____.

4. If you live, you _____.

5. If he's coming back, he's _____.

6. If you like to make-believe, you _____.

7. If it's complicated, _____ it.

8. If you think it's unfair, you should _____.

9. If you want to save it, _____ it.

10. If he finds the dog, give him a _____.

Prefixes and Their Meanings

fore = in front of or before, as in forecast   **over** = above or too much, as in overcome

co, **com**, and **con** = with or together, as in contribute

List Words

postpone
overboard
forecast
conserve
consoled
compete
overcome
cooperate
foresee
committee

Write a List Word to match each definition.

1. over a ship's side _____

2. to put off until later _____

3. comforted _____

4. to enter into a contest _____

5. to predict the weather _____

6. to save _____

7. a group organized to support a cause _____

8. to get the best of _____

9. to work together for a common purpose _____

10. to know beforehand _____

Prefixes and Their Meanings

sub = under, as in subtract   **bi** = two, as in biceps

mid = in the middle part, as in midnight   **tri** = three, as in triangle

List Words

trio
triangle
subject
tripod
triple
midair
middle
midnight
bicycles
subtract

Write a List Word that belongs in each group.

1. duo, quartet, _____

2. single, double, _____

3. camera, film, _____

4. plane, cloud, _____

5. beginning, end, _____

6. course, class, _____

7. add, multiply, _____

8. square, circle, _____

9. cars, trains, _____

10. morning, noon, _____

List Words

transport
discontinue
unusual
insecure
improve
enable
mistrust
protest
preserve
reward
overcome
cooperate
foresee
triangle
midair

Add a prefix from the box to the root or root word and write a List Word on the line.

dis	re	tri	mid	pre
mis	over	pro	in	en
im	un	co	fore	trans

1. angle _____

2. secure _____

3. continue _____

4. able _____

5. test _____

6. serve _____

7. port _____

8. operate _____

9. trust _____

10. usual _____

11. see _____

12. prove _____

13. come _____

14. air _____

15. ward _____

Go for the Goal

Take your Final Replay Test. Then fill in your Scoreboard.
Send any misspelled words to your Word Locker.

SCOREBOARD

number correct	number wrong

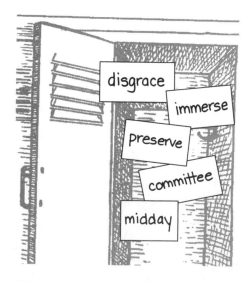

disgrace
immerse
preserve
committee
midday

Clean Out Your Word Locker

Look in your Word Locker. Cross out each word you spelled correctly on your Final Replay Test. Circle the words you're still having trouble with. Add the words you circled to your Spelling Notebook. What do you notice about the words? Watch for those words as you write.

Name _____

Compound Words

Warm Up

Does the word *junk* always mean something ugly?

Beautiful Junk

When we see junk floating on the water, we call it water pollution or the remains of a **shipwreck**. To those in the Far East, however, the sight of junk on the water in the **sunshine** leaves one **spellbound**!

A "junk" is a type of boat. Floating junks are a familiar sight on the rivers and coastal waters of China. In fact, these junks are among the finest sailing vessels in the world.

The first time you see a junk, you might think it is quite odd-looking. It has a flat bottom. Its sails are also unique. The sails look something like giant fans. Huge wooden ribs in the sailcloth make them difficult to hoist. They are easy to lower, however. Lowering the sails of a junk takes only one sailor. That can be important if a storm moves in quickly.

The name *junk* probably comes from the Chinese word *dijong*, which means "boat." The English pronunciation of this word sounds like "junk."

To the sailors who use them to make their living, these vessels are not junk at all. Sometimes a name can fool you!

 Say the boldfaced words in the selection. What do you notice about the way these words are formed?

On Your Mark

Take your Warm Up Test. Then check your spelling with the List Words on the next page.

77

Pep Talk

A compound word is made up of two or more words.

shoe + laces = shoelaces

Some compound words have a hyphen between the words.

forty + six = forty-six

self + control = self-control

A helpful rule: When dividing compound words into syllables, always divide the compound words between the words that form them.

finger • nail   blue • green

LIST WORDS

1. shoelaces
2. paperback
3. haircut
4. jellyfish
5. underwater
6. shipwreck
7. sunshine
8. fingernail
9. cornbread
10. snowdrift
11. hallway
12. kneecap
13. pancakes
14. rainbows
15. blue-green
16. self-control
17. spellbound
18. countdown
19. grapefruit
20. forty-six

Game Plan

Spelling Lineup

Write the List Words on the lines below. Make sure you remember to use hyphens correctly. Then circle the words that make each compound word.

1. _____
2. _____
3. _____
4. _____
5. _____
6. _____
7. _____
8. _____
9. _____
10. _____
11. _____
12. _____
13. _____
14. _____
15. _____
16. _____
17. _____
18. _____
19. _____
20. _____

Word Parts

One of the words that make up each compound word below is also
part of a List Word. Write the List Word.

1. battleship _____

2. kneepads _____

3. watermelon _____

4. cutworm _____

5. downstairs _____

6. raincoat _____

7. sunburn _____

8. himself _____

9. breadboard _____

10. shoemaker _____

11. driftwood _____

12. sixpenny _____

13. notepaper _____

14. fishtail _____

15. bluebird _____

16. cupcakes _____

17. nailhead _____

18. wayside _____

19. outbound _____

20. fruitwood _____

Missing Words

Write the List Word that completes each sentence.

1. The astronauts anxiously awaited the _____ before
the launch.

2. The ocean turns a beautiful shade of _____ in
the sunshine.

3. The _____ , also called the patella, is located at the
front of each leg.

4. It takes a lot of willpower and _____ to diet.

5. A _____ is rich in Vitamin C.

6. A hardcover book is usually more expensive than the
_____ version.

7. In areas where there is heavy snowfall in winter, it is not unusual for a car to

become stuck in a _____ .

8. I haven't been _____ by such an interesting novel
in months.

Flex Your Spelling Muscles

Writing

Have you ever seen or heard about a <u>shipwreck</u>? Recall what you saw or imagine what you might see. Describe or make up how the accident might have occurred. Add details using List Words.

Proofreading

The following story has thirteen mistakes. Fix the mistakes by using the proofreading marks. Write the misspelled List Words correctly on the lines.

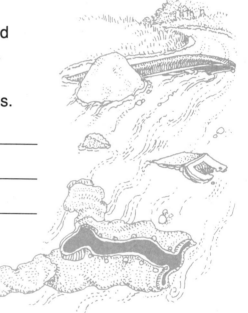

Proofreading Marks	
⬭	spelling mistake
∧	add something

My canoe trip began with a bang I watched the splash of the blugrean water make raynbows in the sunshine. When I saw the huge rock underwater it was too late. What a crash It was an instant shipwreck. My corn-bred paprebak book and jacket fell in the water. My kneekap was scraped and one fingernail was torn. What a mess However I still had enough food to make some pancakes.

1. _____   4. _____

2. _____   5. _____

3. _____   6. _____

Now proofread your description. Fix any mistakes.

Go for the Goal

Take your Final Test. Then fill in your Scoreboard. Send your mistakes to the Word Locker.

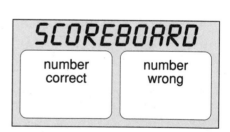

SCOREBOARD

number correct	number wrong

★ ★ ★ ★ ★ ★ ★ ★ **All-Star Words** ★ ★ ★ ★ ★ ★ ★ ★

undersea   broadcast   railway   self-preservation   sixty-four

Write a sentence for each All-Star word. Then erase just the first half or the second half of the compound word. Trade papers with a partner. Fill in the other half of each All-Star Word.

Syllables

Warm Up

In what kinds of races do dogs compete?

Mush!

It's the day of the big race. The competitors are outside in the snow, jumping about, barking, and howling. They're impatient to get started. Finally, the sleds and harnesses are set up. The teams of racers go wild. They can't wait to **perform**. It is a **challenge** for the trainers to hold them at the starting line. Then the **signal** is given. The teams, groups of muscle-bound dogs, pull together. They tow the sleds through the snow, sometimes reaching speeds of up to 20 miles an hour!

A **normal** sled-racing team consists of about seven dogs. The most intelligent and alert dog is the "lead." The second-in-line is the "point-dog." A **partner** to the lead dog, the point dog must know every **command**. It is this dog's job to take over if the lead dog has any trouble. The dogs directly in front of the sled are called "wheel dogs." The strongest ones, placed in the middle, are "team dogs."

The driver uses a few basic command words. "Gee" means "turn right," and "haw" means "left." Rarely does a driver shout the word *mush*. That's because too many people on the sidelines have a habit of yelling this word as the racing team passes. The lead dog could get confused. That could cause a **problem**. Though the sled drivers avoid saying "mush," they do use one form of the word. They call themselves "mushers."

Say the boldfaced words in the selection slowly. Notice how many separate sounds make up each word. Do the words have as many vowel sounds as they do syllables?

On Your Mark

Take your Warm Up Test. Then check your spelling with the List Words on the next page.

81

Words have as many syllables as they do vowel sounds. When you spell a word, think about how each syllable is spelled. When two consonants come between two vowels in a word, the word is usually divided between the two consonants: sug • gest   per • form

LIST WORDS

1. normal
2. problem
3. shallow
4. manners
5. symbol
6. perform
7. suggest
8. fossil
9. scanner
10. expert
11. collect
12. mental
13. forbid
14. signal
15. command
16. cassette
17. rescue
18. challenge
19. partner
20. support

Game Plan

Spelling Lineup

Write the List Words on the lines. Put a • between the two syllables in each word. Look in your dictionary if you need help.

1. _____
2. _____
3. _____
4. _____
5. _____
6. _____
7. _____
8. _____
9. _____
10. _____

11. _____
12. _____
13. _____
14. _____
15. _____
16. _____
17. _____
18. _____
19. _____
20. _____

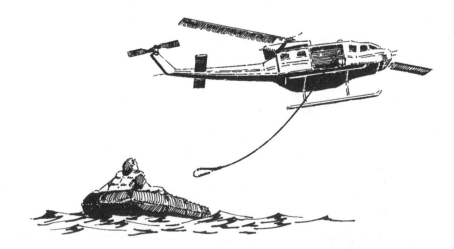

Synonyms and Antonyms

In the first column, write the List Word that is a synonym for each word. In the second column, write the List Word that is an antonym for each word.

Synonyms

1. ways _____

2. gather _____

3. tape _____

4. dare _____

5. save _____

6. act _____

7. help _____

8. order _____

Antonyms

1. solution _____

2. deep _____

3. allow _____

4. physical _____

5. distribute _____

6. beginner _____

7. enemy _____

8. unusual _____

Vocabulary

Write the List Word that best completes each sentence.

1. She practiced until she became

   an _____ pitcher.

2. He will _____ two

   piano pieces at the recital.

3. Exercise is good for both physical

   and _____ health.

4. I have recorded my favorite songs

   on this _____.

Alphabetical Order

Write each group of List Words in alphabetical order.

suggest symbol scanner signal shallow

1. _____

2. _____

3. _____

4. _____

5. _____

command challenge cassette fossil forbid

6. _____

7. _____

8. _____

9. _____

10. _____

Flex Your Spelling Muscles

Writing

Think about a personal <u>challenge</u> that you have experienced. What aspects of the experience made it seem difficult? Write a letter to a friend describing the challenge. Try to use as many List Words as you can.

Proofreading

The following article has fourteen mistakes. Use the proofreading marks to fix the mistakes. Write the misspelled List Words correctly on the lines.

Proofreading Marks	
⬭	spelling mistake
≡	capital letter
ꝑ	take out something

The great working sled dogs are a cymbol of the far far north. Some of of the breeds who meet the chalenge are the alaskan malamute, the eskimo dog, and the siberian husky. These dogs have often often worked with their human parner to rezcue people and and collect supplies. They respond well to every comand and and signal. It's wonderful to watch them purform.

1. _____   4. _____

2. _____   5. _____

3. _____   6. _____

Now proofread your letter. Fix any mistakes.

Go for the Goal

Take your Final Test. Then fill in your Scoreboard. Send your mistakes to the Word Locker.

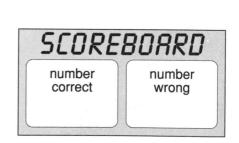

SCOREBOARD

number correct	number wrong

★ ★ ★ ★ ★ ★ ★ ★ ★ **All-Star Words** ★ ★ ★ ★ ★ ★ ★ ★ ★

guilty   advance   sherbet   adhere   mammoth

Write two definitions for each All-Star Word. Make one definition incorrect. Trade papers with a partner. Write the All-Star word next to the corrrect definition.

Name _____

Syllables

Warm Up

Why do people sneeze?

Achoo!

There have been a lot of stories about what a sneeze means. Ancient Greeks believed that a person couldn't sneeze if he or she was lying. A good sneeze was seen as a sign of honesty. What it really means is that the body is getting rid of harmful or irritating bacteria.

What exactly happens when we sneeze? For starters, we create a germ factory. A single sneeze contains over 85 million bacteria. The germs are scattered at a rate of 152 feet a second. If we **cover** our noses and mouths, however, we can reduce spreading germs.

One of the **major** causes of sneezing is hay fever. Hay fever sufferers often resort to medication to **reduce** the amount of sneezing. Hay fever is a type of allergy. People who suffer from hay fever are allergic to the pollen produced by grasses, trees, and weeds.

One of the most common pollen-producing weeds is ragweed, which grows all over the United States. Some communities have tried to come up with **answers** as to how to get rid of the sneeze-producing weed. However, because the wind can carry pollen great distances, removing ragweed has not been a **success** .

Say the boldfaced words in the selection. Each word has two syllables. How many vowel sounds do you hear in each syllable? Which group of letters form each syllable?

On Your Mark

Take your Warm Up Test. Then check your spelling with the List Words on the next page.

Pep Talk

A word has as many syllables as it has vowel sounds. When a single consonant comes between two vowels in a word, the word is usually divided after the consonant if the first vowel is short, and before the consonant if the vowel is long.

short first vowel: <u>mod</u> • <u>ern</u>
long first vowel: <u>ma</u> • <u>jor</u>

Divide a compound word into two words before dividing it into syllables.

compound word: <u>wat</u> • <u>er</u> <u>mel</u> • <u>on</u>

LIST WORDS

1. unit
2. plastic
3. helmet
4. mission
5. rubble
6. splendid
7. cover
8. dozen
9. closet
10. divide
11. major
12. modern
13. grandparents
14. watermelon
15. fingerprints
16. posture
17. silence
18. reduce
19. answers
20. success

Game Plan

Spelling Lineup

Write each List Word under the correct heading. Put a • between the syllables in each word. Use your dictionary for help.

more than one consonant
between two vowels

1. _____
2. _____
3. _____
4. _____
5. _____
6. _____
7. _____
8. _____
9. _____
10. _____
11. _____

single consonant
between two vowels

12. _____
13. _____
14. _____
15. _____
16. _____
17. _____
18. _____
19. _____
20. _____

Dictionary

Use the pronunciation key in the spelling dictionary and the accent marks to say each respelling below. Then write the List Word that goes with that sound-spelling.

1. (yo͞on´it) _____

2. (an´sərs) _____

3. (kuv´ər) _____

4. (mäd´ərn) _____

5. (mā´jər) _____

6. (sək ses´) _____

7. (kläz´ət) _____

8. (duz´ən) _____

9. (rub´əl) _____

10. (hel´mət) _____

11. (plas´tik) _____

12. (mish´en) _____

13. (splen´did) _____

14. (də vīd´) _____

15. (sī´ləns) _____

16. (rē do͞os´) _____

17. (päs´chər) _____

18. (grand´per´ ənts) _____

19. (fiŋ´gər prints) _____

20. (wôt´ər mel ən) _____

Comparing Words

Study the relationship between the first two underlined words. Then write a List Word that has the same relationship with the third underlined word.

1. <u>Two</u> is to <u>pair</u> as <u>twelve</u> is to _____.

2. <u>Little</u> is to <u>big</u> as <u>minor</u> is to _____

3. <u>Ask</u> is to <u>questions</u> as <u>tell</u> is to _____.

4. <u>Add</u> is to <u>subtract</u> as <u>multiply</u> is to _____.

5. <u>Lose</u> is to <u>win</u> as <u>failure</u> is to _____.

6. <u>Old</u> is to <u>new</u> as <u>ancient</u> is to _____.

Flex Your Spelling Muscles

Writing

Write a want ad for an inventor of a hay fever cure or some other possible inventions. Use as many of the List Words as possible in your ad.

Proofreading

This informational article has twelve mistakes. Use the proofreading marks to fix the mistakes. Write the misspelled List Words correctly on the lines.

Proofreading Marks
⬭ spelling mistake
∧ add something

Many people stillbelieve in superstitions their graneparents used tobelieve. Although they may not think superstitions have a place in the modern world, they do not want to redooce their chances of sukkess. Some willnot open an umbrella in the house, while others will not walk undera ladder. Some believe they will have a splended futureif they never break a mirror, while others insist there be only a dozan guests for dinner; thirteenwould be a majer problem.

1. _____   4. _____

2. _____   5. _____

3. _____   6. _____

Now proofread your ad. Fix any mistakes.

Go for the Goal

Take your Final Test. Then fill in your Scoreboard. Send your mistakes to the Word Locker.

SCOREBOARD

number correct	number wrong

★ ★ ★ ★ ★ ★ ★ ★ ★ **All-Star Words** ★ ★ ★ ★ ★ ★ ★ ★ ★

radar   granite   satin   bookkeeper   spoken

Write clues for the All-Star Words. Trade papers with a partner and write the All-Star Word for each clue. Then, compare your clues. Are they similar?

Syllables

Warm Up

What game did Alice play with the Queen of Hearts in
Alice in Wonderland?

Don't Lose Your Head!

If you had ever read Louis Carroll's *Alice in Wonderland*,
you'd certainly **remember** Alice playing croquet with the Queen
of Hearts. Poor Alice had to put up with droopy flamingos for
mallets and hedgehogs for croquet balls. No one waited for
turns, and all that quarrelling and fighting was enough to
make the **horrible** Queen cry, "Off with her head!"

In spite of Louis Carroll's wacky portrayal, croquet has
remained a **popular** outdoor lawn game. Although it's not
terribly **athletic**, croquet can be a lot of fun. To play, you need two
competing sides with one or two players each, a lawn, and, of
course, a croquet set. A set contains mallets, balls, and narrow
arches called wickets. The object is to knock your ball in a
course through the wickets and back again in as few
"strokes" as possible. Sound too easy? It can be quite a
challenge, especially when your opponent can knock
your ball out of the way when he or she chooses.

If you ever have the opportunity
to play, you'll find croquet is fun.
Oh, and don't worry, the chance
of losing your head while playing
is quite **unlikely**.

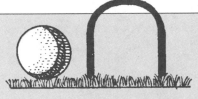

Say the boldfaced words in the selection. Say each
syllable slowly. What do you notice about the spelling of
each syllable?

On Your Mark

Take your Warm Up Test. Then check your spelling with the List Words
on the next page.

Pep Talk

When a vowel is sounded alone in a word, it usually forms a syllable by itself, as in an • i • mal. When a word ends in consonant **-le**, divide the word before that consonant, as in <u>ve</u> • <u>hi</u> • <u>cle</u>. These syllabication rules, and those you have already learned, will help you to spell and pronounce the List Words.

1. history
2. unlikely
3. remember
4. athletic
5. religion
6. citizen
7. animal
8. magazine
9. popular
10. artistic
11. yesterday
12. stadium
13. horrible
14. beautiful
15. serious
16. vehicle
17. opposite
18. impression
19. electric
20. chocolate

Game Plan

Spelling Lineup

Write the List Words on the lines. Put a • between the syllables, as in <u>hol</u> • <u>i</u> • <u>day</u>. Look in your dictionary if you need help.

1. _____
2. _____
3. _____
4. _____
5. _____
6. _____
7. _____
8. _____
9. _____
10. _____

11. _____
12. _____
13. _____
14. _____
15. _____
16. _____
17. _____
18. _____
19. _____
20. _____

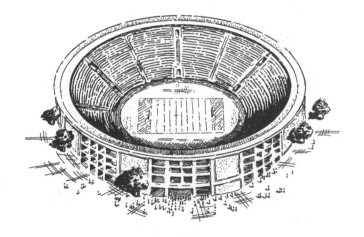

Word Parts

Write the List Word that contains the same root as each word given.

1. beauty _____

2. artist _____

3. day _____

4. electricity _____

5. like _____

6. impress _____

7. horror _____

8. oppose _____

Classification

Write the List Word that belongs in each group.

1. vanilla, strawberry, _____

2. voter, worker, _____

3. newspaper, book, _____

4. dog, cat, _____

5. car, truck, _____

6. strong, active, _____

7. gym, field, _____

Missing Syllables

Fill in the blanks with the missing syllable to form List Words.
Then write the words on the lines.

1. _____ • i • ous

_____

2. re • _____ • ber

_____

3. un • like • _____

_____

4. pop • _____ • lar

_____

5. _____ • co • late

_____

6. re • _____ • gion

_____

7. _____ • le • tic

_____

8. op • _____ • site

_____

9. mag • _____ • zine

_____

10. ve • hi • _____

_____

11. _____ • to • ry

_____

12. _____ • ri • ble

_____

Flex Your Spelling Muscles

Writing

A croquet tournament could be an enjoyable event. Create a poster for an upcoming tournament. Use attention-getting headlines and copy to get people to come. Use as many List Words as you can.

Proofreading

This poem has ten mistakes. Use the proofreading marks to fix the mistakes. Then write the misspelled List Words correctly on the lines.

Isn't ita beautiful sight
Watching baseball played at night
It's quite artistik in a way
To play a game at the end of day.
Canyou feel the electrik air
And the chill that grips your chair
All the players look so seriouse.
And the spectators look so curioes.
Another game is about tostart.
Remember baseball is an art.

Now proofread your poster. Fix any mistakes.

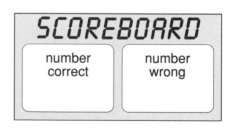

Proofreading Marks	
⬭	spelling mistake
∧	add something

1. _____

2. _____

3. _____

4. _____

Go for the Goal

Take your Final Test. Then fill in your Scoreboard. Send your mistakes to the Word Locker.

SCOREBOARD

number correct	number wrong

★ ★ ★ ★ ★ ★ ★ ★ ★ **All-Star Words** ★ ★ ★ ★ ★ ★ ★ ★ ★

electronic   hamburger   medical   mantle   manager

Decide with a partner how each All-Star Word should be divided into syllables. Trade papers with another team and correct their syllabication, if necessary, using your dictionary. Then write the word in a sentence.

Possessives and Contractions

Warm Up

Do you think there's a plant that can "swallow" houses?

Kudzu

More than a hundred years ago, a plant known as the kudzu plant, was **Japan's** gift to the United States. It was a good gift—one that the farmers really liked. The plant's vines kept topsoil in place. It was also used as cattle feed. All in all, the sturdy plant was welcomed. Then things got a little out of hand.

It seems that the plant liked the Southern climate, especially **Georgia's** warmth. It began to grow and grow. People couldn't control it. It spread across thousands of acres, covering **farmers'** land. The strong vines pulled down telephone wires. In fact, **they've** completely covered forests. It doesn't seem possible but the vines even "swallowed" whole houses! The plant that was once called "Japan's miracle vine" soon became known as "the plant that ate the South!"

Some people feared that kudzu would one day take over the world. Even one of **America's** presidents expressed concern. Jimmy Carter, former President of the United States and Georgia's best known farmer, told people to come down to Georgia, where they would give people all the kudzu they wanted—for free!

 Look back at the boldfaced words in the selection. Each word is spelled with an apostrophe. How are the words alike? How are they different?

On Your Mark

Take your Warm Up Test. Then check your spelling with the List Words on the next page.

LIST WORDS

1. Georgia's
2. class's
3. America's
4. Canada's
5. who'll
6. champion's
7. Japan's
8. women's
9. parent's
10. farmers'
11. college's
12. you'd
13. Kansas'
14. Montreal's
15. governor's
16. senator's
17. mayor's
18. Mexico's
19. they've
20. Texas'

Game Plan

Spelling Lineup

Write each List Word under the correct heading.

Singular Possessives

1. _____
2. _____
3. _____
4. _____
5. _____
6. _____
7. _____
8. _____
9. _____
10. _____
11. _____
12. _____
13. _____
14. _____
15. _____

Plural Possessives

16. _____
17. _____

Contractions

18. _____
19. _____
20. _____

Write the two List Words that add only an apostrophe to form their singular possessives.

21. _____
22. _____

Vocabulary

Write the List Word that best completes each sentence.

1. The team of the college is the _____ team.

2. The stories of the women are the _____ stories.

3. Who will means the same as the contraction _____.

4. The office of the mayor is the _____ office.

5. They have means the same as the contraction _____.

6. The market of the farmers is the _____ market.

7. You would means the same as the contraction _____.

8. The child of the parent is the _____ child.

9. The trophy of the champion is the _____ trophy.

10. The drawings of the class are the _____ drawings.

11. The vote of the senator is the _____ vote.

12. The mansion of the governor is the _____ mansion.

13. The hockey players of Canada are _____ hockey players.

14. The flag of Texas is

_____ flag.

15. The citizens of Japan

are _____ citizens.

Alphabetical Order

Write in alphabetical order the List Words that name cities, states, and countries.

1. _____   5. _____

2. _____   6. _____

3. _____   7. _____

4. _____   8. _____

Flex Your Spelling Muscles

Writing

Do you think a plant could ever become overgrown and take over the world? Write an imaginary news article reporting about what happens. Use your imagination to write an exciting story.

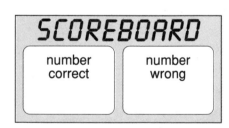

Proofreading

This movie review has ten words that need apostrophes. Use the proofreading mark to fix the mistakes. Write the List Words correctly on the lines.

Proofreading Mark
⌄ add apostrophe

Americas film industry has surpassed even Japans epic monster movies with "Youd Better Hide." The movie features Canadas best actor, a womens softball team, and Georgias beautiful scenery. The giant, green, and hairy monster wipes out farms, towns, and forests even though the governors orders try to stop it. Wholl save the people from this menace? Theyve kept the ending a guarded secret, but some of you might guess that someone turns out to be a hero. A parents advisory is in effect on this film.

Now proofread your news article about the overgrown plant. Fix any mistakes.

1. _____
2. _____
3. _____
4. _____
5. _____
6. _____
7. _____
8. _____
9. _____
10. _____

Go for the Goal

Take your Final Test. Then fill in your Scoreboard. Send your mistakes to the Word Locker.

SCOREBOARD

number correct	number wrong

★ ★ ★ ★ ★ ★ ★ ★ ★ **All-Star Words** ★ ★ ★ ★ ★ ★ ★ ★ ★

you've   she'll   Oregon's   geese's   ladies'

Work with a partner to write a separate paragraph about the same subject using the All Star Words. One partner uses the long form of each All-Star Word (for example: you have; of Oregon). The other uses the All-Star Words. Trade papers and compare the versions.

Instant Replay • Lessons 19–23

Time Out

Look again at how compound words are formed, how words are divided into syllables, and how an apostrophe is used to write possessive nouns and contractions.

Check Your Word Locker

Look at the words in your Word Locker. Write your troublesome words from Lessons 19 through 23.

_____

_____

Practice writing your troublesome words with a partner. Take turns dividing the words into syllables as the other spells them aloud.

Lesson 19

Compound words are made by combining two words, as in <u>snowdrift</u> (<u>snow</u> + <u>drift</u>) and <u>self-control</u> (<u>self</u> + <u>control</u>).

List Words
paperback
haircut
jellyfish
shipwreck
sunshine
snowdrift
hallway
blue-green
countdown
forty-six

Two words in each sentence form a compound List Word. Circle the words and write the compound word on the line.

1. He will cut my hair.   _____

2. The paper is at the back door. _____

3. Show me the way to the hall.   _____

4. Six waiters served forty people. _____

5. Tiny fish swam in the jelly jar. _____

6. Snow will drift in the wind.   _____

7. The sun will shine tomorrow.   _____

8. The house is blue and green.   _____

9. A storm could wreck the ship.   _____

10. Lie down and count to ten.   _____

When two consonants come between two vowels in a word, the word is usually divided between the two consonants, as in <u>scan</u> • <u>ner</u>.

List Words

problem
perform
suggest
expert
collect
forbid
cassette
challenge
partner
support

Combine two syllables from the box to make a List Word. Write the words.

sug	form	for	gest	col	sette	sup	lenge	prob	ner
chal	lem	part	pert	per	lect	cas	port	ex	bid

1. _____   6. _____

2. _____   7. _____

3. _____   8. _____

4. _____   9. _____

5. _____   10. _____

When a consonant comes between two vowels in a word, the word is divided after the consonant if the first vowel is short, as in <u>cov</u> • <u>er</u>. It is divided before the consonant if the vowel is long, as in <u>re</u> • <u>duce</u>.

List Words

helmet
rubble
cover
closet
major
watermelon
fingerprints
silence
answers
success

Write a List Word to match each clue.

1. result of hard work

_____

2. left by an earthquake

_____

3. opposite of minor

_____

4. fun to eat

_____

5. opposite of noise

_____

6. protects your head

_____

7. useful to a detective

_____

8. where you put your coat

_____

9. result of questions

_____

10. top of a jar

_____

A vowel can form its own syllable in a word, as in pop • u • lar. When **le** precedes the last consonant in a word, the word is divided before that consonant, as in hor • ri • ble.

List Words
history
unlikely
remember
athletic
animal
artistic
yesterday
horrible
vehicle
chocolate

Write the List Words that fit each description.

1. What the people do who recall the day before today:

_____   _____

2. What a jogger who paints is:

_____ and _____

3. What a mean bear is: a

_____   _____

4. What the story of cocoa is:

_____   _____

5. What a car with wings is: an

_____   _____

To form a singular or plural possessive, add **'s**; to form the possessive of a plural noun ending in **s**, just add '. Use an apostrophe to stand for letters left out of contractions.

List Words
America's
Canada's
who'll
Japan's
women's
farmers'
you'd
Kansas'
senator's
Mexico's

Write a List Word to complete each sentence.

1. The people of Japan are _____ people.

2. The farms of Kansas are _____ farms.

3. <u>Who will</u> can also be written _____.

4. The flag of America is _____ flag.

5. The vote of the senator is the _____ vote.

6. The food of Mexico is _____ food.

7. <u>You would</u> can also be written _____.

8. The ideas of women are _____ ideas.

9. The rivers of Canada are _____ rivers.

10. The crops of the farmers are the _____ crops.

List Words

Write the List Words in alphabetical order. Then use the letters in the shaded box to solve the riddle.

haircut
jellyfish
shipwreck
forbid
helmet
rubble
major
vehicle
women's
history

1. _ _ _ _ _ _

2. _ _ _ _ _ _ _

3. _ _ _ _ _ _

4. _ _ _ _ _ _ _

5. _ _ _ _ _ _ _ _

6. _ _ _ _

7. _ _ _ _ _

8. _ _ _ _ _ _

9. _ _ _ _ _ _

10. _ _ _ _ _ _

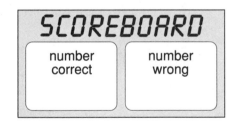

Riddle: Why didn't the orange make it across the road?

Answer: It ran _____ _____ _____.

Go for the Goal

Take your Final Replay Test. Then fill in your Scoreboard.
Send any misspelled words to your Word Locker.

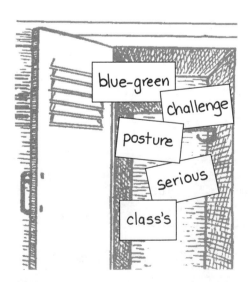

blue-green
challenge
posture
serious
class's

Clean Out Your Word Locker

Look in your Word Locker. Cross out each word you spelled correctly on your Final Replay Test. Circle the words you're still having trouble with. Add the words you circled to your Spelling Notebook. What do you notice about the words? Watch for those words as you write.

Suffixes er, est, or, and ist

Warm Up

What is the loudest sound you've ever heard?

Now Hear This!

How loud is loud? Maybe loudness is a matter of time and place. An alarm clock seems **louder** when it goes off in the morning than it would if it went off during a party. Some sounds are much louder than others.

A **scientist** measures sound in *decibels*. One decibel is the **slightest** sound a human ear can hear. The sound of a vacuum cleaner measures about 70 decibels of sound. Do you prefer the sound of a carpet **sweeper**, which registers low on the decibel scale? A jackhammer scores 100 decibels. A fire-engine siren and a jet engine each reach about 130 decibels. The sound of a rocket blastoff is even **greater** than that. It's about 195 decibels. That's loud enough to hurt your ears. Fortunately, each rocket **inspector** wears special headphones!

There have been a few sounds that are too loud to measure. Over a hundred years ago, a volcano in the South Seas exploded. The mountain was called Krakatoa. When this great mountain blew its top, the sound was heard three-thousand miles away. That's the same as if a person in New York heard a sound that came from California! It is believed that the sound of the volcano was the loudest and **scariest** sound ever made in human history.

Say the boldfaced words in the selection. What suffixes do you find at the end of the words? How are they different?

On Your Mark

Take your Warm Up Test. Then check your spelling with the List Words on the next page.

Pep Talk

A suffix is a word part added to the end of a word. The suffixes **er**, **or**, and **ist** mean <u>something or someone who does something</u>.

sweeper   director   tourist

The suffixes **er** and **est** can also be used with adjectives to show comparison. The suffix **er** means <u>more</u>, as in <u>greater</u>. The suffix **est** means <u>most</u>, as in <u>busiest</u>.

LIST WORDS

1. louder
2. scientist
3. warrior
4. director
5. scariest
6. slightest
7. prisoner
8. sweeper
9. novelist
10. greater
11. emperor
12. busiest
13. tourist
14. drearier
15. interpreter
16. hungrier
17. counselor
18. inspector
19. cartoonist
20. vocalist

Game Plan

Spelling Lineup
Write each List Word under the correct heading.

suffix shows comparison

1. _____
2. _____
3. _____
4. _____
5. _____
6. _____
7. _____

suffix means <u>something or someone who does something</u>

8. _____
9. _____
10. _____
11. _____
12. _____
13. _____
14. _____
15. _____
16. _____
17. _____
18. _____
19. _____
20. _____

Synonyms

Write a List Word that is a synonym for each word given.

1. artist _____

2. advisor _____

3. singer _____

4. smallest _____

5. ruler _____

6. captive _____

7. duller _____

8. noisier _____

9. translator _____

10. fighter _____

11. writer _____

12. traveler _____

13. larger _____

14. most frightening _____

Definitions

Write a List Word to match each definition clue. Then use the numbered letters to solve the riddle. Copy each numbered letter onto the line with the same number.

1. person who directs __ __ __ __ __ __ __ __
                                  15   1 7

2. one who sweeps __ __ __ __ __ __ __
                             3 8   16

3. most active __ __ __ __ __ __ __
                              13 14

4. detective __ __ __ __ __ __ __ __ __
                                            2

5. least __ __ __ __ __ __ __ __
            9   12   5

6. more needy of food __ __ __ __ __ __ __ __
                                6   10 11

7. expert in science __ __ __ __ __ __ __ __ __
                                 4   17

Riddle: Why did the girl sleep with a ruler next to her bed?

Answer: She wanted __ __ __ __ __ __ __ __ __ __ __ __
                         1 2   3 4 5   6 7 8   9 2 10 11

__ __ __ __ __ __ __ __ !
14 12 13 14 9 15 16 17

Flex Your Spelling Muscles

Writing

You're a reporter for a TV news program. Your assignment is to interview a <u>scientist</u> who has just witnessed a volcano erupt. Write a list of questions that you would ask.

Proofreading

This movie review has ten mistakes. Use the proofreading marks to fix the mistakes. Write the misspelled List Words correctly on the lines.

Proofreading Marks

⬭   spelling mistake

≡   capital letter

⊙   add period

Rush to your nearest theater to see "Volcano II." The direckter, B. J williams, has created the skaryest movie this reviewer has ever seen. The sound effects are lowdor and the special effects are grator than those in "volcano I." The scene with the lost tourest will have you biting your nails I don't have the slittist doubt that you will find "Volcano II" explosive entertainment. I give it five stars.

1. _____

2. _____

3. _____

4. _____

5. _____

6. _____

Volcano II

They saved the townspeople in Volcano I. Can they do it again?

Now proofread your interview questions. Fix any mistakes.

Go for the Goal

Take your Final Test. Then fill in your Scoreboard. Send your mistakes to the Word Locker.

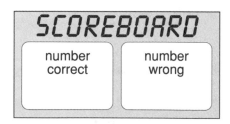

SCOREBOARD

number correct	number wrong

★ ★ ★ ★ ★ ★ ★ ★ ★ **All-Star Words** ★ ★ ★ ★ ★ ★ ★ ★ ★

realist   aviator   fanciest   harsher   voter

Create a crossword puzzle that contains the All-Star Words. Write clues and draw a blank grid. Trade puzzles with a partner. Can you solve each other's puzzle?

Suffixes <u>ee</u>, <u>eer</u>, <u>ent</u>, and <u>ant</u>

LESSON
26

Warm Up

What do you think happens at the world's biggest puppet parade?

Puppet Parade

For most of the year, this Vermont valley is quiet. Then on one weekend, 10,000 people stream in for the biggest puppet pageant in the world. Puppets as tall as 20 feet amble through the open-air theater, star in plays, and mingle freely with the guests.

These puppets are part of the **excellent** Bread and Puppet Theater. The puppeteers believe theater should be "as basic as bread." The people who work at the theater, both as volunteers and employees, write scripts, create sets, and handle the giant puppets.

Unlike hand-held puppets, it takes five or six people to work these papier-mâché giants. They practically require a puppet **engineer**! A chief **puppeteer** holds the stick that supports the puppet's body. Each **assistant** controls an arm or a leg.

The two-day event begins with a parade and circus. There are sideshows with giant animals. You'll see immense witches, Trojan horses, and even fire-breathing dragons! Later in the evening is the pageant. It's usually a play with an orchestra and hundreds of singing people. Of course, there are also the unforgettable puppets. Whether you're a **resident** or a tourist, if you are lucky enough to see this spectacle, you'll never forget it.

Say the boldfaced words in the selection. How many suffixes can you find? What pattern do you see in the way the words end?

On Your Mark

Take your Warm Up Test. Then check your spelling with the List Words on the next page.

The suffixes **ee**, **eer**, **ent**, and **ant** usually mean <u>one who</u>:
   <u>absentee</u> means <u>one who is absent</u>
   <u>mountaineer</u> means <u>one who climbs mountains</u>
   <u>resident</u> means <u>one who resides</u>
   <u>assistant</u> means <u>one who assists</u>

The suffixes **ent** and **ant** can also mean
<u>that which</u>:
   <u>excellent</u> means <u>that which excels</u>
   <u>abundant</u> means <u>that which abounds</u>

LIST WORDS

1. employee
2. mountaineer
3. absentee
4. excellent
5. reliant
6. volunteer
7. puppeteer
8. engineer
9. payee
10. participant
11. resident
12. pleasant
13. competent
14. violent
15. assistant
16. accountant
17. repellent
18. abundant
19. dominant
20. applicant

Game Plan

Spelling Lineup

Write each List Word under the correct heading.

words with the suffix **ee**

1. _____
2. _____
3. _____

words with the suffix **ent**

4. _____
5. _____
6. _____
7. _____
8. _____

words with the suffix **eer**

9. _____
10. _____
11. _____
12. _____

words with the suffix **ant**

13. _____
14. _____
15. _____
16. _____
17. _____
18. _____
19. _____
20. _____

Word Parts

Create List Words by circling a suffix to add to each root or root word.
Write the words on the lines.

1. mountain   eer _____
            or

2. reli   ent _____
      ant

3. puppet   or _____
         eer

4. particip   ant _____
           ent

5. engin   or _____
        eer

6. viol   ent _____
      ant

7. repell   ent _____
        ant

8. abund   ent _____
        ant

Definitions

Write the List Word that matches each definition.

1. one who is absent _____

2. one who is employed _____

3. one who is paid _____

4. one who assists _____

5. that which is pleasing _____

6. that which dominates _____

7. one who works for free _____

8. one who does accounting _____

9. one who is capable _____

10. one who resides _____

11. that which excels _____

12. one who applies _____

Flex Your Spelling Muscles

Writing

What job would you like to perform in a Puppet Theater? Write a letter convincing the theater manager that you should be hired for that job. Tell why you would make an <u>excellent</u> <u>employee</u>. List any <u>volunteer</u> experience.

Proofreading

These how-to directions for putting on a puppet show have eleven mistakes. Use the proofreading marks to fix the mistakes. Write the misspelled List Words correctly on the lines.

Proofreading Marks
⬯ spelling mistake
ℓ take out something
/ make small letter

Follow these simple directions to be an exsellant pupetier.

1. Turn a finger into a puppet in an instant. Put the top of an Acorn on a a finger to make a hat. Draw a face.
2. An old sock can make a puppet, too. Just sew on some button eyes and and yarn hair.
3. Ask a supermarket Manager or imploye to give you you a carton. Cut out an opening to make a puppet theater.
4. Ask a friend to to vulintear to be an asistent backstage.

1. _____   4. _____

2. _____   5. _____

3. _____

Now proofread your letter. Fix any mistakes.

Go for the Goal

Take your Final Test. Then fill in your Scoreboard. Send your mistakes to the Word Locker.

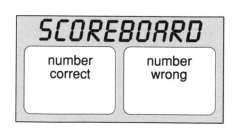

SCOREBOARD

number correct	number wrong

★ ★ ★ ★ ★ ★ ★ ★ ★ **All-Star Words** ★ ★ ★ ★ ★ ★ ★ ★ ★

appointee   auctioneer   absorbent   occupant   persistent

Divide the words between you and a partner. Write both a real and a fake definition for each of your words. Trade papers. Write your partner's words and circle the meanings that you think are correct.

Suffixes _ward_, _en_, _ize_, _ful_, and _ness_

Warm Up

What animal is the shyest animal in the ocean?

Shy Guy

Despite its fearsome appearance, the octopus is a lonely creature. It's the sea's most bashful inhabitant. The octopus's **shyness** shows. When an octopus spies another animal—even another octopus—it hides. It might slip under a large rock or a sunken ship. When frightened, it will squirt a cloud of ink to confuse its enemy. Afterward, it will scoot away to some dark place. It might even **darken** or lighten its color, or camouflage itself, so that no one will **recognize** it.

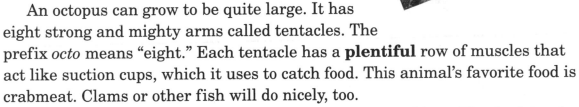

The octopus is a very delightful animal to watch, if you can get a glimpse of one! An octopus swims by drawing water into its body and expelling it, which moves the octopus **backward**.

An octopus can grow to be quite large. It has eight strong and mighty arms called tentacles. The prefix _octo_ means "eight." Each tentacle has a **plentiful** row of muscles that act like suction cups, which it uses to catch food. This animal's favorite food is crabmeat. Clams or other fish will do nicely, too.

What should you do if an octopus grabs you? Just tickle it. That's right. An octopus hates to be tickled. It will take off before you can count to octo.

 Say the boldfaced words in the selection. Notice how each word ends. Can you find the five different suffixes? How are they different?

On Your Mark

Take your Warm Up Test. Then check your spelling with the List Words on the next page.

Pep Talk

The suffix **ward** means <u>in the direction of</u>. The suffix **en** means <u>made of</u> or <u>to make</u>. The suffix **ize** means <u>to make</u> or <u>to become</u>. The suffix **ful** means <u>full of</u>. The suffix **ness** means <u>quality</u> or <u>condition of being</u>.

LIST WORDS

1. shyness
2. peaceful
3. forward
4. cheerful
5. afterward
6. darken
7. plentiful
8. loudness
9. backward
10. tighten
11. politeness
12. sharpen
13. memorize
14. wonderful
15. recognize
16. shameful
17. friendliness
18. alphabetize
19. delightful
20. wilderness

Game Plan

Spelling Lineup

Write each List Word under the correct heading.

words with the suffix **ward**

1. _____
2. _____
3. _____

words with the suffix **en**

4. _____
5. _____
6. _____

words with the suffix **ize**

7. _____
8. _____
9. _____

words with the suffix **ful**

10. _____
11. _____
12. _____
13. _____
14. _____
15. _____

words with the suffix **ness**

16. _____
17. _____
18. _____
19. _____
20. _____

Alphabetical Order

Number each column of words to show their alphabetical order. Write the words in alphabetical order on the lines.

___ afterward   1. _____

___ delightful   2. _____

___ darken   3. _____

___ alphabetize   4. _____

___ cheerful   5. _____

___ loudness   6. _____

___ peaceful   7. _____

___ politeness   8. _____

___ memorize   9. _____

___ plentiful   10. _____

___ tighten   1. _____

___ shameful   2. _____

___ shyness   3. _____

___ wonderful   4. _____

___ sharpen   5. _____

___ backward   6. _____

___ wilderness   7. _____

___ forward   8. _____

___ recognize   9. _____

___ friendliness   10. _____

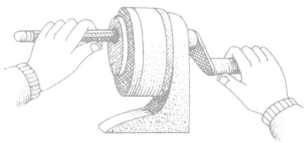

Synonyms and Antonyms

In the first column, write the List Word that is a synonym for each word given. In the second column, write the List Word that is an antonym for each word given. There are two List Words that are antonyms for one of the words.

Synonyms		**Antonyms**	
1. calm	_____	1. loosen	_____
2. later	_____	2. rudeness	_____
3. disgraceful	_____	3. sad	_____
4. shade	_____	4. softness	_____
5. identify	_____	5. lacking	_____
6. bashfulness	_____	6. forward	_____
7. ahead	_____	7. terrible	_____

Flex Your Spelling Muscles

Writing

Make yourself the superhero of a <u>delightful</u> tall tale that you write. It takes place in the sea. Exaggerate the <u>wonderful</u> feats that you accomplish. Don't forget to create one or more <u>shameful</u> villains.

Proofreading

This TV listing has ten mistakes. Use the proofreading marks to fix the mistakes. Write the misspelled List Words correctly on the lines.

Proofreading Marks
⌒ spelling mistake
/ make a small letter

8:00 Channel 89: Wonnarfull Willderniss
The Host, Shirley Chin, takes a delitefull underwater tour suitable for the whole family. Time-lapse Photography lets the viewer see some unusual sights. You can actually see how a Shark's reserve teeth move foreword to replace lost ones. You'll see a starfish lose an arm, and afterword, grow a new one. You'll watch camouflage in action as Fish darkin their color to blend in with their background.

1. _____   4. _____

2. _____   5. _____

3. _____   6. _____

Now proofread your tall tale. Fix any mistakes.

Go for the Goal

Take your Final Test. Then fill in your Scoreboard. Send your mistakes to the Word Locker.

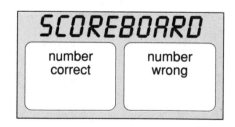

SCOREBOARD
number correct	number wrong

★ ★ ★ ★ ★ ★ ★ ★ **All-Star Words** ★ ★ ★ ★ ★ ★ ★ ★ ★

shoreward   thicken   minimize   resourceful   stiffness

Work with a partner to list at least one synonym or antonym for each All-Star Word. Use a thesaurus or dictionary to check your work. How many additional synonyms or antonyms can you find?

Name _____

Suffixes hood, ship, ment, able, and ible

Warm Up

How can you sky dive without jumping from a plane?

Flyaway

Sky divers have long known the thrill of free falling. Now even people who have never been in a plane can get to know what it's like. A new invention, called the "Flyaway," makes it **possible**.

Flyaway is really a high, padded room. Its floor is made of a DC-4 jet engine covered with a safety grate. The engineer generates winds of up to 120 miles per hour. While the wind is blowing upward, you jump in. The wind takes care of keeping you off the floor. You just have to remember to keep your chin up, keep your knees bent, your back arched, and your arms spread. This has all the **excitement** of sky diving, but there's less **likelihood** of an accident.

People who fly in Flyaways are called *aeronauts*. Aeronauts must wear crash helmets, kneepads, ear plugs, goggles, and a special jump suit. They may not be **comfortable**, but they're well protected.

A regular sky dive from a plane lasts only about 60 seconds. The average Flyaway dive lasts five minutes. Even a sky diver who has won the world **championship** has never stayed aloft that long!

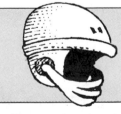

Say the boldfaced words in the selection. Notice how each word ends. Can you find the five different suffixes? How are they different?

On Your Mark

Take your Warm Up Test. Then check your spelling with the List Words on the next page.

Pep Talk

The suffixes **hood**, **ship**, and **ment** mean the state or condition of being, as in motherhood, leadership, and statement.

The suffixes **able** and **ible** usually mean able to be or full of, as in agreeable and sensible.

LIST WORDS

1. possible
2. excitement
3. terrible
4. neighborhood
5. leadership
6. membership
7. equipment
8. profitable
9. ownership
10. falsehood
11. championship
12. statement
13. sensible
14. motherhood
15. dependable
16. comfortable
17. visible
18. likelihood
19. agreeable
20. durable

Game Plan

Spelling Lineup
Write each List Word under the correct heading. Circle the suffix in each word.

words with the suffixes
able or **ible**

1. _____
2. _____
3. _____
4. _____
5. _____
6. _____
7. _____
8. _____
9. _____

words with the suffixes
hood, **ship**, or **ment**

10. _____
11. _____
12. _____
13. _____
14. _____
15. _____
16. _____
17. _____
18. _____
19. _____
20. _____

Word Parts

Write the List Word that contains the same root as each word given.

1. neighborly _____

2. equipped _____

3. sensitive _____

4. champions _____

5. dependent _____

6. motherly _____

7. terror _____

8. duration _____

9. comforting _____

10. leading _____

11. profits _____

12. members _____

13. impossible _____

14. excitable _____

15. owners _____

16. likely _____

17. agreement _____

18. stated _____

19. visual _____

20. falsely _____

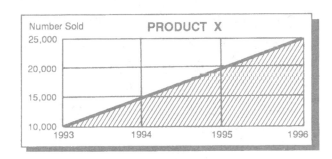

Vocabulary

Write the List Word that matches each definition.

1. lasting in spite of hard wear _____

2. able to be seen _____

3. fearful; frightful; dreadful _____

4. legal right of possession _____

5. the position of being the one who guides or shows the way _____

6. showing financial gain _____

7. at ease in body or mind _____

8. having or showing sound judgment _____

9. able to happen or be done _____

10. the state of belonging to a group or organization _____

Flex Your Spelling Muscles

Writing

Imagine that you have just opened an amusement park that has a "Flyaway." Create a poster that convinces people to visit your park. Make them think that they will find loads of <u>excitement</u> there.

Proofreading

This campaign poster has eleven mistakes. Use the proofreading marks to fix the mistakes. Write the misspelled List Words correctly on the lines.

Proofreading Marks
⬭ spelling mistake
∧ add something

Jane Smith for Town Council!
Jane Smith willprovide the leadaship that our neaghberhod needs. She is dependible reliable and sensibul. You can trust her judgment. You will reconise an obvious difference in the way our schools parks, and libraries are run. Vote for Smith andmake change possible. Join the exsitement!

1. _____   4. _____

2. _____   5. _____

3. _____   6. _____

Now proofread your poster. Fix any mistakes.

Go for the Goal

Take your Final Test. Then fill in your Scoreboard. Send your mistakes to the Word Locker.

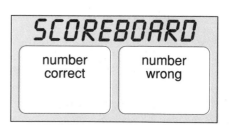

SCOREBOARD

number correct	number wrong

★ ★ ★ ★ ★ ★ ★ ★ ★ **All-Star Words** ★ ★ ★ ★ ★ ★ ★ ★ ★

brotherhood   scholarship   settlement   washable   legible

Write one question for each All-Star Word. Then trade questions with a partner and write the answers. Be sure to include the All-Star Words in your responses.

Suffixes ion, tion, ance, ence, ity, and ive

Warm Up

What would it be like to be blind and go skiing?

Brave and Bold

Two girls stand on a snowy slope. One is the ski instructor. The other is a student. The instructor clearly describes the conditions.

"The surface is powdery, and it's a wide, easy slope with no bumps. Try to get up some speed. Go for it!"

When the student reaches the bottom of the hill, she beams with **confidence** because of her demonstration of **independence**.

These two skiers are part of a group called BOLD. The letters stand for "Blind Outdoor Leisure Development." The young instructor is a volunteer. It's her job to help her blind student experience the thrill of skiing.

Guides are carefully trained to give each **direction** clearly. They also ski closely to the students, paying attention to every bump and hill. They know the **importance** of winning a student's trust.

BOLD was begun by Jean Eymere, whose friends taught him to ski after he became blind. He realized that it would help blind people to be less **selective** about sports in which they participate.

What is a blind skier's **opinion** of this activity? One said it all. "I can do something I never thought was possible and feel an **equality** with other ski enthusiasts."

Look back at the boldfaced words in the selection. Notice how each word ends. How are the suffixes alike? How are they different?

On Your Mark

Take your Warm Up Test. Then check your spelling with the List Words on the next page.

Pep Talk

The suffixes **ion** and **tion** usually mean <u>the act of</u> or <u>the condition of being</u>, as in <u>protection</u>. The suffixes **ance**, **ence**, and **ity** usually mean <u>quality</u> or <u>fact of being</u>, as in <u>importance</u> and <u>equality</u>. The suffix **ive** usually means <u>likely</u> or <u>having to do with</u>, as in <u>selective</u>.

LIST WORDS

1. direction
2. protection
3. allowance
4. equality
5. selective
6. population
7. massive
8. captive
9. humidity
10. vacation
11. importance
12. opinion
13. election
14. humanity
15. objection
16. confidence
17. imitation
18. attendance
19. originality
20. independence

Game Plan

Spelling Lineup

Write each List Word under the correct heading.

words with the suffix ive

1. _____
2. _____
3. _____

words with the suffix tion or ion

4. _____
5. _____
6. _____
7. _____
8. _____
9. _____
10. _____
11. _____

words with the suffix ence

12. _____
13. _____

words with the suffix ity

14. _____
15. _____
16. _____
17. _____

words with the suffix ance

18. _____
19. _____
20. _____

Vocabulary

Write the List Word that best completes each sentence.

1. People who are not dependent show _____.

2. People who select carefully are _____.

3. People who direct give a lot of _____.

4. A person who objects has an _____.

5. People who protect give _____.

6. If you confide, or trust, in people, you

    have _____ in them.

7. People who elect officials vote in an _____.

8. A person who opines or thinks, has an _____.

9. People who are equal have _____.

10. People are humans and are part of _____.

11. People call objects that are large and have a lot

     of mass _____.

12. People who are original and creative show _____.

13. People vacate, or leave, home to go on a _____.

14. What people notice about humid, or damp, weather

     is the _____.

15. A person who imitates shows an _____.

Hidden Words

Each word below is hidden in a List Word. Write the List Words.

1. cap _____

2. pop _____

3. pin _____

4. mass _____

5. allow _____

6. depend _____

7. port _____

8. tend _____

9. man _____

10. den _____

Flex Your Spelling Muscles

Writing

Imagine that you are a BOLD instructor trying to convince a student to try skiing. Write the dialogue that might take place between you and that student. What could you say to help that student gain the <u>confidence</u> to try?

Proofreading

The plaque honoring BOLD and its instructors has ten mistakes. Use the proofreading marks to fix the mistakes. Write the misspelled List Words correctly on the lines.

Proofreading Marks	
⬭	spelling mistake
≡	capital letter

The Mayor's Helping Huminaty Award

Under the direcshion of jean Eymere, BOLD instructors have helped further the indipendanse and confidance of others. our citizens recognize the importince of one person reaching out to help another, and, therefore, the city of lynbrook awards this plaque. In our upinion, BOLD instructors are heroes.

mayor Juanita Daquino

---

1. _____

2. _____

3. _____

4. _____

5. _____

6. _____

Now proofread your dialogue. Fix any mistakes.

Go for the Goal

Take your Final Test. Then fill in your Scoreboard. Send your mistakes to the Word Locker.

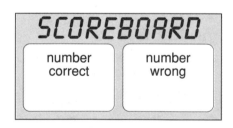

SCOREBOARD

number correct	number wrong

★ ★ ★ ★ ★ ★ ★ ★ **All-Star Words** ★ ★ ★ ★ ★ ★ ★ ★

adoption   violence   acceptance   sincerity   relative

Write one definition for each All-Star Word. Work with a partner to check your work using your dictionary. Circle the suffix in each All-Star Word and place a star next to any words that have more than one meaning.

Instant Replay Lessons 25–29

Time Out

Look again at the suffixes and their meanings. How do suffixes change the meaning of words?

Check your Word Locker

Look at the words in your Word Locker. Write your most troublesome words from Lessons 25 through 29.

_____

_____

Practice writing your troublesome words with a partner. Circle the suffix in each word and tell its meaning.

Lesson 25

The suffixes **er**, **or**, and **ist** mean <u>something or someone who does something</u>, as in <u>counselor</u>. The suffixes **er** and **est** can be added to adjectives to show comparison, as in <u>hungrier</u>.

List Words
louder
warrior
scariest
slightest
novelist
greater
emperor
busiest
inspector
vocalist

Write the two List Words that fit each description.

1. A better writer of books:

   the _____ _____

2. The detective with the most to do:

   the _____ _____

3. The most frightening fighter:

   the _____ _____

4. The least important king:

   the _____ _____

5. The singer who can be heard far away:

   the _____ _____

121

Suffixes and Their Meanings

ee, **eer**, **ent**, and **ant** = one who   **ent** and **ant** = that which

List Words

employee
mountaineer
engineer
participant
resident
competent
assistant
accountant
repellent
abundant

Write the List Word that relates best to the word given.

1. helper _____

2. apartment _____

3. conductor _____

4. Alps _____

5. member _____

6. bugs _____

7. capable _____

8. plenty _____

9. numbers _____

10. worker _____

Suffixes and Their Meanings

ward = in the direction of   **ize** = to make, become   **ful** = full of
en = made of or to make   **ness** = quality, condition of being

List Words

peaceful
forward
cheerful
afterward
darken
loudness
politeness
sharpen
memorize
recognize

Write a List Word to complete each sentence.

1. You _____ a friend you know.

2. You _____ a pencil.

3. You _____ a poem to recite it.

4. You are _____ when you sleep.

5. You arrive _____ when you're late.

6. You are _____ when you're happy.

7. You hold your ears because of the _____.

8. You _____ the room to go to sleep.

9. Your _____ shows you have manners.

10. You move _____ to get ahead.

Suffixes and Their Meanings

hood, ship, ment = the state or condition of being   **able** and **ible** = able to be, or full of

List Words

possible
excitement
membership
equipment
statement
sensible
dependable
comfortable
likelihood
durable

Write five List Words that could be found listed between each set of the dictionary guide words given. Write the words in alphabetical order.

agreeable/falsehood

1. _____
2. _____
3. _____
4. _____
5. _____

leadership/terrible

6. _____
7. _____
8. _____
9. _____
10. _____

Suffixes and Their Meanings

ion and **tion** = the act of, the condition of being   **ive** = likely, having to do with
ance, **ence**, and **ity** = quality, fact of being

List Words

direction
allowance
equality
selective
population
objection
confidence
imitation
attendance
originality

Write the List Word that means the same as the word given.

1. creativity _____

2. particular _____

3. inhabitants _____

4. way _____

5. payment _____

6. fairness _____

7. disapproval _____

8. fake _____

9. sureness _____

10. presence _____

List Words

warrior
scariest
slightest
engineer
resident
competent
forward
politeness
recognize
possible
equipment
durable
direction
allowance
selective

Write a List Word to answer each clue.

1. having ability; capable _____

2. quality of having good manners _____

3. lasting _____

4. choosy _____

5. one who runs a locomotive _____

6. soldier _____

7. one who lives in a place _____

8. able to happen _____

9. at the front _____

10. things needed for some special purpose _____

11. to know something you've seen before _____

12. a sum of money _____

13. the most frightening _____

14. a point to move toward _____

15. the smallest _____

Go for the Goal

Take your Final Replay Test. Then fill in your Scoreboard.
Send any misspelled words to your Word Locker.

SCOREBOARD

number correct	number wrong

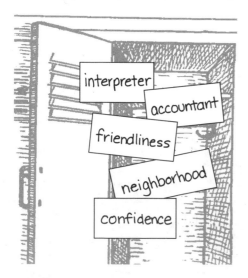

interpreter
accountant
friendliness
neighborhood
confidence

Clean Out Your Word Locker

Look in your Word Locker. Cross out each word you spelled
correctly on your Final Replay Test. Circle the words you're
still having trouble with. Add the words you circled to your
Spelling Notebook. What do you notice about the words?
Watch for those words as you write.

Doubling Final Consonants; Adding Suffixes to Words Ending in <u>e</u>

Warm Up

How do you think shredded wheat was invented?

Champion of Breakfasts

Good things often happen in the **strangest** ways. Especially if you have an active **imagination**. So it was with one of America's favorite breakfast cereals—**shredded** wheat.

It all began in 1892. Henry Perkey was having breakfast in a hotel. A fellow guest was enjoying an unusual dish—boiled corn in milk. That gave Perkey an idea. His first thought was of producing a cereal made from dried corn. He looked around for a machine to press the corn into flakes. Instead, he found a wheat presser—one that could turn the wheat grain into thin strips. The strips could easily be made into biscuits. Even though he had **planned** to use corn, he **decided** to switch to shredded wheat. Soon he was **shipping** his new food far and wide.

As business grew, he opened a huge bakery so he could produce the biscuits himself. The bakery was equipped with several large ovens and, of course, the wheat shredder.

Moral: Even if your plan doesn't work out, you can still succeed by altering your plans and working hard.

Look back at the boldfaced words in the selection. Find the root word in each boldfaced word. What happened to the root word when the suffixes were added?

On Your Mark

Take your Warm Up Test. Then check your spelling with the List Words on the next page.

Pep Talk

Some short-vowel words end in a single consonant. If you add a suffix beginning with a vowel to them, first double the final consonant:

spin + ing = spinning; shred + ed = shredded.

Some words end in a silent **e**. If you add a suffix beginning with a vowel to them, first drop the silent **e**:

imagine + ation = imagination.

LIST WORDS

1. shredded
2. planned
3. pledged
4. throbbing
5. spinning
6. hoping
7. decided
8. strangest
9. shipping
10. usable
11. valuable
12. pleasing
13. scraping
14. skidded
15. imagination
16. introducing
17. disapproved
18. unforgivable
19. persuaded
20. amazing

Game Plan

Spelling Lineup

Add a suffix, or a prefix and a suffix, to each word given to make a List Word.

1. amaze
   _____

2. strange
   _____

3. forgive
   _____

4. approve
   _____

5. decide
   _____

6. imagine
   _____

7. introduce
   _____

8. persuade
   _____

9. please
   _____

10. use
    _____

11. value
    _____

12. skid
    _____

13. plan
    _____

14. ship
    _____

15. hope
    _____

16. throb
    _____

17. spin
    _____

18. shred
    _____

19. scrape
    _____

20. pledge
    _____

Synonyms

Write a List Word that is a synonym for each word given.

1. oddest _____

2. mailing _____

3. promised _____

4. wishing _____

5. astonishing _____

6. beating _____

7. presenting _____

8. slipped _____

Classification

Write the List Word that belongs in each group.

1. chopped, cut, _____

2. disfavored, rejected, _____

3. dreams, fantasy, _____

4. useful, fit, _____

5. turning, twisting, _____

6. set up, arranged, _____

Syllables

Write each List Word under the correct number of syllables.

1 syllable

1. _____

2. _____

2 syllables

3. _____

4. _____

5. _____

6. _____

7. _____

8. _____

9. _____

10. _____

11. _____

3 syllables

12. _____

13. _____

14. _____

15. _____

16. _____

4 syllables

17. _____

18. _____

5 syllables

19. _____

20. _____

Flex Your Spelling Muscles

Writing

What's the one food whose pleasing taste you can't get out of your mind? Write a letter to the producer or farmer of that food. Be sure to tell why you decided to write and why you picked that particular food.

Proofreading

This menu from a diner for animals has ten mistakes. Use the proofreading marks to correct them. Write the List Words correctly on the lines.

Proofreading Marks
⬭ spelling mistake
⌄ add apostrophe

Fido's Diner: Weve always pledgd to give your pets the finest service. We're hopping that youll become a regular customer.

Fishburgers Your cat will love the amazeing taste of shreaded fish. $3.95

Chicken Biscuit Pie Why dont you consider introduseing your pet to Fidos newest creation? $2.75

Table Scraps Fido uses her imagennation and leftovers to create this homestyle treat. $2.50

1. _____
2. _____
3. _____
4. _____
5. _____
6. _____

Now proofread your letter. Fix any mistakes.

Go for the Goal

Take your Final Test. Then fill in your Scoreboard. Send your mistakes to the Word Locker.

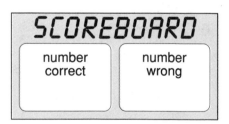

SCOREBOARD

number correct	number wrong

★ ★ ★ ★ ★ ★ ★ ★ ★ **All-Star Words** ★ ★ ★ ★ ★ ★ ★ ★ ★

strutted   rotting   observation   advanced   forgivable

Write a sentence for each word. Instead of writing the All-Star Word, write the root word. Trade papers with a partner, add the suffixes, and write each All-Star Word.

Adding Suffixes to Words Ending in y

LESSON

32

Warm Up

Why do we say "hello" when we answer the telephone?

Hello!

Alexander Graham Bell invented the telephone, but the greeting "hello" was coined by another inventor, Thomas Alva Edison.

Because the telephone was invented as a tool for **supplying** communication for businesses, the proper word had to be found. It needed to be a greeting as well as a phrase that would let people know someone was on the line. Mr. Bell chose the greeting "ahoy!" but it was not accepted by telephone users. The phrase, "What is wanted?" was later suggested. But this greeting wasn't popular either. Mr. Edison felt that a shorter and **friendlier** greeting was needed. He insisted on "hello." And since it was Mr. Edison who set up the first telephone offices, dozens of telephone operators found themselves **obeying** his orders.

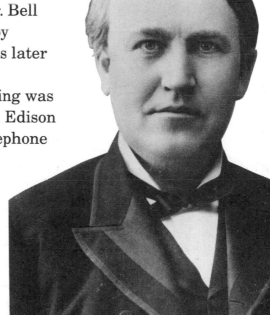

Actually, the word *hello* comes from a nineteenth century British expression, "hullo," that was used as an expression of surprise, as in "Hullo, what have we here?" Mr. Edison changed "hullo" to "hello." As a result, every day, millions of people find themselves **cheerily** answering "hello" when the telephone rings.

Look back at the boldfaced words in the selection. Say the root word for each boldfaced word. What happens to root words that end in **y** when a suffix is added?

On Your Mark

Take your Warm Up Test. Then check your spelling with the List Words on the next page.

Pep Talk

When a final **y** follows a consonant, change the **y** to **i** before adding a suffix, <u>unless</u> the suffix is **ing**.

worr<u>y</u>   worr<u>i</u>ed   worr<u>i</u>er   worr<u>y</u>ing

When a final y follows a vowel, just add a suffix.

ob<u>ey</u>   ob<u>ey</u>ed   ob<u>ey</u>ing

LIST WORDS

1. envied
2. worrying
3. friendlier
4. obeying
5. sunniest
6. readily
7. stickiest
8. hastily
9. heavier
10. noisily
11. sturdier
12. greedily
13. sleepiest
14. merrily
15. occupying
16. supplying
17. classified
18. magnifying
19. angrily
20. cheerily

Game Plan

Spelling Lineup

Write each List Word below its root word. Circle the suffix in each List Word.

1. greedy

_____

2. sunny

_____

3. noisy

_____

4. envy

_____

5. cheery

_____

6. sticky

_____

7. magnify

_____

8. hasty

_____

9. friendly

_____

10. sleepy

11. angry

_____

12. sturdy

_____

13. ready

_____

14. worry

_____

15. supply

_____

16. heavy

_____

17. merry

_____

18. obey

_____

19. classify

_____

20. occupy

Word Parts

Write the List Word that contains the same root as each word given.

1. hastiest _____

2. obeyed _____

3. merrier _____

4. magnifier _____

5. greediest _____

6. sunnier _____

7. readying _____

8. cheerier _____

9. stickier _____

10. friendliest _____

11. sleepily _____

12. angriest _____

13. sturdily _____

14. envying _____

15. worrier _____

16. supplied _____

17. heavily _____

18. classifying _____

19. occupied _____

20. noisier _____

Missing Words

Write a List Word to complete each sentence.

1. Job seekers read the _____ ads in the newspaper.

2. If he hadn't been in a hurry and written the word so

_____, he may not have made the spelling mistake.

3. A _____ glass will allow you to see small objects

in more detail.

4. As a political candidate, her ambition and honesty were

_____ by others.

5. This plant will thrive in not just any sunny spot, but the

_____ spot in the room.

6. She has a very easy filing system, so she can

_____ provide you with

the information.

Flex Your Spelling Muscles

Writing

Write a newspaper advertisement for a telephone that might have appeared in 1876, the year Bell completed his famous invention. Try to convince people that they will be envied by others if they purchase one.

Proofreading

The following conversation has ten mistakes. Use the proofreading marks to correct them. Write the misspelled List Words correctly on the lines.

Proofreading Marks	
⬭	spelling mistake
≡	capital letter
⋀	add something

"I have the stickyest problem," said Uncle edward. "It's been ocuepying my mind for days. I need to name the number 1 followed by one hundred zeros."

"stop worreying," his nine-year-old nephew milton said cheeryly. "Why not call it a googol"

"That's it," said Uncle Edward merriely. "Thanks for souplying me with that perfectly wonderful word."

1. _____   4. _____

2. _____   5. _____

3. _____   6. _____

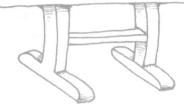

Now proofread your advertisement. Fix any mistakes.

Go for the Goal

Take your Final Test. Then fill in your Scoreboard. Send your mistakes to the Word Locker.

SCOREBOARD

number correct	number wrong

★ ★ ★ ★ ★ ★ ★ ★ ★ **All-Star Words** ★ ★ ★ ★ ★ ★ ★ ★ ★

modified   levying   surveying   tardiest   displayed

Create a newspaper headline for each All-Star Word, leaving a blank line where that word belongs. Feel free to use your dictionary. Trade papers with a partner. Can you fill in the missing words?

Plurals of Words Ending in y

Warm Up

How can sails be used to power spacecraft?

Sailing Into the Future

For **centuries**, adventurers have used sails to propel their ships to unknown lands. In the future, sails may also be the tools to drive crafts on **journeys** through space.

Scientists from several **countries** are working on the idea. They believe that they can propel a spacecraft by reflecting sunlight off of a giant sail. The proposed spacecraft would be launched by rocket into the earth's orbit. There, high above the atmosphere, a huge sail would be unfurled. The sail is meant to catch the gentle push of photons from the sun. Scientists estimate that the effect of these photons of sunlight on the sail is very slight. But in the vacuum of outer space, it will be enough to propel a ship without a drop of fuel. Scientists will most likely visit Mars first, as they are eager to unlock the many **mysteries** of this red planet.

Perhaps someday soon, great sailing ships will once again travel the trade routes. But this time it could be between Earth, Mars, and beyond.

Look back at the boldfaced words in the selection. How are the words alike? What do you notice about their spelling?

On Your Mark

Take your Warm Up Test. Then check your spelling with the List Words on the next page.

Pep Talk

Follow these rules to write the plural form of words ending in **y**:

• If the letter before the **y** is a consonant, change the **y** to **i** and add **es**, as in <u>victories</u>.

• If the letter before the **y** is a vowel, just add **s**, as in <u>relays</u>.

LIST WORDS

1. centuries
2. groceries
3. countries
4. journeys
5. families
6. delays
7. kidneys
8. decoys
9. bakeries
10. libraries
11. cavities
12. cranberries
13. mysteries
14. activities
15. injuries
16. apologies
17. secretaries
18. authorities
19. victories
20. relays

Game Plan

Spelling Lineup

Write each List Word below its singular form.

1. victory
   _____

2. apology
   _____

3. country
   _____

4. grocery
   _____

5. mystery
   _____

6. relay
   _____

7. century
   _____

8. family
   _____

9. library
   _____

10. cavity
    _____

11. injury
    _____

12. journey
    _____

13. delay
    _____

14. authority
    _____

15. activity
    _____

16. decoy
    _____

17. secretary
    _____

18. kidney
    _____

19. cranberry
    _____

20. bakery
    _____

Classification

Write the List Word that belongs in each group.

1. years, decades, _____

2. cities, states, _____

3. wins, triumphs, _____

4. parents, children, _____

5. schools, museums, _____

6. hearts, lungs, _____

7. scrapes, cuts, _____

8. secrets, clues, _____

9. lures, traps, _____

10. pastries, breads, _____

11. clerks, typists, _____

12. regrets, sorrows, _____

13. trips, travels, _____

14. apples, grapes, _____

Definitions

Write a List Word to match each definition clue. Then use the numbered letters to solve the riddle. Copy each numbered letter on the line with the same number.

1. long waits __ __ __ __ __ __
7

2. decay in teeth __ __ __ __ __ __ __ __
3

3. actions, movements __ __ __ __ __ __ __ __ __ __
4

4. groups of related people __ __ __ __ __ __ __ __
6

5. sorry! sorry! sorry! __ __ __ __ __ __ __ __ __
510

6. those who enforce laws __ __ __ __ __ __ __ __ __ __ __
911 2

7. kinds of races __ __ __ __ __ __
1

8. food and supplies __ __ __ __ __ __ __ __ __
8

Riddle: What do you need before you can have a dozen bakeries?

Answer: __ __ __ __ __ __ __ __ __ __ __
1 2 3 4 5 6 7 8 9 10 11

Flex Your Spelling Muscles

Writing

Imagine that you are vacationing on Mars several <u>centuries</u> in the future. What will life be like? Will there be towns with <u>bakeries</u>, schools, and <u>libraries</u>? Write a postcard home describing your visit.

Proofreading

This futuristic advertisement has ten mistakes. Use the proofreading marks to correct them. Write the misspelled List Words correctly on the lines.

Proofreading Marks	
⬭	spelling mistake
≡	capital letter
⋀	add something

Acme Spacewagons: Go on journies to Jupiter mars, or pluto in comfort in an Acme Spacewagon with an autopilot feature. All of our spacewagons come with airbags to prevent injories during rough landings. Available in shocking pink electric blue, and ruby red. Remember, Acme has been making the best spacewagons for centarys. Our engineers are the best authoratys in the galaxy on space travel. Please accept our apollogyes in advance for any delayes in shipping.

1. _____

2. _____

3. _____

4. _____

5. _____

6. _____

Now proofread your postcard from Mars. Fix any mistakes.

Go for the Goal

Take your Final Test. Then fill in your Scoreboard. Send your mistakes to the Word Locker.

SCOREBOARD

number correct	number wrong

★ ★ ★ ★ ★ ★ ★ ★ ★ **All-Star Words** ★ ★ ★ ★ ★ ★ ★ ★ ★

attorneys   missionaries   alloys   walkways   theories

Write a sentence for each All-Star Word. Trade papers with a partner. Take turns telling how the plural form of the word is formed.

Irregular Plurals

Warm Up

Which animal is related to the deer and has a baby called a calf?

Moose on the Loose

Meet the moose family. There's papa moose. He's called a bull. Mama moose goes by the name of cow. Their children are **calves**. This family is the same **species** as the deer family, but moose are much larger. A bull moose can weigh as much as 1,800 pounds.

Moose are mammals of many talents. They can dive into water from an 18-foot high cliff. They can easily swim for 12 miles. On land, they can run at 35 miles an hour. Moose feed on twigs, leaves, pondweeds, and water lilies. They do not feed on **trout** or **salmon**. Each adult eats about 40 to 60 pounds of food a day.

Perhaps the most fascinating feature of the moose is the antlers. Only bulls have them. On some bulls, their crowns measure six feet across. Every winter, the male sheds its antlers. He grows them back each spring. Male moose use their antlers to attract females. Occasionally, two males will fight each other by ramming their antlers together. They rarely hurt each other this way, but there is a danger of their antlers locking.

The female has a unique characteristic, too. It's her strange call, which has been described as a bellowing a-e-i-o-u! When a male hears the call, he'll follow the sound for miles.

Look back at the boldfaced words in the selection. Say the singular form of each plural word. What do you notice about the spelling of some plural forms of words?

On Your Mark

Take your Warm Up Test. Then check your spelling with the List Words on the next page.

LIST WORDS

1. moose
2. trout
3. salmon
4. wolves
5. calves
6. halves
7. scarves
8. broccoli
9. spaghetti
10. radios
11. tomatoes
12. sheriffs
13. cuffs
14. potatoes
15. beliefs
16. chiefs
17. volcanoes
18. species
19. igloos
20. tornadoes

Game Plan

Spelling Lineup

Write each List Word below its singular form.

1. volcano

2. spaghetti

3. tomato

4. tornado

5. broccoli

6. sheriff

7. potato

8. salmon

9. belief

10. scarf

11. cuff

12. trout

13. calf

14. chief

15. radio

16. igloo

17. half

18. wolf

19. species

20. moose

Classification

Write the List Words that belong under each heading.

vegetables/fruits	mammals	fish
1. _____	4. _____	7. _____
2. _____	5. _____	8. _____
3. _____	6. _____	

Comparing Words

Study the relationship between the first two underlined words. Then write a List Word that has the same relationship with the third underlined word.

1. Reading is to books as listening is to _____.

2. Peas are to vegetables as _____ is to pasta.

3. Wood is to pencils as ice is to _____.

4. Snow is to blizzards as wind is to _____.

5. Kings are to countries as _____ are to tribes.

6. Belts are to waists as _____ are to necks.

7. Nickels are to dimes as _____

   are to wholes.

8. Water is to hoses as lava is to _____.

9. Collars are to necks as

   _____ are to wrists.

Missing Words

Write a List Word to complete each sentence.

1. Scientists study many _____ of insects.

2. _____ are in charge of law and order in a county.

3. _____ often look and act like their cousins, dogs.

4. People differ in opinion because they don't share the same _____.

5. For dinner, I had a big plate of _____ and meatballs.

Flex Your Spelling Muscles

Writing

You are lost deep in the woods in <u>moose</u> country. What will you eat? Who will you contact for help, and how? Write how you would survive until you are rescued.

Proofreading

This naturalist's journal entry has ten mistakes. Use the proofreading marks to correct them. Write the misspelled List Words correctly on the lines.

Proofreading Marks	
⌐	spelling mistake
≡	capital letter
∧	add something

ellesmere Island, the Arctic, may 19:

A pack of wolfs attacked a herd of musk oxen. The adults formed a circle around the calfes. The pack killed aweak musk ox. The pack leaders, who are like the chieves of their group, ate first. People hold mistaken believes about wolves. They feel that they are a threat to the survival of the musk ox. Actually, they help this speeces by weeding out the sick animals. we put transmitter radioes on three musk oxen so that we can keep track of them.

1. _____
2. _____
3. _____
4. _____
5. _____
6. _____

Now proofread your survival plan. Fix any mistakes.

Go for the Goal

Take your Final Test. Then fill in your Scoreboard. Send your mistakes to the Word Locker.

SCOREBOARD

number correct	number wrong

★ ★ ★ ★ ★ ★ ★ ★ ★ **All-Star Words** ★ ★ ★ ★ ★ ★ ★ ★ ★

loaves   torpedoes   thieves   piccolos   pliers

Create a simple sketch for each All-Star Word. If you need help, use your dictionary. Trade drawings with a partner. Can you write the word that matches each picture clue?

Hurdle Words

Warm Up

What is the world's most famous portrait?

Lisa's Smiles

In the 1500s, there lived a woman named Lisa del Giocondo. Her home was Florence, Italy, where her husband was a merchant. Today, this woman is **famous** the world over. The name she is known by is Mona Lisa. That's Italian for "my Lisa."

The Mona Lisa may be the world's most well-known portrait. It took the artist, Leonardo da Vinci, five years to finish painting it. What makes this **familiar** picture so special?

Most people agree that it's Lisa's smile that sets her apart. There are interesting things about her time that you can learn by looking at this portrait, too. For one thing, Lisa has no eyebrows. In her day, it was the **fashion** for women to shave them off. Also, the portrait shows her from the waist up. Until Leonardo did this work, no artist had **chosen** to portray more than the subject's head in a portrait.

Scientists have X-rayed through the top layer of the painting. They have found some **surprises** beneath the paint. There are three **separate** portraits of Lisa under the final one. All of them were painted by Leonardo.

Look back at the boldfaced words in the selection. Say the words. Do you notice anything unusual about their spelling?

On Your Mark

Take your Warm Up Test. Then check your spelling with the List Words on the next page.

Pep Talk

Some words don't follow the usual spelling rules. The best way to become familiar with these unexpected spellings is to practice using them as often as you can.

yolk   stomach   forfeit

LIST WORDS

1. yolk
2. familiar
3. separate
4. weird
5. February
6. column
7. surprises
8. islands
9. misspelled
10. ballet
11. fashion
12. stomach
13. recommend
14. famous
15. prairie
16. forfeit
17. wisdom
18. chosen
19. weather
20. punctuation

Game Plan

Spelling Lineup

Write each List Word below the unexpected spelling it contains.

1. fei

_____

2. liar

_____

3. rpr

_____

4. ach

_____

5. wea

_____

6. wei

_____

7. punc

_____

8. lk

_____

9. mous

_____

10. sspe

_____

11. ose

_____

12. par

_____

13. umn

_____

14. wis

_____

15. let

_____

16. rair

_____

17. isl

_____

18. hion

_____

19. mmen

_____

20. bru

_____

Classification

Write the List Word that belongs in each group.

1. usual, known, _____

2. style, clothes, _____

3. continents, peninsulas, _____

4. shell, egg, _____

5. well-known, popular, _____

6. give up, lose, _____

7. picked, selected, _____

8. strange, unusual, _____

9. waltz, tap-dance, _____

10. snow, heat, _____

11. learning, knowledge, _____

12. misread, miscopied, _____

13. divide, split, _____

14. row, list, _____

15. suggest, offer, _____

16. March, April, _____

17. plain, plateau, _____

18. heart, liver, _____

19. wonders, marvels, _____

20. period, comma, _____

Vocabulary

A thesaurus is a reference book that contains synonyms and antonyms.
Write a List Word to match the synonyms and antonyms given.

1. **synonyms**: intelligence, knowledge
   antonyms: unintelligence, stupidity

   _____

2. **synonyms**: suggest, advise
   antonyms: warn against, caution

   _____

3. **synonyms**: disconnect, part
   antonyms: unite, come together

   _____

4. **synonyms**: prominent, renowned
   antonyms: unknown, obscure

   _____

5. **synonyms**: uncommon, odd
   antonyms: common, typical

   _____

6. **synonyms**: selected, preferred
   antonyms: rejected, excluded

   _____

Flex Your Spelling Muscles

Writing

Write a dialogue that might have taken place between Lisa del Giocondo and Leonardo da Vinci. Did they talk about everyday subjects such as the <u>weather</u>? Did they know that one day they would both be <u>famous</u>?

Proofreading

This biography has ten mistakes. Use the proofreading marks to fix the mistakes. Write the misspelled List Words correctly on the lines.

Proofreading Marks	
⬯	spelling mistake
⊙	add period
ℛ	take out something

Leonardo da Vinci (1452–1519) created several notebooks filled with with suprizes At first glance, the writing looks wierd. That's because Leonardo had had chozen to write backwards. His famus books can only be read with a mirror. Many of the drawings in the notebooks will look famillar to us today They include sketches of a parachute and a simple helicopter. Despite his great wizdum, his designs for flying machines are not workable. They all have flapping wings that require too much effort to be effective.

1. _____   4. _____

2. _____   5. _____

3. _____   6. _____

Now proofread your dialogue. Fix any mistakes.

Go for the Goal

Take your Final Test. Then fill in your Scoreboard. Send your mistakes to the Word Locker.

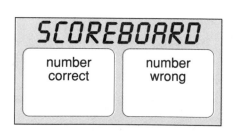

★ ★ ★ ★ ★ ★ ★ ★ ★   **All-Star Words**   ★ ★ ★ ★ ★ ★ ★ ★ ★

eerie   seize   orchid   conscience   basically

Create an exclamatory sentence using each word. Then erase a few letters of each All-Star Word. Trade sentences with a partner and fill in the missing letters.

Name _____

Instant Replay • Lessons 31–35

Time Out

Look again at how words are spelled when suffixes are added to words that end in **e** or **y,** how plurals are formed, and hurdle words.

Check Your Word Locker

Look at the words in your Word Locker. Write your most troublesome words from Lessons 31 through 35.

_____

_____

Practice writing your troublesome words with a partner. Underline the letters that change when adding a suffix or when forming the plural of the word.

Lesson 31

Before adding a suffix to a word, sometimes you need to double the final consonant, as in <u>planned</u>, or drop the final **e**, as in <u>amazing</u>.

List Words
planned
spinning
hoping
decided
strangest
usable
valuable
pleasing
imagination
amazing

Add a suffix to each root word to form a List Word. Write the word on the line.

1. decide + ed _____

2. plan + ed _____

3. amaze + ing _____

4. imagine + ation _____

5. please + ing _____

6. value + able _____

7. strange + est _____

8. hope + ing _____

9. use + able _____

10. spin + ing _____

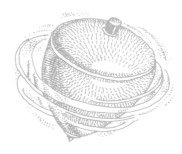

145

Before adding a suffix to a word that ends in **y**, sometimes you need to change the **y** to **i**, as in <u>noisily</u>.

List Words

sturdier
cheerily
worrying
greedily
hastily
sleepiest
heavier
magnifying
sunniest
noisily

Write a List Word that is an antonym for the word given.

1. reducing _____

2. generously _____

3. weaker _____

4. sadly _____

5. slowly _____

6. lighter _____

7. quietly _____

8. most awake _____

9. relaxing _____

10. cloudiest _____

Use the following rules to make words that end in **y** plural:
• If a consonant precedes the **y**, add **es**, as in <u>centuries</u>.
• If a vowel precedes the **y**, add **s**, as in <u>kidneys</u>.

List Words

delays
cavities
injuries
victories
kidneys
cranberries
journeys
bakeries
mysteries
families

Write a List Word that matches each clue.

1. wounds; harm done to people _____

2. groups of related people _____

3. trips, excursions _____

4. the opposite of losses _____

5. areas of decay in teeth _____

6. places to buy baked goods _____

7. pair of major body organs _____

8. unexplained things; secrets _____

9. postponements _____

10. sour, red berries grown in a marsh _____

Lesson 34

Some words don't change in the plural form. For some words that end in **f** or **fe**, change **f** or **fe** to **v** and add **es**; for others, just add **s**. Some words that end in **o** take an **es**; others just take an **s**.

List Words

wolves
calves
broccoli
spaghetti
radios
tomatoes
sheriffs
beliefs
species
igloos

Fill in List Words to complete the sentences.

1. _____ are assisted by deputies.

2. _____, _____, and _____ are things you eat.

3. _____ and _____ have four legs.

4. People listen to music and news on _____.

5. _____ are built out of blocks of ice.

6. What we believe in are our _____.

7. There are numerous _____ of animals.

Lesson 35

There are some words that you just need to practice using to become familiar with their spellings.

List Words

yolk
column
stomach
separate
islands
misspelled
weather
February
ballet
punctuation

Write a List Word to complete each sentence.

1. A comma is a kind of _____.

2. A word with letters missing is _____.

3. The yellow center of an egg is a _____.

4. The month after January is _____.

5. A dance performed on toes is _____.

6. Places surrounded by water are _____.

7. A vertical list of numbers is a _____.

8. Another word for divide is _____.

9. Rain and snow are kinds of _____.

10. Food is digested in a person's _____.

List Words

planned
strangest
valuable
worrying
heavier
delays
bakeries
spaghetti
tomatoes
yolk
separate
islands
punctuation

Write a List Word to match each clue.

1. strange + est _____

2. yellow of an egg _____

3. plural of delay _____

4. value + able _____

5. plural of bakery _____

6. worry + ing _____

7. plural of spaghetti _____

8. heavy + er _____

9. plural of tomato _____

10. areas surrounded by water _____

11. ! ? " _____

12. plan + ed _____

13. divide _____

Go for the Goal

Take your Final Replay Test. Then fill in your Scoreboard.
Send any misspelled words to your Word Locker.

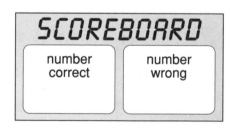

SCOREBOARD

number correct	number wrong

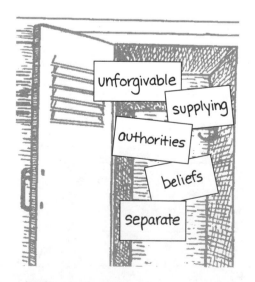

unforgivable
supplying
authorities
beliefs
separate

Clean Out Your Word Locker

Look in your Word Locker. Cross out each word you spelled
correctly on your Final Replay Test. Circle the words you're
still having trouble with. Add the words you circled to your
Spelling Notebook. What do you notice about the words?
Watch for those words as you write.

Writing and Proofreading Guide

1. Choose a topic to write about.
2. Write your ideas. Don't worry about mistakes.
3. Now organize your writing so that it makes sense.
4. Proofread your work.
   Use these proofreading marks to make changes.

> **Proofreading Marks**
> ⬭ spelling mistake
> ≡ capital letter
> ⊙ add period
> ∧ add something
> ⌄ add apostrophe
> ℒ take out something
> ¶ indent paragraph
> / make small letter

tomorrow well interview the (auther) of of our favorite Mystery story⊙

5. Write your final copy.

   Tomorrow we'll interview the author of our favorite mystery story.

6. Share your writing.

Using Your Dictionary

The Spelling Workout Dictionary shows you
many things about your spelling words.

The **respelling** tells how
to pronounce the word.

The **entry word** listed in
alphabetical order is the
word you are looking up.

The **part of speech** is
given as an abbreviation.

im·prove (im prōōv′) **v.** 1 to make or become better
[Business has *improved*.] 2 to make good use of [She
improved her spare time by reading.] — **im·proved′,
im·prov′ing**

Sample sentences or phrases
show how to use the word.

Other **forms** of the
word are given.

The **definition** tells what the
word means. There may be
more than one definition.

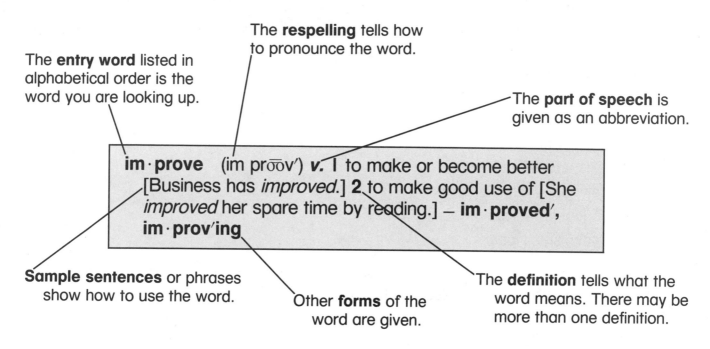

Pronunciation Key

SYMBOL	KEY WORDS	SYMBOL	KEY WORDS	SYMBOL	KEY WORDS	SYMBOL	KEY WORDS
a	ask, fat	ōō	look, pull	b	bed, dub	t	top, hat
ā	ape, date	ou	ooze, tool	d	did, had	v	vat, have
ä	car, lot		out, crowd	f	fall, off	w	will, always
				g	get, dog	y	yet, yard
e	elf, ten	u	up, cut	h	he, ahead	z	zebra, haze
ē	even, meet	ʉ	fur, fern	j	joy, jump		
				k	kill, bake		
i	is, hit	ə	a in ago	l	let, ball	ch	chin, arch
ī	ice, fire		e in agent	m	met, trim	ŋ	ring, singer
			e in father	n	not, ton	sh	she, dash
ō	open, go		i in unity	p	put, tap	th	thin, truth
ô	law, horn		o in collect	r	red, dear	*th*	then, father
oi	oil, point		u in focus	s	sell, pass	zh	s in pleasure

An Americanism is a word or usage of a word that was born in this country. An open star before an
entry word or definition means that the word or definition is an Americanism.

These dictionary entries are taken, by permission, in abridged or modified form from *Webster's New World
Dictionary*. Copyright © 1992 by Simon & Schuster Inc.

Aa

ab·sen·tee (ab sən tē′) **n.** a person who is absent, as from school, work, etc. ◆**adj.** living far away from land or a building that one owns [an *absentee* landlord].

ab·sorb·ent (ab sôr′bənt *or* ab zôr′bent) **adj.** able to absorb moisture, light, etc. [*absorbent* cotton].

a·bun·dant (ə bun′dənt) **adj. 1** very plentiful; more than enough [The farmers had an *abundant* crop of grain last year.] **2** rich; well-supplied [a lake *abundant* in fish].

ac·cept·ance (ak sep′təns) **n. 1** the act of accepting [the actor's *acceptance* of the award] **2** the condition of being accepted [his *acceptance* as a member of the club] **3** approval or belief [a theory that has the *acceptance* of most scientists].

ac·count·ant (ə kount′nt) **n.** a person whose work is keeping or examining accounts, or business records.

ac·cu·mu·late (ə kyo͞om′yo͞o lāt′) **v.** to pile up, collect, or gather over a period of time [Junk has *accumulated* in the garage. Our school has *accumulated* a large library.] —**ac·cu′mu·lat·ed, ac·cu′mu·lat·ing**

ache (āk) **v. 1** to have or give a dull, steady pain [My head *aches*.] **2** to want very much; long: *used only in everyday talk* [She is *aching* to take a trip.] —**ached, ach′ing**

a·chieve (ə chēv′) **v. 1** to do; succeed in doing; accomplish [He *achieved* very little while he was mayor.] **2** to get or reach by trying hard; gain [She *achieved* her ambition to be a lawyer.] —**a·chieved′, a·chiev′ing**

a·cre (āk′ər) **n. 1** a measure of land equal to 43,560 square feet. **2** **acres,** *pl.* lands or fields [golden *acres* of grain].

ac·tiv·i·ty (ak tiv′ə tē) **n. 1** the condition of being active; action; motion [There was not much *activity* in the shopping mall today.] **2** normal power of mind or body; liveliness; alertness [His mental *activity* at age eighty was remarkable.] **3** something that one does besides one's regular work [We take part in many *activities* after school.] —*pl.* **ac·tiv′i·ties**

ad·here (ad hir′) **v. 1** to stick and not come loose; stay attached [This stamp won't *adhere* to the envelope.] **2** to follow closely or faithfully [to *adhere* to a plan]. —**ad·hered′, ad·her′ing**

ad·min·is·tra·tion (əd min′i strā′shən) **n. 1** an administering; management; direction. **2** *often* **Administration,** the president and the other people who work in the executive branch of a government [The *Administration* was criticized for its foreign policy.] **3** their term of office [Johnson was vice-president during Kennedy's *administration*.] **4** the people who manage a company, school, or other organization. —**ad·min′is·tra′tive adj.**

a·dopt (ə däpt′) **v. 1** to take into one's family by a legal process [to *adopt* a child] **2** to take and use as one's own [He *adopted* her teaching methods for his own classroom.] **3** to choose or follow [to *adopt* a plan of action]. —**a·dop′tion n.**

ad·vance (ad vans′) **v. 1** to go or bring forward; move ahead [The trail became rougher as we *advanced*.] **2** to make or become higher; increase [Prices continue to *advance*.] —**ad·vanced′, ad·vanc′ing**

af·ter·ward (af′tər wərd) or **af·ter·wards** (af′tər wərdz) **adv.** at a later time; later [We had dinner and went for a walk *afterward*.]

a·gree·a·ble (ə grē′ə bəl) **adj. 1** pleasing or pleasant [an *agreeable* odor]. **2** willing or ready to say "yes" [The principal was *agreeable* to our plan.] —**a·gree′a·bly adv.**

a·gree·ment (ə grē′mənt) **n. 1** the fact of agreeing or being similar [The news report was not in *agreement* with the facts.] **2** a fixing of terms between two or more people, countries, etc., as in a treaty [The U.S. has trade *agreements* with many nations.]

aisle (īl) **n. 1** an open way for passing between sections of seats, as in a theater. **2** a part of a church along the inside wall, set off by a row of pillars.

a·lign (ə līn′) **v. 1** to put into a straight line [*Align* the chairs along the wall.] —**a·ligned′, a·lign′ing**

al·low·ance (ə lou′əns) **n. 1** an amount of money, food, etc. given regularly to a child or to anyone who depends on others for support. **2** an amount added or taken off to make up for something [We give an *allowance* of $5 on your used tire when you buy a new one.]

al·loy (al′oi) **n.** a metal that is a mixture of two or more metals, or of a metal and something else [Bronze is an *alloy* of copper and tin.]

al·pha·bet·ize (al′fə bə tīz) **v.** to arrange in alphabetical order. —**al′pha·bet·ized′, al′pha·bet·iz′ing**

a·maz·ing (ə māz′iŋ) **adj.** causing amazement; astonishing. —**a·maz′ing·ly adv.**

A·mer·i·ca (ə mer′ə kə) **1** either North America or South America. **2** North America and South America together. ☆**3** the United States of America.

America

a	ask, fat
ā	ape, date
ä	car, lot
e	elf, ten
ē	even, meet
i	is, hit
ī	ice, fire
ō	open, go
ô	law, horn
oi	oil, point
o͞o	look, pull
o͞o	ooze, tool
ou	out, crowd
u	up, cut
ʉ	fur, fern
ə	a in ago
	e in agent
	e in father
	i in unity
	o in collect
	u in focus
ch	chin, arch
ŋ	ring, singer
sh	she, dash
th	thin, truth
th	then, father
zh	s in pleasure

an·ces·tor (an′ses tər) *n.* 1 a person who comes before one in a family line, especially someone earlier than a grandparent; forefather [Their *ancestors* came from Poland.] 2 an early kind of animal from which later kinds have developed [The *ancestor* of the elephant was the mammoth.]

an·gri·ly (aŋ′grə lē) *adv.* in an angry manner.

an·gry (aŋ′grē) *adj.* 1 feeling or showing anger [*angry* words; an *angry* crowd]. 2 wild and stormy [an *angry* sea]. —**an′gri· er, an′gri·est**

an·i·mal (an′ə məl) *n.* 1 any living being that can move about by itself, has sense organs, and does not make its own food as plants do from inorganic matter [Insects, snakes, fish, birds, cattle, and people are all *animals*.] 2 any such being other than a human being; especially, any four-footed creature; beast.

an·i·mat·ed (an′ə māt′əd) *adj.* vigorous; lively [an *animated* conversation]. —**an′i· mat′ed·ly** *adv.*

☆**animated cartoon** *n.* a motion picture made by filming a series of drawings, each changed slightly from the one before. The drawn figures seem to move when the drawings are shown on a screen, one quickly after the other.

an·swer (an′sər) *n.* 1 something said, written, or done in return to a question, argument, letter, action, etc.; reply; response [The only *answers* required for the test were "true" or "false." His *answer* to the insult was to turn his back.] 2 a solution to a problem, as in arithmetic. ◆*v.* to give an answer; reply or react, as to a question or action.

a·pol·o·gy (ə päl′ə jē) *n.* a statement that one is sorry for doing something wrong or being at fault [Please accept my *apology* for sending you the wrong book.] —*pl.* **a· pol′o·gies**

ap·pli·cant (ap′li kənt) *n.* a person who applies or asks for something [*applicants* for a job].

ap·point·ee (ə poin tē′) *n.* a person who has been appointed to some position.

a·pri·cot (ap′rə kät′ *or* ā′prə kät′) *n.* 1 a pale orange fruit that is a little like a peach, but smaller. 2 the tree it grows on. 3 a pale orange color.

ar·e·a (er′ē ə) *n.* 1 the amount or size of a surface, measured in square units [If a floor is 10 meters wide and 20 meters long, its *area* is 200 square meters.] 2 a part of the earth's surface; region [Our family lives mostly in rural *areas*.] 3 a space used for a special purpose [a picnic *area*].

ar·row (er′ō) *n.* 1 a slender rod that is shot from a bow. Arrows usually have a point at the front end and feathers at the back end. 2 anything that looks or is used like an arrow; especially, a sign (←) used to point out a direction or place.

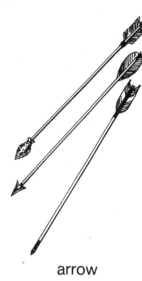

arrow

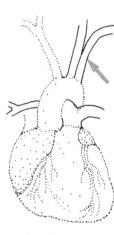

artery

ar·ter·y (är′tər ē) *n.* 1 any of the tubes that carry blood from the heart to all parts of the body. 2 a main road or channel [a railroad *artery*]. —*pl.* **ar′ter·ies**

ar·tis·tic (är tis′tik) *adj.* 1 of art or artists. 2 done with skill and a good sense of color, form, design, etc. [an *artistic* job of redecorating]. 3 knowing and enjoying what is beautiful. —**ar·tis′ti·cal·ly** *adv.*

as·sign (ə sīn′) *v.* 1 to set apart for a special purpose; designate [Let's *assign* a day for the trip.] 2 to place at some task or work [Two pupils were *assigned* to write the report.] 3 to give out as a task; allot [The teacher *assigned* some homework.]

as·sist·ant (ə sis′tənt) *n.* a person who assists or helps another; helper; aid [an *assistant* to the president]. ◆*adj.* assisting or helping the person under whom one works [an *assistant* principal].

as·so·ci·ate (ə sō′shē āt′ *or* ə sō′sē āt′) *v.* 1 to connect in one's mind; think of together [We *associate* the taste of something with its smell.] 2 to bring or come together as friends or partners [Don't *associate* with people who gossip.] —**as· so′ci·at·ed, as·so′ci·at·ing** ◆*n.* (ə sō′shē ət *or* ə sō′sē ət) a person with whom one is joined in some way; friend, partner, or fellow worker.

ath·let·ic (ath let′ik) *adj.* 1 of or for athletes or athletics. 2 like an athlete; physically strong and active. —**ath·let′i·cal·ly** *adv.*

at·mos·phere (at′məs fir) *n.* 1 all the air around the earth. 2 the gases around any planet or star. 3 the air in any particular place.

at·tach·ment (ə tach′mənt) *n.* 1 the act of attaching something. 2 anything used for attaching; fastening. 3 strong liking or love; friendship; affection.

at·tend·ance (ə ten′dəns) *n.* 1 the act of attending. 2 people present [The *attendance* at the ball game was 36,000.]

at·ti·tude (at′ə tōōd *or* at′ə tyōōd) *n.* 1 the position of the body in doing a particular thing [We knelt in an *attitude* of prayer.] 2 a way of acting or behaving that shows what one is thinking or feeling [a friendly *attitude*].

at·tor·ney (ə tʉr′nē) *n.* a person whose profession is giving advice on law or acting for others in lawsuits. —*pl.* **at·tor′neys**

auc·tion·eer (ôk shə nir′ *or* äk shə nir′) *n.* a person whose work is selling things at auctions.

au·di·ence (ô′dē əns *or* ä′dē əns) *n.* a group of persons gathered together to hear and see a speaker, a play, or a concert [The *audience* cheered the singer.]

au·thor (ô′thər *or* ä′thər) *n.* 1 a person who writes something, as a book or story [The Brontë sisters were the *authors* of novels.] 2 a person who makes or begins something; creator [the *author* of a new plan for peace]. ◆*v.* to be the author of.

au·thor·i·ty (ə thôr′ə tē) *n.* **1** the right to give orders, make decisions, or take action [Do you have the *authority* to spend the money?] **2** a person or agency that has the right to govern or the power to enforce laws [The city *authorities* have approved the plan.] **3** a person, book, etc. that can be trusted to give the right information or advice [an *authority* on rare diseases]. —*pl.* **au·thor′i·ties**

au·to·graph (ôt′ə graf *or* ät′ə graf) *n.* something written in a person's own handwriting, especially that person's name. ◆*v.* to write one's name on [Please *autograph* this baseball.]

a·vi·a·tor (ā′vē āt′ər) *n.* a person who flies airplanes; pilot.

a·void (ə void′) *v.* **1** to keep away from; get out of the way of; shun [to *avoid* crowds]. **2** to keep from happening [Try to *avoid* spilling the milk.] —**a·void′a·ble** *adj.* —**a·void′ance** *n.*

awe (ô *or* ä) *n.* deep respect mixed with fear and wonder [The starry sky filled them with *awe*.]

aw·ful·ly (ô′fəl ē *or* ä′fəl ē) *adv.* **1** in an awful way. ☆**2** very; extremely: *used only in everyday talk* [I'm *awfully* glad you came.]

awk·ward (ôk′wərd *or* äk′wərd) *adj.* **1** not having grace or skill; clumsy; bungling [an *awkward* dancer; an *awkward* writing style]. **2** hard to use or manage; not convenient [an *awkward* tool]. **3** uncomfortable; cramped [sitting in an *awkward* position]. **4** embarrassed or embarrassing [an *awkward* remark]. —**awk′ward·ly** *adv.* —**awk′ward·ness** *n.*

Bb

back·ward (bak′wərd) *adv.* **1** toward the back; behind [to look *backward*]. **2** with the back toward the front [If a man rides *backward*, he can see where he has been.] **3** in a way opposite to the usual way [Noel is Leon spelled *backward*.]

☆**bak·er·y** (bāk′ər ē) *n.* a place where bread, cakes, etc. are baked or sold. —*pl.* **bak′er·ies**

bal·let (bal′ā *or* ba lā′) *n.* **1** a dance performed on a stage, usually by a group of dancers in costume. It often tells a story by means of its graceful, fixed movements. **2** a group of such dancers.

bas·i·cal·ly (bā′sik lē) *adv.* in a basic way.

beau·ti·ful (byōō′ti fəl) *adj.* very pleasant to look at or hear; giving delight to the mind [a *beautiful* face]. —**beau′ti·ful·ly** *adv.*

be·hav·ior (bē hāv′yər) *n.* the way a person or thing behaves, or acts; conduct or action [His *behavior* at the dance was rude. The Curies studied the *behavior* of radium.]

be·lief (bē lēf′) *n.* **1** a believing or feeling that certain things are true or real; faith [You cannot destroy my *belief* in the honesty of most people.] **2** trust or confidence [I have *belief* in Pat's ability.] **3** anything believed or accepted as true; opinion [What are your religious *beliefs*?]

be·lieve (bē lēv′) *v.* **1** to accept as true or real [Can we *believe* that story?] **2** to have religious faith [to *believe* in life after death]. **3** to have trust or confidence [I know you will win; I *believe* in you.] **4** to suppose; guess. —**be·lieved′, be·liev′ing** —**be·liev′a·ble** *adj.* —**be·liev′er** *n.*

ben·e·fit (ben′ə fit) *n.* **1** help or advantage; also, anything that helps [Speak louder for the *benefit* of those in the rear.] **2** *often* **benefits**, *pl.* money paid by an insurance company, the government, etc. as during old age or sickness, or for death. **3** any public event put on to raise money for a certain person, group, or cause [The show is a *benefit* for children.]

be·tray (bē trā′) *v.* to fail to keep a promise, secret, or agreement; be unfaithful [My cousin *betrayed* my trust by wasting my money.] —**be·trayed′, be·tray′ing**

bi·ceps (bī′seps) *n.* the large muscle in the front of the upper arm.

bi·cy·cle (bī′si kəl) *n.* a vehicle to ride on that has two wheels, one behind the other. It is moved by foot pedals and steered by a handlebar. ◆*v.* to ride a bicycle. —**bi′cy·cled, bi′cy·cling** —**bi·cy·clist** (bī′si klist) *n.*

bi·fo·cals (bī′fō kəlz) *pl.n.* eyeglasses in which each lens has two parts, one for reading and seeing nearby objects and the other for seeing things far away.

bi·og·ra·phy (bī äg′rə fē) *n.* the story of a person's life written by another person. —*pl.* **bi·og′ra·phies** —**bi·o·graph·i·cal** (bī′ə graf′i kəl) *adj.*

bi·sect (bī sekt′ *or* bī′sekt) *v.* **1** to cut into two parts [Budapest is *bisected* by the Danube River.] **2** to divide into two equal parts [A circle is *bisected* by its diameter.]

blue (blōō) *adj.* having the color of the clear sky or the deep sea.

blue-green (blōō′grēn) *adj.* having a combination of the colors blue and green

boast (bōst) *v.* **1** to talk about with too much pride and pleasure; praise too highly; brag [We tired of hearing him *boast* of his bravery.] **2** to be proud of having [Our city *boasts* a fine new zoo.] —**boast′er** *n.*

a	ask, fat
ā	ape, date
ä	car, lot
e	elf, ten
ē	even, meet
i	is, hit
ī	ice, fire
ō	open, go
ô	law, horn
oi	oil, point
͝oo	look, pull
͞oo	ooze, tool
ou	out, crowd
u	up, cut
u	fur, fern
ə	a in ago
	e in agent
	e in father
	i in unity
	o in collect
	u in focus
ch	chin, arch
ŋ	ring, singer
sh	she, dash
th	thin, truth
th	then, father
zh	s in pleasure

153

bureau

bond (bänd) *n.* **1** anything that binds or ties [Handcuffs or shackles are called *bonds.*] **2** an agreement that binds one, as to pay certain sums or to do or not do certain things. **3** a certificate sold by a government or business as a way of raising money. It promises to return the money to the buyer by a certain date, along with interest [The city issued *bonds* to build a subway.]

book·keep·er (book′kēp ər) *n.* a person whose work is to keep accounts for a business.

bor·row (bär′ō *or* bôr′ō) *v.* **1** to get to use something for a while by agreeing to return it later [You can *borrow* that book from the library.] **2** to take another's word, idea, etc. and use it as one's own [The Romans *borrowed* many Greek myths.]

bot·a·ny (bät′n ē) *n.* the science that studies plants and how they grow. —**bot′a·nist** *n.*

bound·a·ry (boun′drē *or* boun′dər ē) *n.* a line or thing that marks the outside edge or limit [The Delaware River forms the eastern *boundary* of Pennsylvania.] —*pl.* **bound′a·ries**

braid (brād) *v.* **1** to weave together three or more strands of hair, straw, ribbon, etc. **2** to make by weaving such strands [to *braid* a rug]. ◆*n.* **1** a length of braided hair. **2** a band of braided cloth, ribbon, etc. used for trimming or decoration.

breathe (brēth) *v.* **1** to take air into the lungs and then let it out. **2** to live [While I *breathe*, you are safe.] **3** to speak quietly; whisper [Don't *breathe* a word of it to anyone.] **4** to stop for breath; rest [to *breathe* a horse after a long run]. —**breathed, breath′ing**

brief (brēf) *adj.* **1** not lasting very long; short in time [a *brief* visit] **2** using just a few words; concise [a *brief* news report].

broad·cast (brôd′kast) *v.* to send over the air by means of radio or television [to *broadcast* a program]. —**broad′cast** *or* **broad′cast·ed, broad′cast·ing**

broc·co·li (bräk′ə lē) *n.* a vegetable whose tender shoots and loose heads of tiny green buds are cooked for eating.

broil (broil) *v.* **1** to cook or be cooked close to a flame or other high heat [to *broil* steaks over charcoal]. **2** to make or be very hot [a *broiling* summer day]. ◆*n.* the act or state of broiling.

broth·er·hood (bruth′ər hood) *n.* the tie between brothers or between people who feel they all belong to one big family.

bu·reau (byoor′ō) *n.* ☆**1** a chest of drawers for holding clothes. It usually has a mirror. **2** an office, as for a certain part of a business [an information *bureau*]. ☆**3** a department of the government [The *Bureau* of Internal Revenue is in charge of collecting Federal taxes.] —*pl.* **bu′reaus** *or* **bu·reaux** (byoor′ōz)

bus·y (biz′ē) *adj.* **1** doing something; active; at work; not idle [The students are *busy* at their desks.] **2** full of activity; with much action or motion [a *busy* morning; a *busy* store]. —**bus′i·er, bus′i·est** —**bus′ied, bus′y·ing** *v.* —**bus′y·ness** *n.*

cab·i·net (kab′i nət) *n.* **1** a case or cupboard with drawers or shelves for holding or storing things [a china *cabinet*; a medicine *cabinet*]. ☆**2** *often* **Cabinet**, a group of officials who act as advisers to the head of a nation. Our president's cabinet is made up of the heads of the departments of our government.

calf (kaf) *n.* **1** a young cow or bull. **2** a young elephant, whale, hippopotamus, seal, etc. —*pl.* **calves**

cam·paign (kam pān′) *n.* **1** a series of battles or other military actions having a special goal [Napoleon's Russian *campaign* ended in his defeat.] **2** a series of planned actions for getting something done [a *campaign* to get someone elected]. ◆*v.* to take part in a campaign. —**cam·paign′er** *n.*

Can·a·da (kan′ə də) a country in the northern part of North America.

can·cel (kan′səl) *v.* **1** to cross out with lines or mark in some other way [Postage stamps and checks are *canceled* to show that they have been used.] **2** to do away with; wipe out; say that it will no longer be [to *cancel* an order]. **3** to balance something so that it has no effect [My gains and losses *cancel* each other.] —**can′celed** *or* **can′celled, can′cel·ing** *or* **can′cel·ling**

ca·pac·i·ty (kə pas′ə tē) *n.* **1** the amount of space that can be filled; room for holding [a jar with a *capacity* of 2 quarts; a stadium with a seating *capacity* of 80,000]. **2** the ability to be, learn, become, etc.; skill or fitness [the *capacity* to be an actor]. **3** position or office [He made the decision in his *capacity* as president.] —*pl.* **ca·pac′i·ties**

cap·il·lar·y (kap′i ler′ē) *n.* **1** a tube that is very narrow inside [The ordinary thermometer is a *capillary*.] **2** any of the tiny blood vessels joining the arteries and the veins. —*pl.* **cap′il·lar′ies**

cap·tion (kap′shən) *n.* ☆a title at the head of an article or below a picture, as in a newspaper.

cap·tive (kap′tiv) *n.* a person caught and held prisoner, as in war. ◆*adj.* **1** held as a prisoner. ☆**2** forced to listen, whether wanting to or not [a *captive* audience].

carbon dioxide *n.* a gas made up of carbon and oxygen, that has no color and no smell and is heavier than air. It is breathed out of the lungs and is taken in by plants, which use it to make their food.

ca·reer (kə rir′) *n.* **1** the way one earns one's living; profession or occupation [Have you thought of teaching as a *career*?] **2** one's progress through life or in one's work [a long and successful *career* in politics].

car·toon (kär tōn′) *n.* **1** a drawing, as in a newspaper or magazine, that shows how the editor or artist feels about some person or thing in the news. It is often a caricature that criticizes or praises. **2** a humorous drawing. ☆**3** *same as* **comic strip.** ☆**4** *same as* **animated cartoon.** ◆☆*v.* to draw cartoons. —**car·toon′ist** *n.*

cas·sette (kə set′) *n.* **1** a case with a roll of film in it, for loading a camera quickly and easily. **2** a case with recording tape in it, for quick, easy use in a tape recorder.

cas·u·al (kazh′ o̅o̅ əl) *adj.* **1** happening by chance; not planned [a *casual* visit] **2** for wear at times when dressy clothes are not needed [*casual* sports clothes]. —**cas′u·al·ly** *adv.* —**cas′u·al·ness** *n.*

cat·a·log or **cat·a·logue** (kat′ə lôg *or* kat′ə läg) *n.* ☆**1** a card file in alphabetical order giving a complete list of things in a collection, as of all the books in a library. **2** a book or paper listing all the things for sale or on display. ◆*v.* to make a list of or put into a list. —**cat′a·loged** or **cat′a·logued, cat′a·log·ing** or **cat′a·logu·ing**

cau·li·flow·er (kôl′ə flou′ər *or* käl′ə flou′ər) *n.* a kind of cabbage with a head of white, fleshy flower clusters growing tightly together. It is eaten as a vegetable.

cau·tion (kô′shən *or* kä′shən) *n.* **1** the act of being careful not to get into danger or make mistakes [Use *caution* in crossing streets.] **2** a warning [Let me give you a word of *caution.*] ◆*v.* to warn; tell of danger [The sign *cautioned* us to slow down.]

cav·i·ty (kav′i tē) *n.* **1** a hollow place, such as one caused by decay in a tooth. **2** a natural hollow space in the body [the chest *cavity*]. —*pl.* **cav′i·ties**

cel·e·brate (sel′ə brāt) *v.* **1** to honor a victory, the memory of something, etc. in some special way [to *celebrate* a birthday with a party; to *celebrate* the Fourth of July with fireworks]. **2** to honor or praise widely [Aesop's fables have been *celebrated* for centuries.] **3** to perform a ceremony in worshiping [to *celebrate* Mass]. **4** to have a good time: *used only in everyday talk* [Let's *celebrate* when we finish painting the garage.] —**cel′e·brat·ed, cel′e·brat·ing** —**cel′e·bra′tion** *n.*

cen·tu·ry (sen′chər ē) *n.* **1** any of the 100-year periods counted forward or backward from the beginning of the Christian Era [From 500 to 401 B.C. was the fifth *century* B.C. From 1901 to 2000 is the twentieth *century* A.D.] **2** any period of 100 years [Mark Twain was born over a *century* ago.] —*pl.* **cen′tu·ries**

cer·e·mo·ny (ser′ə mō′nē) *n.* **1** an act or set of acts done in a special way, with all the right details [a wedding *ceremony* in church; the *ceremony* of inaugurating the President]. **2** very polite behavior that follows strict rules; formality [The special dinner was served with great *ceremony*.] —*pl.* **cer′e·mo′nies**

cer·tain (sʉrt′n) *adj.* **1** without any doubt or question; sure; positive [Are you *certain* of your facts?] **2** bound to happen; not failing or missing [to risk *certain* death; the soldier's *certain* aim]. **3** not named or described, though perhaps known [It happened in a *certain* town out west.]

cer·tif·i·cate (sʉr tif′i kət) *n.* a written or printed statement that can be used as proof of something because it is official [A birth *certificate* proves where and when someone was born.]

chal·lenge (chal′ənj) *v.* **1** to question the right or rightness of; refuse to believe unless proof is given [to *challenge* a claim; to *challenge* something said or the person who says it]. **2** to call to take part in a fight or contest; dare [He *challenged* her to a game of chess.] **3** to refuse to let pass unless a certain sign is given [The sentry waited for the password after *challenging* the soldier.] **4** to call for skill, effort, or imagination [That puzzle will really *challenge* you.] —**chal′lenged, chal′leng·ing**

cham·pi·on (cham′pē ən) *n.* **1** a person or thing that wins first place or is judged to be best, as in a contest or sport [a spelling *champion*; a tennis *champion*]. **2** a person who fights for another or for a cause; defender [a *champion* of the poor].

cham·pi·on·ship (cham′pē ən ship′) *n.* **1** the position or title of a champion; first place. **2** the act of championing, or defending.

chan·nel (chan′əl) *n.* **1** the bed of a river or stream. **2** the deeper part of a river, harbor, etc. **3** a body of water joining two larger bodies of water [The English *Channel* links the Atlantic Ocean to the North Sea.] **4** the band of frequencies on which a single radio or television station sends out its programs. —**chan′neled** or **chan′nelled, chan′nel·ing** or **chan′nel·ling** *v.*

cassette

a	ask, fat
ā	ape, date
ä	car, lot
e	elf, ten
ē	even, meet
i	is, hit
ī	ice, fire
ō	open, go
ô	law, horn
oi	oil, point
o̅o̅	look, pull
o̅o̅	ooze, tool
ou	out, crowd
u	up, cut
ʉ	fur, fern
ə	a in ago
	e in agent
	e in father
	i in unity
	o in collect
	u in focus
ch	chin, arch
ŋ	ring, singer
sh	she, dash
th	thin, truth
th	then, father
zh	s in pleasure

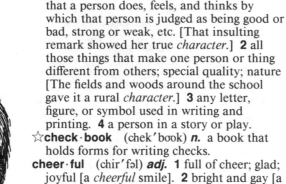

chimpanzee

char·ac·ter (kär′ək tər) *n.* **1** all the things that a person does, feels, and thinks by which that person is judged as being good or bad, strong or weak, etc. [That insulting remark showed her true *character*.] **2** all those things that make one person or thing different from others; special quality; nature [The fields and woods around the school gave it a rural *character*.] **3** any letter, figure, or symbol used in writing and printing. **4** a person in a story or play.

☆**check·book** (chek′book) *n.* a book that holds forms for writing checks.

cheer·ful (chir′fəl) *adj.* **1** full of cheer; glad; joyful [a *cheerful* smile]. **2** bright and gay [a *cheerful* room]. **3** willing; glad to help [a *cheerful* worker]. —**cheer′ful·ly** *adv.* —**cheer′ful·ness** *n.*

cheer·y (chir′ē) *adj.* cheerful; lively and happy [They gave us a *cheery* welcome.] —**cheer′i·er, cheer′i·est** —**cheer′i·ly** *adv.* —**cheer′i·ness** *n.*

chem·i·cal (kem′i kəl) *adj.* **1** of or in chemistry [a *chemical* process]. **2** made by or used in chemistry [*chemical* compounds]. —**chem′i·cal·ly** *adv.*

chief (chēf) *n.* the leader or head of some group [an Indian *chief*; the *chief* of a hospital staff]. ◆*adj.* **1** having the highest position [the *chief* foreman]. **2** main; most important [Jill's *chief* interest is golf.]

chim·pan·zee (chim′pan zē′ *or* chim pan′zē) *n.* an ape of Africa that is smaller than a gorilla and is a very intelligent animal: *the word is often shortened to* **chimp** (chimp).

chin·chil·la (chin chil′ə) *n.* **1** a small, ratlike animal found in the Andes Mountains in South America. **2** its soft, gray fur, which is very expensive. **3** a heavy wool cloth with a rough surface, used for making coats.

Chi·nese (chī nēz′) *n.* **1** a member of a people whose native country is China. —*pl.* **Chi·nese′** **2** the language of China. ◆*adj.* of China, its people, language, or culture.

choc·o·late (chôk′lət *or* chäk′lət *or* chôk′ə lət *or* chäk′ə lət) *n.* **1** a paste, powder, syrup, or bar made from cacao seeds that have been roasted and ground. **2** a drink made of chocolate, sugar, and milk or water. **3** a candy made of chocolate or covered with chocolate. **4** reddish brown. ◆*adj.* made of or flavored with chocolate.

choir (kwīr) *n.* **1** a group of people trained to sing together, especially as part of a church service. **2** the part of a church where the choir sits or stands.

choose (chooz) *v.* **1** to pick out one or more from a number or group [*Choose* a subject from this list.] **2** to make up one's mind; decide or prefer [She *chose* to stay home.] —**chose, cho′sen, choos′ing**

cho·sen (chō′zən) *past participle of* **choose.** ◆*adj.* picked out carefully, as for a special purpose [A *chosen* few soldiers formed the king's guard.]

chinchilla

cir·cus (sur′kəs) *n.* **1** a traveling show held in tents or in a hall, with clowns, trained animals, acrobats, etc. ☆**2** a very funny or entertaining person or thing: *used only in everyday talk.* **3** a stadium or arena in ancient Rome, where games or races were held.

cir·rus (sir′əs) *n.* a kind of cloud that looks like thin strips of woolly curls. —*pl.* **cir′rus**

cit·i·zen (sit′i zən) *n.* **1** a person who is a member of a country or state either because of being born there or having been made a member by law. Citizens have certain duties to their country and are entitled to certain rights. **2** a person who lives in a particular city or town [the *citizens* of Atlanta].

class (klas) *n.* **1** a number of people or things thought of as a group because they are alike in certain ways [Whales belong to the *class* of mammals. She is a member of the working *class*.] ☆**2** a group of students meeting together to be taught; also, a meeting of this kind [My English *class* is held at 9 o'clock.] ☆**3** a group of students who are or will be graduating together [the *class* of 1981]. **4** a division or grouping according to grade or quality [to travel first *class*].

clas·si·fy (klas′i fī′) *v.* to arrange by putting into classes or groups according to some system [Plants and animals are *classified* into various orders, families, species, etc.] —**clas′si·fied, clas′si·fy·ing**

cli·ent (klī′ənt) *n.* **1** a person or company for whom a lawyer, accountant, etc. is acting. **2** a customer.

clos·et (kläz′ət *or* klôz′ət) *n.* a small room or cupboard for clothes, linens, supplies, etc. ◆*v.* to shut up in a room for a private talk [The president was *closeted* with his close advisers.]

☆**cloud·burst** (kloud′burst) *n.* a sudden, very heavy rain.

coast (kōst) *n.* **1** land along the sea; seashore. ☆**2** a slide or ride downhill, as on a sled. ◆*v.* **1** to sail along a coast. ☆**2** to ride or slide downhill, as on a sled. ☆**3** to keep on moving after the driving power is cut off [We ran out of gas, but the car *coasted* into the gas station.]

co·coa (kō′kō) *n.* **1** a powder made from roasted cacao seeds, used in making chocolate. **2** a drink made from this powder by adding sugar and hot water or milk. **3** a light, reddish brown.

co·co·nut *or* **co·coa·nut** (kō′kə nut) *n.* the large, round fruit of a tall, tropical palm tree (called the **coconut palm** or **coco palm**). Coconuts have a thick, hard, brown shell that has an inside layer of sweet white matter used as a food. The hollow center is filled with a sweet, milky liquid.

col·lect (kə lekt′) **v. 1** to gather in one place; assemble [*Collect* the rubbish and burn it. Water *collects* around the drain.] **2** to gather things as a hobby [She *collects* stamps.] **3** to call for and get money owed [The building manager *collects* the rent.]

col·lege (käl′ij) **n. 1** a school that one can go to after high school for higher studies. Colleges give degrees to students when they graduate. A college is often a part of a university, which may have a number of special colleges, as of law or medicine. **2** a school where one can get training in some special work [a business *college*].

co·logne (kə lōn′) **n.** a sweet-smelling liquid like perfume, but not so strong.

co·lon (kō′lən) **n.** the main part of the large intestine, that leads to the rectum.

col·umn (käl′əm) **n. 1** a long, generally round, upright support; pillar. Columns usually stand in groups to hold up a roof or other part of a building, but they are sometimes used just for decoration. **2** any long, upright thing like a column [a *column* of water; the spinal *column*]. **3** any of the long sections of print lying side by side on a page and separated by a line or blank space [Each page of this book has two *columns*.] **4** any of the articles by one writer or on a special subject, that appear regularly in a newspaper or magazine [a chess *column*].

com·fort·a·ble (kumf′tər bəl *or* kum′fər tə bəl) **adj. 1** giving comfort or ease; not giving pain [a *comfortable* pair of shoes]. **2** feeling comfort; not uneasy [Are you *comfortable* in that chair?] —**com′fort·a·bly adv.**

com·ic (käm′ik) **adj. 1** having to do with comedy. **2** funny or amusing; making one laugh. ◆**n.** ☆**comics,** *pl.* a section of comic strips, as in a newspaper.

com·mand (kə mand′) **v. 1** to give an order to; direct [I *command* you to halt!] **2** to be in control of [Captain Stone *commands* Company B.] **3** to deserve to have [Her courage *commands* our respect.] ◆**n. 1** an order or direction [He obeyed the queen's *commands*.] **2** the power or ability to control or command; control [Who is in *command* here? He has no *command* of his temper.]

com·mence (kə mens′) **v.** to begin or start [The trial will *commence* at noon.] —**com·menced′, com·menc′ing**

com·mend (kə mend′) **v. 1** to mention with approval; praise [a ballet company *commended* by all the dance critics]. **2** to put in someone's care or keeping; commit. —**com·men·da·tion** (käm′ən dā′shən) **n.**

com·mit·tee (kə mit′ē) **n.** a group of people chosen to study some matter or to do a certain thing [a *committee* to plan the party].

com·pan·ion (kəm pan′yən) **n. 1** a person who goes along with another; especially, one who often shares or supports the other's activities; comrade; associate. **2** either one of a pair of matched things [Where is the *companion* to this glove?]

com·pa·ny (kum′pə nē) **n. 1** a group of people; especially, a group joined together in some work or activity [a *company* of actors; a business *company*]. **2** a group of soldiers that is usually under the command of a captain. **3** the state of being companions; companionship [We enjoy each other's *company*.] **4** friends or companions [One is judged by the *company* one keeps.] **5** a guest or guests [We invited *company* for dinner.] —*pl.* **com′pa·nies**

com·pen·sa·tion (käm′pən sā′shən) **n. 1** the act of compensating. **2** something given or done to make up for something else [She was given an expensive gift as extra *compensation* for her services.]

com·pete (kəm pēt′) **v.** to take part in a contest; be a rival for something [Two hundred students *competed* for the scholarship.] —**com·pet′ed, com·pet′ing**

com·pe·tent (käm′pə tənt) **adj.** having enough ability to do what is needed; capable [a *competent* typist]. —**com′pe·tent·ly adv.**

com·plain (kəm plān′) **v. 1** to find fault with something or show pain or displeasure [Everyone *complained* about the poor food in the cafeteria.] **2** to make a report about something bad [We *complained* to the police about the noisy party next door.]

con·ceive (kən sēv′) **v. 1** to form or develop in the mind; think of; imagine [I have *conceived* a plan for making a fortune.] **2** to understand [It is difficult to *conceive* how this motor works.] **3** to become pregnant. —**con·ceived′, con·ceiv′ing**

con·cern (kən surn′) **v.** to have a relation to; be important to; involve [This matter *concerns* all of us.] —**con·cerned′, con·cern′ing** ◆**n.** worry or anxiety [He felt great *concern* over his wife's health.]

con·cert (kän′sərt) **n.** a musical program, especially one in which a number of musicians perform together.

con·den·sa·tion (kän′dən sā′shən) **n. 1** the act of condensing. **2** the condition of being condensed. **3** something condensed [This book is a *condensation* of the novel.]

con·di·tion (kən dish′ən) **n. 1** the particular way a person or thing is [What is the *condition* of the patient? Weather *conditions* won't allow us to go.] **2** the right or healthy way to be [The whole team is in *condition*.] **3** anything which must be or must happen before something else can take place [Her parents made it a *condition* that she had to do her homework before she could watch TV.]

column

a	ask, fat
ā	ape, date
ä	car, lot
e	elf, ten
ē	even, meet
i	is, hit
ī	ice, fire
ō	open, go
ô	law, horn
oi	oil, point
͏oo	look, pull
o͞o	ooze, tool
ou	out, crowd
u	up, cut
u͏	fur, fern
ə	a in ago
	e in agent
	e in father
	i in unity
	o in collect
	u in focus
ch	chin, arch
ŋ	ring, singer
sh	she, dash
th	thin, truth
th	then, father
zh	s in pleasure

con·fi·dence (kän′fi dəns) *n.* **1** strong belief or trust in someone or something; reliance [They have *confidence* in my skill.] **2** a belief in oneself; self-confidence [I began to play the piano with *confidence.*] **3** trust in another to keep one's secret [She told it to him in strict *confidence.*] **4** a secret [Don't burden me with your *confidences.*]

con·gress (käŋ′grəs) *n.* **1** a coming together; meeting; convention. ☆**2 Congress,** the group of elected officials in the United States government that makes the laws. It consists of the Senate and the House of Representatives.

con·gru·ent (käŋ′grōō ənt) *adj.* in agreement or harmony; corresponding.

con·nect (kə nekt′) *v.* **1** to join together; unite [Several bridges *connect* Ohio and Kentucky.] **2** to relate in some way; think of together [Do you *connect* his silence with her arrival?] —**con·nect′ed, con·nect′ing**

con·quer (käŋ′kər) *v.* **1** to get or gain by using force, as by winning a war [The Spaniards *conquered* Mexico.] **2** to overcome by trying hard; get the better of; defeat [She *conquered* her bad habits.] —**con′quer·or** *n.*

con·science (kän′shəns) *n.* a sense of right and wrong; feeling that keeps one from doing bad things [My *conscience* bothers me after I tell a lie.]

con·serve (kən surv′) *v.* to keep from being hurt, lost, or wasted [to *conserve* one's energy]. —**con·served′**

con·sid·er·ate (kən sid′ər ət) *adj.* thoughtful of other people's feelings; kind [It was *considerate* of you to invite her too.] —**con·sid′er·ate·ly** *adv.*

con·sole (kən sōl′) *v.* to make less sad or troubled; comfort [A toy *consoled* the lost child.] —**con·soled′, con·sol′ing**

con·sti·tu·tion (kän′sti tōō′shən *or* kän′sti tyōō′shən) *n.* **1** the act of setting up, forming, establishing, etc. **2** the way in which a person or thing is formed; makeup; structure [My strong *constitution* keeps me from catching cold.] **3** the system of basic laws or rules of a government, society, etc. **4** a document in which these laws and rules are written down [The *Constitution* of the U.S. is the supreme law here.]

con·trib·ute (kən trib′yōōt) *v.* **1** to give together with others [I *contribute* to my church.] **2** to write an article, poem, etc. as for a magazine or newspaper. —**con·trib′ut·ed, con·trib′ut·ing**

con·vex (kän veks′ *or* kän′veks) *adj.* curving outward like the outside of a ball [a *convex* lens]. —**con·vex′i·ty** *n.* —**con·vex′ly** *adv.*

cook (kook) *v.* **1** to prepare food by heating; boil, roast, bake, etc. **2** to be cooked [The roast should *cook* longer.]

co·op·er·ate (kō äp′ər āt′) *v.* to work together to get something done [If we all *cooperate,* we can finish sooner.] —**co·op′er·at·ed, co·op′er·at·ing** —**co·op′er·a′tion** *n.*

☆**corn bread** *n.* bread made with cornmeal.

cor·rect (kə rekt′) *v.* **1** to make right; get rid of mistakes in [*Correct* your spelling before turning in your papers.] **2** to point out the mistakes of; sometimes, to punish or scold for such mistakes [to *correct* a child's behavior]. ◆*adj.* **1** without a mistake; right; true [a *correct* answer]. **2** agreeing with what is thought to be proper [*correct* behavior]. —**cor·rect′ly** *adv.* —**cor·rect′ness** *n.*

cough (kôf *or* käf) *v.* to force air from the lungs with a sudden, loud noise —**coughed, cough′ing** ◆*n.* the act or sound of coughing [I have a bad *cough.*]

coun·se·lor *or* **coun·sel·lor** (koun′sə lər) *n.* **1** a person who advises; adviser. **2** a lawyer. **3** a person in charge of children at a camp.

count (kount) *v.* **1** to name numbers in a regular order [I'll *count* to five.] **2** to add up so as to get a total [*Count* the people here.] **3** to take account of; include [There are ten here, *counting* you.] **4** to be taken into account; have importance, value, etc. [Every bit of help *counts.*]

☆**count·down** (kount′doun) *n.* the schedule of things that take place in planned order just before the firing of a rocket, the setting off of a nuclear explosion, etc.; also, the counting backward in units of time while these things take place.

coun·try (kun′trē) *n.* **1** an area of land; region [wooded *country*]. **2** the whole land of a nation [The *country* of Japan is made up of islands.] **3** the people of a nation [The speech was broadcast to the whole *country.*] **4** the nation to which one belongs ["My *country,* 'tis of thee"] —*pl.* **coun′tries**

cou·ple (kup′əl) *n.* **1** two things of the same kind that go together; pair [a *couple* of book ends]. **2** a man and woman who are married, engaged, or partners, as in a dance. ◆*v.* to join together; unite; connect [to *couple* railroad cars]. —**cou′pled, cou′pling**

cou·pon (kōō′pän *or* kyōō′pän) *n.* **1** a ticket or part of a ticket that gives the holder certain rights [The *coupon* on the cereal box is worth 10¢ toward buying another box.] **2** a part of a bond which is cut off at certain times and turned in for payment of interest. **3** a part of a printed advertisement that can be used for ordering goods, samples, etc.

cou·ra·geous (kə rā′jəs) *adj.* having or showing courage; brave.

cour·te·ous (kur′tē əs) *adj.* polite and kind; thoughtful of others.

cous·in (kuz′ən) *n.* **1** the son or daughter of one's uncle or aunt: *also called* **first cousin**. You are a *second cousin* to the children of your parents' first cousins, and you are a *first cousin once removed* to the children of your first cousins. **2** a distant relation.

cov·er (kuv′ər) *v.* **1** to place one thing over another; spread over [*Cover* the bird cage at night. *Cover* the wall with white paint. Water *covered* the fields.] **2** to keep from being seen or known; hide [He tried to *cover* up the scandal.] **3** to protect, as from harm or loss [Are you *covered* by insurance?] **4** to provide for; take care of [Is this case *covered* by the rules?] **5** to have to do with; be about; include [This book *covers* the Civil War.]

☆**cran·ber·ry** (kran′ber′ē) *n.* **1** a hard, sour, red berry used in sauces and jellies. **2** the marsh plant it grows on. —*pl.* **cran′ber′ries**

crea·ture (krē′chər) *n.* a living being; any person or animal.

cred·it (kred′it) *n.* **1** belief; trust [I give little *credit* to what he says.] **2** praise or approval [I give her *credit* for trying.] **3** official recognition in a record [You will receive *credit* for your work on this project.] **4** a person or thing that brings praise [She is a *credit* to the team.] **5** trust that a person will be able and willing to pay later [That store doesn't give *credit*, so you have to pay cash.]

crim·i·nal (krim′i nəl) *adj.* **1** being a crime; that is a crime [a *criminal* act]. **2** having to do with crime [*criminal* law]. ◆*n.* a person guilty of a crime. —**crim′i·nal·ly** *adv.*

crowd (kroud) *n.* **1** a large group of people together [*crowds* of Christmas shoppers]. **2** the common people; the masses. ☆**3** a group of people having something in common; set: *used only in everyday talk* [My brother's *crowd* is too old for me.] ◆*v.* **1** to push or squeeze [Can we all *crowd* into one car?] **2** to come together in a large group [People *crowded* to see the show.]

cu·cum·ber (kyōō′kum bər) *n.* **1** a long vegetable with green skin and firm, white flesh. It is used in salads and made into pickles. **2** the vine that it grows on. —**cool as a cucumber,** calm; not excited.

cuff (kuf) *n.* **1** a band at the wrist of a sleeve, either fastened to the sleeve or separate. **2** a fold turned up at the bottom of a trouser leg. **3** a handcuff.

cu·mu·lus (kyōōm′yə ləs) *n.* a kind of cloud in which round masses are piled up on each other.

cur·rant (kur′ənt) *n.* **1** a small, sweet, black raisin, used in cooking. **2** a small, sour berry used in jams and jellies; also, the bush it grows on.

cus·tom·er (kus′tə mər) *n.* **1** a person who buys, especially one who buys regularly [I have been a *customer* of that shop for many years.] **2** any person with whom one has dealings: *used only in everyday talk.*

Dd

dan·ger·ous (dān′jər əs) *adj.* full of danger; likely to cause injury, pain, etc.; unsafe [This shaky old bridge is *dangerous.*] —**dan′ger·ous·ly** *adv.*

Dan·ube (dan′yōōb) a river in southern Europe, flowing from southwestern Germany eastward into the Black Sea.

dark (därk) *adj.* **1** having little or no light [a *dark* room; a *dark* night]. **2** closer to black than to white; deep in shade; not light [*dark* green]. **3** hidden; full of mystery [a *dark* secret]. **4** gloomy or hopeless [Things look *dark* for Lou.] —**dark′ly** *adv.* —**dark′ness** *n.*

dark·en (där′kən) *v.* to make or become dark.

daugh·ter (dôt′ər *or* dät′ər) *n.* **1** a girl or woman as she is related to a parent or to both parents. **2** a girl or woman who is influenced by something in the way that a child is by a parent [a *daughter* of France].

de·cay (dē kā′) *v.* **1** to become rotten by the action of bacteria [The fallen apples *decayed* on the ground.] **2** to fall into ruins; become no longer sound, powerful, rich, beautiful, etc. [Spain's power *decayed* after its fleet was destroyed.] **3** to break down so that there are fewer radioactive atoms.

de·ceit (dē sēt′) *n.* **1** a deceiving or lying. **2** a lie or a dishonest act or acts.

de·ceive (dē sēv′) *v.* to make someone believe what is not true; fool or trick; mislead [The queen *deceived* Snow White by pretending to be her friend.] —**de·ceived′, de·ceiv′ing** —**de·ceiv′er** *n.*

de·cid·ed (dē sīd′əd) *adj.* **1** clear and sharp; definite [a *decided* change in the weather]. **2** sure or firm; without doubt [Clem has very *decided* ideas on the subject.] —**de·cid′ed·ly** *adv.*

de·code (dē kōd′) *v.* to figure out the meaning of something written in code. —**de·cod′ed, de·cod′ing**

dec·o·ra·tive (dek′ə rə tiv *or* dek′ə rā′tiv) *adj.* that serves to decorate; ornamental.

de·coy (dē′koi *or* dē koi′) *n.* **1** an artificial bird or animal used to attract wild birds or animals to a place where they can be shot or trapped; also, a live bird or animal used in the same way. **2** a thing or person used to lure someone into a trap.

cucumber

a	ask, fat
ā	ape, date
ä	car, lot
e	elf, ten
ē	even, meet
i	is, hit
ī	ice, fire
ō	open, go
ô	law, horn
oi	oil, point
ōō	look, pull
ōō	ooze, tool
ou	out, crowd
u	up, cut
ʉ	fur, fern
ə	a in ago
	e in agent
	e in father
	i in unity
	o in collect
	u in focus
ch	chin, arch
ŋ	ring, singer
sh	she, dash
th	thin, truth
th	then, father
zh	s in pleasure

de·gree (dē grē′) *n.* **1** a step in a series; stage in the progress of something [He advanced by *degrees* from office boy to president.] **2** a unit used in measuring temperature that is shown by the symbol °. The boiling point of water is 100° Celsius or 212° Fahrenheit. **3** a unit used in measuring angles and arcs of circles [There are 360 *degrees* in the circumference of a circle.] **4** a rank given by a college to a student who has satisfactorily completed a course of study, or to an outstanding person as an honor [a B.A. *degree*].

de·lay (dē lā′) *v.* **1** to put off to a later time; postpone [The bride's illness will *delay* the wedding.] **2** to make late; hold back; keep from going on [We were *delayed* by the storm.]

de·light·ful (dē līt′fəl) *adj.* giving delight or pleasure; very pleasing [a *delightful* party]. —**de·light′ful·ly** *adv.*

de·part·ment (dē pärt′mənt) *n.* a separate part or branch, as of a government or business [the police *department*; the shipping *department*; the *department* of mathematics in a college]. —**de·part·men·tal** (dē′part ment′l) *adj.*

de·pend·a·ble (dē pen′də bəl) *adj.* that can be depended on; reliable [a *dependable* friend]. —**de·pend′a·bil′i·ty** *n.*

de·pos·it (dē päz′it) *v.* **1** to place for safekeeping, as money in a bank. **2** to give as part payment or as a pledge [They *deposited* $500 on a new car.] **3** to lay down [I *deposited* my books on the chair. The river *deposits* tons of mud at its mouth.] ◆*n.* **1** something placed for safekeeping, as money in a bank. **2** money given as a pledge or part payment.

de·scend·ant (dē sen′dənt) *n.* a person who is descended from a certain ancestor.

de·sign (dē zīn′) *v.* **1** to think up and draw plans for [to *design* a new model of a car]. **2** to arrange the parts, colors, etc. of [Who *designed* this book?] **3** to set apart for a certain use; intend [This chair was not *designed* for hard use.] ◆*n.* **1** a drawing or plan to be followed in making something [the *designs* for a house]. **2** the arrangement of parts, colors, etc.; pattern or decoration [the *design* in a rug].

de·stroy (dē stroi′) *v.* to put an end to by breaking up, tearing down, ruining, or spoiling [The flood *destroyed* 300 homes.] —**de·stroyed′, de·stroy′ing**

de·tec·tor (dē tek′tər) *n.* a person or thing that detects; especially, a device used to show that something is present.

di·am·e·ter (dī am′ət ər) *n.* **1** a straight line passing through the center of a circle or sphere, from one side to the other. **2** the length of such a line [The *diameter* of the moon is about 2,160 miles.]

di·a·ry (dī′ə rē) *n.* **1** a record written day by day of some of the things done, seen, or thought by the writer. **2** a book for keeping such a record. —*pl.* **di′a·ries**

dic·tion·ar·y (dik′shə ner′ē) *n.* **1** a book in which some or most of the words of a language, or of some special field, are listed in alphabetical order with their meanings, pronunciations, etc. [a school *dictionary*; a medical *dictionary*]. **2** a book like this in which words of one language are explained in words of another language [a Spanish-English *dictionary*]. —*pl.* **dic′tion·ar′ies**

dig·it (dij′it) *n.* **1** any number from 0 through 9. **2** a finger or toe.

di·plo·ma (di plō′mə) *n.* a certificate given to a student by a school or college to show that the student has completed a required course of study.

di·rec·tion (də rek′shən) *n.* **1** a directing or managing; control [The choir is under the *direction* of Ms. Jones.] **2** an order or command. **3** *usually* **directions**, *pl.* instructions on how to get to some place or how to do something [*directions* for driving to Omaha; *directions* for building a model boat]. **4** the point toward which something faces or the line along which something moves or lies ["North," "up," "forward," and "left" are *directions*.] —**di·rec′tion·al** *adj.*

di·rec·tor (də rek′tər) *n.* **1** a person who directs or manages the work of others [the *director* of a play, a band, a government bureau]. **2** a member of a group chosen to direct the affairs of a business. —**di·rec′tor·ship** *n.*

dis·ap·pear (dis ə pir′) *v.* to stop being seen or to stop existing; vanish [The car *disappeared* around a curve. Dinosaurs *disappeared* millions of years ago.] —**dis′ap·pear′ance** *n.*

dis·ap·prove (dis ə prōōv′) *v.* to refuse to approve; have an opinion or feeling against; think to be wrong [The Puritans *disapproved* of dancing.] —**dis′ap·proved′, dis′ap·prov′ing** —**dis′ap·prov′ing·ly** *adv.*

dis·be·lief (dis bə lēf′) *n.* the state of not believing; lack of belief [The guide stared at me in *disbelief.*]

dis·con·tin·ue (dis′kən tin′yōō) *v.* to stop doing, using, etc.; give up [to *discontinue* a subscription to a magazine]. —**dis′con·tin′ued, dis′con·tin′u·ing**

dis·cov·er (di skuv′ər) *v.* **1** to be the first to find, see, or learn about [Marie and Pierre Curie *discovered* radium.] **2** to come upon, learn, or find out about [I *discovered* my name on the list.] **3** to be the first person who is not a native to come to or see a continent, river, etc. [De Soto *discovered* the Mississippi River.]

dis·grace (dis grās′) *n.* **1** loss of favor, respect, or honor; dishonor; shame [She is in *disgrace* for cheating on the test.] **2** a person or thing bringing shame [Slums are a *disgrace* to a city.] ◆*v.* to bring shame or dishonor upon; hurt the reputation of [My cousin's crime has *disgraced* our family.] —**dis·graced′, dis·grac′ing**

dis·mal (diz′məl) *adj.* 1 causing gloom or misery; sad [a *dismal* story] 2 dark and gloomy [a *dismal* room]. —**dis′mal·ly** *adv.*

dis·play (di splā′) *v.* to put or spread out so as to be seen; exhibit [to *display* a collection of stamps] —**dis·played′, dis·play′ing** ◆*n.* something that is displayed [a *display* of jewelry].

dis·tance (dis′təns) *n.* 1 the length of a line between two points [The *distance* between New York and Chicago is 713 miles.] 2 the condition of being far apart in space or time; remoteness ["*Distance* lends charm." There was quite a *distance* between their views.] 3 a place far away [viewing things from a *distance*]. —**dis′tanced, dis′tanc·ing** ◆*v.*

dis·turb (di sturb′) *v.* 1 to break up the quiet or calm of [The roar of motorcycles *disturbed* the peace.] 2 to make worried or uneasy; upset [They are *disturbed* by their parents' divorce.] 3 to put into disorder; mix up [Someone *disturbed* the books on my shelf.]

di·vide (də vīd′) *v.* 1 to separate into parts; split up [a classroom *divided* by a movable wall]. 2 to separate into equal parts by arithmetic [If you *divide* 12 by 3, you get 4.] 3 to put into separate groups; classify [Living things are *divided* into plants and animals.] 4 to make separate or keep apart [A stone wall *divides* their farms.]

dol·phin (dôl′fin) *n.* a water animal related to the whale but smaller. The common dolphin has a long snout and many teeth.

dom·i·nant (däm′ə nənt) *adj.* most important or most powerful; ruling, controlling [a *dominant* world power].

dou·ble (dub′əl) *adj.* 1 having two parts that are alike [a *double* house; a *double* door; gun with a *double* barrel]. 2 being of two kinds [Sometimes a word is used in a joke because it has a *double* meaning and can be understood in two different ways.] 3 twice as much, as many, as great, as fast, etc. [a *double* portion; *double* time]. 4 made for two [a *double* bed; a *double* garage]. ◆*adv.* two at one time; in a pair [to ride *double* on a bicycle]. —**dou′bled, doub′ling** *v.*

doz·en (duz′ən) *n.* a group of twelve. —*pl.* **doz′ens** or, *especially after a number,* **doz′en.**

drain (drān) *v.* 1 to make flow away [*Drain* the water from the potatoes.] 2 to draw off water or other liquid from; make empty [to *drain* a swamp; to *drain* one's glass]. 3 to flow off [Water won't *drain* from a flat roof.] 4 to become empty or dry [Our bathtub *drains* slowly.] 5 to flow into [The Ohio River *drains* into the Mississippi.]

dra·ma (drä′mə *or* dram′ə) *n.* 1 a story that is written to be acted out, as on a stage; play. 2 the art of writing or performing plays. 3 a series of interesting or exciting events [the *drama* of the American Revolution].

draw·er (drô′r) *n.* 1 a person or thing that draws. 2 (drôr) a box that slides in and out of a table, chest, desk, etc.

drear·y (drir′ē) *adj.* without happiness or cheer; gloomy, sad, or dull [a long, *dreary* tale]. —**drear′i·er, drear′i·est** —**drear′i·ly** *adv.* —**drear′i·ness** *n.*

du·ra·ble (door′ə bəl *or* dur′ə bəl) *adj.* lasting in spite of hard wear or much use. —**du′ra·bil′i·ty** *n.* —**du′ra·bly** *adv.*

Ee

earth·quake (urth′kwāk) *n.* a shaking or trembling of the ground, caused by the shifting of underground rock or by the action of a volcano.

ea·sel (ē′zəl) *n.* a standing frame for holding an artist's canvas or a picture.

ee·rie or **ee·ry** (ir′ē) *adj.* giving a person a feeling of fear or mystery; weird [an *eerie* house that looked haunted].

ef·fort (ef′ərt) *n.* 1 the use of energy to get something done; a trying hard with the mind or body [It took great *effort* to climb the mountain.] 2 a try or attempt [They made no *effort* to be friendly.] 3 something done with effort [My early *efforts* at poetry were not published.]

eight·een (ā′tēn′) *n., adj.* the cardinal number between seventeen and nineteen; 18.

eight·y (āt′ē) *n., adj.* eight times ten; the number 80. —*pl.* **eight′ies** —**the eighties,** the numbers or years from 80 through 89.

ei·ther (ē′thər *or* ī′thər) *adj.* 1 one or the other of two [Use *either* exit.] 2 both one and the other; each [She had a tool in *either* hand.] ◆*pron.* one or the other of two [*Either* of the suits will fit you.]

e·lec·tion (ē lek′shən) *n.* the act of choosing or the fact of being chosen, especially by voting.

e·lec·tric (ē lek′trik) *adj.* 1 of or having to do with electricity [*electric* current; *electric* wire]. 2 making or made by electricity [an *electric* generator; *electric* lighting]. 3 worked by electricity [an *electric* toothbrush].

e·lec·tron·ic (ē lek′trän′ik *or* el′ek trän′ik) *adj.* working or produced by the action of electrons [*electronic* equipment].

el·e·va·tion (el′ə vā′shən) *n.* 1 a raising up or being raised up [her *elevation* to the position of principal]. 2 a higher place or position [The house is on a slight *elevation*.] 3 height above the surface of the earth or above sea level [The mountain has an *elevation* of 20,000 feet.]

em·per·or (em′pər ər) *n.* a man who rules an empire.

dolphin

a	ask, fat
ā	ape, date
ä	car, lot
e	elf, ten
ē	even, meet
i	is, hit
ī	ice, fire
ō	open, go
ô	law, horn
oi	oil, point
͞oo	look, pull
o͞o	ooze, tool
ou	out, crowd
u	up, cut
u	fur, fern
ə	a in ago
	e in agent
	e in father
	i in unity
	o in collect
	u in focus
ch	chin, arch
ŋ	ring, singer
sh	she, dash
th	thin, truth
th	then, father
zh	s in pleasure

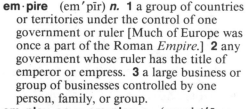

endangered species

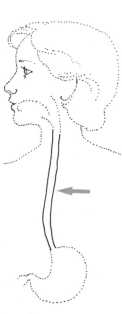

esophagus

em·pire (em′pīr) *n.* **1** a group of countries or territories under the control of one government or ruler [Much of Europe was once a part of the Roman *Empire*.] **2** any government whose ruler has the title of emperor or empress. **3** a large business or group of businesses controlled by one person, family, or group.

em·ploy·ee or **em·ploy·e** (em ploi′ē *or* em′ploi ē′) *n.* a person who works for another in return for pay.

en·a·ble (en ā′bəl) *v.* to make able; give the means or power to [A loan *enabled* Lou to go to college.] —**en·a′bled, en·a′bling**

en·cour·age (en kʉr′ij) *v.* to give courage or hope to; make feel more confident [Praise *encouraged* the children to try harder.] —**en·cour′aged, en·cour′ag·ing**

en·cy·clo·pe·di·a or **en·cy·clo·pae·di·a** (en sī′klə pē′dē ə) *n.* a book or set of books that gives information on all branches of knowledge or, sometimes, on just one branch of knowledge. It is made up of articles usually in alphabetical order.

en·dan·ger (en dān′jər) *v.* to put in danger or peril [to *endanger* one's life].

en·dan·gered species (en dān′jərd) *n.* a species of animal or plant in danger of becoming extinct, or dying off [The whooping crane is an *endangered species*.]

en·dure (en dŏŏr′ *or* en dyŏŏr′) *v.* **1** to hold up under pain, weariness, etc.; put up with; bear; stand [to *endure* torture; to *endure* insults]. **2** to go on for a long time; last; remain [The Sphinx has *endured* for ages.] —**en·dured′, en·dur′ing** —**en·dur′a·ble** *adj.*

en·force (en fôrs′) *v.* **1** to force people to pay attention to; make people obey [to *enforce* traffic laws]. **2** to bring about by using force or being strict [He is unable to *enforce* his views on others.] —**en·forced′, en·forc′ing** —**en·force′ment** *n.*

en·gage (en gāj′) *v.* **1** to promise to marry [Harry is *engaged* to Grace.] **2** to promise or undertake to do something [She *engaged* to tutor the child after school.] **3** to get the right to use something or the services of someone; hire [to *engage* a hotel room; to *engage* a lawyer]. **4** to take part or be active [I have no time to *engage* in dramatics.] —**en·gaged′, en·gag′ing**

en·gi·neer (en′jə nir′) *n.* **1** a person who is trained in some branch of engineering. **2** a person who runs an engine, as the driver of a railroad locomotive. **3** a soldier whose special work is the building or wrecking of roads, bridges, etc.

en·joy·a·ble (en joi′ə bəl) *adj.* giving joy or pleasure; delightful [What an *enjoyable* concert!]

e·nough (ē nuf′) *adj.* as much or as many as needed or wanted; sufficient [There is *enough* food for all.] ◆*n.* the amount needed or wanted [I have heard *enough* of that music.] ◆*adv.* as much as needed; to the right amount [Is your steak cooked *enough*?]

en·rich (en rich′) *v.* to make richer in value or quality [Music *enriches* one's life.] —**en·riched′, en·rich′ing**

en·ter·prise (en′tər prīz) *n.* **1** any business or undertaking, especially one that takes daring and energy. **2** willingness to undertake new or risky projects [They succeeded because of their *enterprise*.]

en·tire (en tīr′) *adj.* **1** including all the parts: whole; complete [I've read the *entire* book.] **2** not broken, not weakened, not lessened, etc. [We have his *entire* support.] —**en·ire′ly** *adv.*

en·vi·ron·ment (en vī′rən mənt) *n.* the things that surround anything; especially, all the conditions that surround a person, animal, or plant and affect growth, actions, character, etc. [Removing pollution from water and air will improve our *environment*.] —**en·vi′ron·men′tal** *adj.*

en·vy (en′vē) *n.* **1** jealousy and dislike felt toward another having some thing, quality, etc. that one would like to have [He glared at the winner with a look of *envy*.] **2** the person or thing one has such feelings about [Their new car is the *envy* of the neighborhood.] —*pl.* **en′vies** ◆*v.* to feel envy toward or because of [to *envy* a person for her wealth]. —**en′vied, en′vy·ing**

e·qual (ē′kwəl) *adj.* **1** of the same amount, size, or value [The horses were of *equal* height.] **2** having the same rights, ability, or position [All persons are *equal* in a court of law in a just society.] ◆*v.* **1** to be equal to; match [His long jump *equaled* the school record. Six minus two *equals* four.] **2** to do or make something equal to [You can *equal* my score easily.] —**e′qualed** or **e′qualled, e′qual·ing** or **e′qual·ling** —**e′qual·ly** *adv.*

e·qual·i·ty (ē kwôl′ə tē) *n.* the condition of being equal, especially of having the same political, social, and economic rights and duties.

e·quip·ment (ē kwip′mənt) *n.* **1** the special things needed for some purpose; outfit, supplies, etc. [fishing *equipment*]. **2** the act of equipping.

er·rand (er′ənd) *n.* a short trip to do a thing, often for someone else [I'm going downtown on an *errand* for my sister.]

e·soph·a·gus (e säf′ə gəs) *n.* the tube through which food passes from the throat to the stomach.

e·vap·o·rate (e vap′ə rāt) **v. 1** to change into vapor [Heat *evaporates* water. The perfume in the bottle has *evaporated*.] **2** to disappear like vapor; vanish [Our courage *evaporated* when we saw the lion.] **3** to make thicker by heating so as to take some of the water from [to *evaporate* milk].
—**e·vap′o·rat·ed, e·vap′o·rat·ing**
—**e·vap′o·ra′tion** *n.*

ev·i·dence (ev′ə dəns) *n.* something that shows or proves, or that gives reason for believing; proof or indication [The footprint was *evidence* that someone had been there. Clear skin gives *evidence* of a good diet.] ◆*v.* to show clearly; make plain [His smile *evidenced* his joy.] —**ev′i·denced, ev′i·denc·ing**

ex·act·ly (eg zakt′lē) *adv.* **1** in an exact way; precisely [That's *exactly* the bike I want.] **2** quite true; I agree: *used as an answer to something said by another.*

ex·ceed (ek sēd′) *v.* **1** to go beyond what is allowed [to *exceed* the speed limit] **2** to be more or better than [Her success *exceeded* her own wildest dreams.] —**ex·ceed′ed, ex·ceed′ing**

ex·cel·lent (ek′sə lənt) *adj.* better than others of its kind; very good [Their cakes are fairly good, but their pies are *excellent*.] —**ex′cel·lent·ly** *adv.*

ex·change (eks chānj′) *v.* **1** to give in return for something else; trade [She *exchanged* the bicycle for a larger one.] **2** to give each other similar things [The bride and groom *exchanged* rings during the ceremony.]
—**ex·changed′, ex·chang′ing** ◆*n.* **1** a giving of one thing in return for another; trade [I'll give you my pen in *exchange* for that book.] **2** a giving to one another of similar things [Our club has a gift *exchange* at Christmas time.]

ex·cite·ment (ek sīt′mənt) *n.* **1** the condition of being excited [The hotel fire caused great *excitement* in the town.] **2** anything that excites.

ex·claim (eks klām′) *v.* to speak out suddenly and with strong feeling, as in surprise, anger, etc. ["I won't go!" she *exclaimed*.]

ex·haust (eg zôst′ *or* eg zäst′) *v.* **1** to use up completely [Our drinking water was soon *exhausted*.] **2** to let out the contents of; make completely empty [The leak soon *exhausted* the gas tank.] **3** to use up the strength of; tire out; weaken [They are *exhausted* from playing tennis.] ◆*n.* **1** the used steam or gas that comes from the cylinders of an engine; especially, the fumes from the gasoline engine in an automobile.

ex·ist (eg zist′) *v.* **1** to be; have actual being [The unicorn never really *existed*.] **2** to occur or be found [Tigers do not *exist* in Africa.] **3** to live [Fish cannot *exist* long out of water.]

ex·pe·di·tion (ek′spə dish′ən) *n.* **1** a long journey or voyage by a group of people, as to explore a region or to take part in a battle. **2** the people, ships, etc. making such a trip. **3** speed or quickness with little effort or waste [We finished our task with *expedition*.] —**ex′pe·di′tion·ar′y** *adj.*

ex·pe·ri·ence (ek spir′ē əns) *n.* **1** the fact of living through a happening or happenings [*Experience* teaches us many things.] **2** something that one has done or lived through [This trip was an *experience* that I'll never forget.] **3** skill that one gets by training, practice, and work [a lawyer with much *experience*]. —**ex·pe′ri·enced, ex·pe′ri·enc·ing** *v.*

ex·pert (eks′pərt *or* ek spurt′) *adj.* **1** having much special knowledge and experience; very skillful [an *expert* golfer]. **2** of or from an expert [*expert* advice]. ◆*n.* (ek′spert) an expert person; authority [an *expert* in art].

ex·plain (ek splān′) *v.* **1** to make clear or plain; give details of [He *explained* how the engine works.] **2** to give the meaning of [The teacher *explained* the story.] **3** to give reasons for [Can you *explain* your absence?]

ex·port (ek spôrt′) *v.* to send goods from one country for sale in another [Japan *exports* many radios.] ◆*n.* (eks′pôrt) **1** the act of exporting [Brazil raises coffee for *export*.] **2** something exported [Oil is Venezuela's chief *export*.] —**ex′por·ta′tion** *n.* —**ex·port′er** *n.*

ex·pres·sion (ek spresh′ən) *n.* **1** an expressing, or putting into words [This note is an *expression* of my gratitude.] **2** a way of speaking, singing, or playing something that gives it real meaning or feeling [to read with *expression*]. **3** the act of showing how one feels, what one means, etc. [Laughter is an *expression* of joy.]

ex·tend (ek stend′) *v.* **1** to make longer; stretch out [Careful cleaning *extends* the life of a rug.] **2** to lie or stretch [The fence *extends* along the meadow.] **3** to make larger or more complete; enlarge; increase [to *extend* one's power]. **4** to offer or give [May I *extend* congratulations to the winner?] —**ex·tend′ed** *adj.*

ex·tinc·tion (ek stiŋk′shən) *n.* **1** the fact of becoming extinct, or dying out [The California condor faces *extinction*.] **2** a putting an end to or wiping out [the *extinction* of all debts]. **3** an extinguishing, or putting out [the *extinction* of a fire].

a	ask, fat
ā	ape, date
ä	car, lot
e	elf, ten
ē	even, meet
i	is, hit
ī	ice, fire
ō	open, go
ô	law, horn
oi	oil, point
͝oo	look, pull
͞oo	ooze, tool
ou	out, crowd
u	up, cut
u	fur, fern
ə	a in ago
	e in agent
	e in father
	i in unity
	o in collect
	u in focus
ch	chin, arch
ŋ	ring, singer
sh	she, dash
th	thin, truth
th	then, father
zh	s in pleasure

163

Ff

feather

faint (fānt) *adj.* **1** weak; not strong or clear; dim or feeble [a *faint* whisper; a *faint* odor; *faint* shadows]. **2** weak and dizzy, as if about to swoon. **3** not very certain; slight [a *faint* hope]. ◆*n.* a condition in which one becomes unconscious because not enough blood reaches the brain, as in sudden shock. ◆*v.* to fall into a faint; swoon. —**faint′ly** *adv.*

false·hood (fôls′hoͧod) *n.* a lie or the telling of lies.

fa·mil·iar (fə mil′yər) *adj.* **1** friendly; intimate; well-acquainted [a *familiar* face in the crowd]. **2** too friendly; intimate in a bold way [We were annoyed by the *familiar* manner of our new neighbor.] **3** knowing about; acquainted with [Are you *familiar* with this book?] **4** well-known; common; ordinary [Car accidents are a *familiar* sight.] ◆*n.* a close friend.

fam·i·ly (fam′ə lē) *n.* **1** a group made up of two parents and all of their children. **2** the children alone [a widow who raised a large *family*]. **3** a group of people who are related by marriage or a common ancestor; relatives; clan. **4** a large group of related plants or animals [The robin is a member of the thrush *family*.] —*pl.* **fam′i·lies**

fa·mous (fā′məs) *adj.* much talked about as being outstanding; very well known.

fan·cy (fan′sē) *adj.* having much design and decoration; not plain; elaborate [a *fancy* dress]. —**fan′ci·er, fan′ci·est**

farm (färm) *n.* **1** a piece of land used to raise crops or animals; also, the house, barn, orchards, etc. on such land. **2** any place where certain things are raised [An area of water for raising fish is a fish *farm*.]

farm·er (fär′mər) *n.* a person who owns or works on a farm.

fash·ion (fash′ən) *n.* **1** the popular or up-to-date way of dressing, speaking, or behaving; style [It was once the *fashion* to wear powdered wigs.] **2** the way in which a thing is done, made, or formed [tea served in the Japanese *fashion*]. ◆*v.* to make, form, or shape [Bees *fashion* honeycombs out of wax.]

fau·cet (fô′sət *or* fä′sət) *n.* a device with a valve which can be turned on or off to control the flow of a liquid, as from a pipe; tap; cock.

feath·er (fe*th*′ər) *n.* **1** any of the parts that grow out of the skin of birds, covering the body and filling out the wings and tail. Feathers are soft and light. **2** anything like a feather in looks, lightness, etc. **3** the same class or kind [birds of a *feather*]. —**feath′er·y** *adj.*

Feb·ru·ar·y (feb′roͧo er′ē *or* feb′yoͧo er′ē) *n.* the second month of the year. It usually has 28 days but in leap year it has 29 days: abbreviated **Feb.**

fed·er·al (fed′ər əl) *adj.* **1** of or describing a union of states having a central government. **2** of such a central government [a *federal* constitution]. ☆**3** *usually* **Federal,** of the central government of the U.S. [the *Federal* courts]. —**fed′er·al·ist** *adj., n.*

fel·low·ship (fel′ō ship′) *n.* **1** friendship; companionship. **2** a group of people having the same activities or interests. **3** money given to a student at a university or college to help him or her study for a higher degree.

fer·ry (fer′ē) *v.* to take or go across a river or bay in a boat or raft. [They *ferried* our cars to the island.] —**fer′ried, fer′ry·ing**

fes·ti·val (fes′tə vəl) *n.* **1** a happy holiday [The Mardi Gras in New Orleans is a colorful *festival*.] **2** a time of special celebration or entertainment [Our town holds a garlic *festival* every spring.]

fierce (firs) *adj.* **1** wild or cruel; violent; raging [a *fierce* dog; a *fierce* wind]. **2** very strong or eager [a *fierce* effort]. —**fierc′er, fierc′est** —**fierce′ly** *adv.* —**fierce′ness** *n.*

fi·nal (fī′nəl) *adj.* **1** coming at the end; last; concluding [the *final* chapter in a book]. **2** allowing no further change; deciding [The decision of the judges is *final*.] ◆*n.* **1** anything final. **2 finals,** *pl.* the last set in a series of games, tests, etc. —**fi′nal·ly** *adv.*

fi·nance (fi nans′ *or* fī′nans) *n.* **1 finances,** *pl.* all the money or income that a government, company, person, etc. has ready for use. **2** the managing of money matters [Bankers are often experts in *finance*.] ◆*v.* to give or get money for [loans to *finance* new business]. —**fi·nanced′, fi·nanc′ing**

fin·ger·nail (fiŋ′gər nāl) *n.* the hard, tough cover at the top of each finger tip.

fin·ger·print (fiŋ′gər print) *n.* the mark made by pressing the tip of a finger against a flat surface. The fine lines and circles form a pattern that can be used to identify a person. ◆*v.* to take the fingerprints of someone by pressing the finger tips on an inked surface and then on paper.

flaw (flô *or* flä) *n.* **1** a break, scratch, crack, etc. that spoils something; blemish [There is a *flaw* in this diamond.] **2** any fault or error [a *flaw* in one's reasoning]. —**flaw′less** *adj.* —**flaw′less·ly** *adv.*

flur·ry (flʉr′ē) *n.* ☆**1** a sudden, short rush of wind, or a sudden, light fall of rain or snow. **2** a sudden, brief excitement or confusion. —*pl.* **flur′ries** ◆*v.* to confuse or excite [New drivers get *flurried* when they are in heavy traffic.] —**flur′ried, flur′ry·ing**

foam·y (fōm′ē) *adj.* foaming, full of foam, or like foam [the *foamy* water in the rapids]. —**foam′i·er, foam′i·est** —**foam′i·ness** *n.*

for·bid (fər bid′) **v.** to order that something not be done; not allow; prohibit [The law *forbids* you to park your car there. Talking out loud is *forbidden* in the library.] —**for·bade′** or **for·bad′, for·bid′den, for·bid′ding**

fore·arm (fôr′ ärm) **v.** to arm beforehand; get ready for trouble before it comes.

fore·cast (fôr′kast) **v.** to tell or try to tell how something will turn out; predict [Rain is *forecast* for tomorrow.] —**fore′cast** or **fore′cast·ed, fore′cast·ing** ◆**n.** a telling of what will happen; prediction [a weather *forecast*]. —**fore′cast·er n.**

for·eign (fôr′in *or* fär′in) **adj. 1** that is outside one's own country, region, etc. [a *foreign* land]. **2** of, from, or dealing with other countries [*foreign* trade; *foreign* languages; *foreign* policy]. **3** not belonging; not a natural or usual part [conduct *foreign* to one's nature; *foreign* matter in the eye].

fore·see (fôr sē′) **v.** to see or know beforehand [to *foresee* the future]. —**fore·saw′, fore·seen′, fore·see′ing**

fore·sight (fôr′sīt) **n.** the ability to look ahead and plan for the future [Amy had the *foresight* to bring a snack on our hike.]

fore·warn (fôr wôrn′) **v.** to warn ahead of time [We were *forewarned* we wouldn't get tickets later.]

for·feit (fôr′fit) **v.** to give up or lose something because of what one has done or has failed to do [Because our team was late in arriving, we had to *forfeit* the game.] ◆**n.** the thing that is forfeited; penalty.

for·giv·a·ble (fər giv′ə bəl) **adj.** deserving to be forgiven; excusable [*forgivable* anger].

for·give (fər giv′) **v.** to give up feeling angry or wanting to punish; show mercy to; excuse or pardon [She *forgave* him for his unkindness to her.] —**for·gave′, for·giv′en, for·giv′ing** —**for·giv′a·ble adj.**

for·ty six (fôrt′ē siks) **n.** the cardinal number equal to four times ten plus six; 46.

for·ward (fôr′wərd) **adj. 1** at, toward, or of the front. **2** ahead of others in ideas, growth, progress, etc.; advanced. **3** ready or eager; prompt [She was *forward* in helping.] **4** too bold or free in manners; rude or impudent. —**for′ward·ness n.**

fos·sil (fäs′əl) **n. 1** any hardened remains or prints, as in rocks or bogs, of plants or animals that lived many years ago. **2** a person who is very set or old-fashioned in his or her ideas or ways. ◆**adj. 1** of or like a fossil. **2** taken from the earth [Coal and oil are *fossil* fuels.]

freight (frāt) **n. 1** a load of goods shipped by train, truck, ship, airplane, etc. **2** the cost of shipping such goods. **3** the shipping of goods in this way [Send it by *freight*.]

French (french) **adj.** of France, its people, etc. ◆**n.** the language of France. —**the French,** the people of France.

friend·ly (frend′lē) **adj. 1** of, like, to, or from a friend; kindly [some *friendly* advice]. **2** showing good and peaceful feelings; ready to be a friend [a *friendly* nation]. —**friend′li·er, friend′li·est** ◆**adv.** in a friendly way [to act *friendly*]. —**friend′li·ness n.**

fright·en (frīt′n) **v. 1** to make or become suddenly afraid; scare. **2** to force to do something by making afraid [He was *frightened* into confessing.]

frol·ic (fräl′ik) **n.** a lively game or party; merry play. ◆**v.** to play or romp about in a happy and carefree way. —**frol′icked, frol′ick·ing**

fu·el (fyo͞o′əl) **n. 1** anything that is burned to give heat or power [Coal, gas, oil, and wood are *fuels*.] **2** anything that makes a strong feeling even stronger [Their teasing only added *fuel* to her anger.] ◆**v. 1** to supply with fuel. **2** to get fuel. —**fu′eled** or **fu′elled, fu′el·ing** or **fu′el·ling**

fund (fund) **n. 1** an amount of money to be used for a particular purpose [a scholarship *fund*]. **2 funds**, *pl.* money on hand, ready for use. **3** a supply; stock [a *fund* of good will].

fu·ture (fyo͞o′chər) **adj. 1** in the time to come; after the present time [a *future* date; my *future* happiness]. **2** showing time to come ["Shall" and "will" are used with a verb to express *future* tense.] ◆**n. 1** the time that is to come [We'll buy a new car sometime in the *future*.] **2** what is going to be [We all have some control over the *future*.] **3** chance to succeed [She has a great *future* as a lawyer.] —**fu′tur·is′tic adj.**

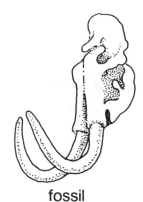

fossil

gadg·et (gaj′ət) **n. 1** a small, mechanical thing having some special use [a *gadget* for opening cans]. **2** any interesting but not very useful device.

gain (gān) **n. 1** a thing or amount added; increase or addition [a *gain* in weight]. **2** *often* **gains**, *pl.* profit or winnings [the *gains* from our business]. **3** the act of getting something, especially money [A love of *gain* can make a person greedy.] ◆**v. 1** to get as an increase or advantage [He *gained* ten pounds in two months.] **2** to become better; improve [She *gained* in health.] —**gained, gaining**

gall·blad·der (gôl′blad ər) **n.** a small sac attached to the liver: the gall, or bile, is stored in it.

ga·rage (gər äzh′ *or* gər äj′) **n. 1** a closed place where automobiles are sheltered. **2** a place where automobiles are repaired.

a	ask, fat
ā	ape, date
ä	car, lot
e	elf, ten
ē	even, meet
i	is, hit
ī	ice, fire
ō	open, go
ô	law, horn
oi	oil, point
oo	look, pull
o͞o	ooze, tool
ou	out, crowd
u	up, cut
u	fur, fern
ə	a in ago
	e in agent
	e in father
	i in unity
	o in collect
	u in focus
ch	chin, arch
ŋ	ring, singer
sh	she, dash
th	thin, truth
th	then, father
zh	s in pleasure

gorilla

graduate

gen·er·al (jen′ər əl) *adj.* **1** of, for, or from the whole or all, not just a part or some [to promote the *general* welfare]. **2** widespread or common [The *general* opinion of him is unfavorable.] **3** having to do with the main parts but not with details [the *general* features of a plan]. **4** not special or specialized [*general* science; a *general* store]. **5** highest in rank; most important [the attorney *general*].

gen·er·a·tion (jen′ər ā′shən) *n.* **1** a single stage in the history of a family [Grandmother, mother, and son are three *generations*.] **2** all the people born at about the same time [Most of his *generation* of men spent time in the army.] **3** the average time between the birth of one generation and the birth of the next, about 30 years.

gen·er·ous (jen′ər əs) *adj.* **1** willing to give or share; not selfish or stingy; openhanded. **2** large; great in amount [*generous* helpings of dessert]. **3** not mean; noble and forgiving [To forgive your enemy is a *generous* act.] —**gen′er·ous·ly** *adv.* —**gen′er·ous·ness** *n.*

ge·og·ra·phy (jē ôg′rə fē *or* jē ä′grə fē) *n.* **1** the study of the surface of the earth and how it is divided into continents, countries, seas, etc. Geography also deals with the climates, plants, animals, minerals, etc. of the earth. **2** the natural features of a certain part of the earth [the *geography* of Ohio]. —**ge·og′ra·pher** *n.*

ge·ol·o·gy (jē ä′lə jē) *n.* the study of the earth's crust and of the way in which its layers were formed. It includes the study of rocks and fossils. —**ge·ol′o·gist** *n.*

ge·om·e·try (jē äm′ə trē) *n.* the branch of mathematics that deals with lines, angles, surfaces, and solids, and with their measurement.

Geor·gia (jôr′jə) **1** a State in the southeastern part of the U.S.: abbreviated **Ga., GA** **2** a republic in the southwestern part of the U.S.S.R. —**Geor′gian** *adj., n.*

ges·ture (jes′chər) *n.* **1** a motion made with some part of the body, especially the hands or arms, to show some idea or feeling. **2** anything said or done to show one's feelings; sometimes, something done just for effect, and not really meant [Our neighbor's gift was a *gesture* of friendship.] ◆*v.* to make a gesture or gestures. —**ges′tured, ges′tur·ing**

gi·gan·tic (jī gan′tik) *adj.* like a giant in size; very big; huge; enormous [a *gigantic* building].

gnaw (nô *or* nä) *v.* **1** to bite and wear away bit by bit with the teeth [The rat *gnawed* the rope in two. The dog *gnawed* on the bone.] **2** to make by gnawing [to *gnaw* a hole]. **3** to keep on troubling for a long time [Jealousy *gnawed* at her heart.] —**gnawed, gnaw′ing, gnaws**

goose (gōōs) *n.* a swimming bird that is like a duck but has a larger body and a longer neck; especially, the female of this bird: the male is called a *gander.* —*pl.* **geese**

gorge (gôrj) *n.* a narrow pass or valley between steep cliffs or walls ◆*v.* to stuff with food in a greedy way [to *gorge* oneself with cake]. —**gorged, gorg′ing**

☆**go·ril·la** (gə ril′ə) *n.* the largest and strongest of the apes, found in African jungles.

gov·er·nor (guv′ər nər) *n.* ☆**1** the person elected to be head of a State of the United States. **2** a person appointed to govern a province, territory, etc. **3** any of the persons who direct some organization [the board of *governors* of a hospital]. **4** a device in an engine, etc. that automatically controls its speed. —**gov′er·nor·ship′** *n.*

grad·u·ate (gra′jōō ət) *n.* a person who has finished a course of study at a school or college and has been given a diploma or degree. ◆*adj.* **1** that is a graduate [*Graduate* students work for degrees above the bachelor's.] ☆**2** of or for graduates [*graduate* courses]. ◆*v.* (gra′jōō āt′) **1** to make or become a graduate of a school or college. **2** to mark off with small lines for measuring [A thermometer is a tube *graduated* in degrees.] —**grad′u·at·ed, grad′u·at·ing** —**grad′u·a′tion** *n.*

grand·par·ent (grand′per ənt) *n.* a grandfather or grandmother.

gran·ite (gran′it) *n.* a very hard rock used for buildings and monuments.

grape·fruit (grāp′frōōt) *n.* a large, round citrus fruit with a yellow rind and a juicy, somewhat sour pulp.

grate·ful (grāt′fəl) *adj.* **1** feeling thankful or showing thanks; appreciative. **2** pleasing or welcome [a *grateful* blessing]. —**grate′ful·ly** *adv.* —**grate′ful·ness** *n.*

great (grāt) *adj.* **1** much above the average in size, degree, power, etc.; big or very big; much or very much [the *Great* Lakes; a *great* distance; *great* pain]. **2** very much of a [a *great* reader]. **3** very important; noted; remarkable [a *great* composer; a *great* discovery]. **4** older or younger by a generation: *used in words formed with a hyphen* [my *great*-aunt; my *great*-niece]. —**great′er, great′est** —**great′ly** *adv.* —**great′ness** *n.*

greed·y (grēd′ē) *adj.* wanting or taking all that one can get with no thought of what others need [The *greedy* girl ate all the cookies.] —**greed′i·er, greed′i·est** —**greed′i·ly** *adv.* —**greed′i·ness** *n.*

green (grēn) *adj.* having the color of grass [*green* peas].

grief (grēf) *n.* **1** deep and painful sorrow, as that caused by someone's death. **2** something that causes such sorrow.

grieve (grēv) *v.* to feel grief; be sad [She is *grieving* over a lost cat.] —**grieved, griev′ing**

gro·cer·y (grō′sər ē) *n.* ☆**1** a store selling food and household supplies. **2 groceries,** *pl.* the goods sold by a grocer.

guest (gest) *n.* **1** a person who is visiting another's home, or who is being treated to a meal, etc. by another. **2** any paying customer of a hotel or restaurant. **3** any person invited to appear on a program.

guilt·y (gil′tē) *adj.* **1** having done something wrong; being to blame for something [She is often *guilty* of telling lies.] **2** judged in court to be a wrongdoer [The jury found him *guilty* of robbery.] —**guilt′i·er, guilt′i·est** —**guilt′i·ly** *adv.* —**guilt′i·ness** *n.*

gust (gust) *n.* **1** a strong and sudden rush of air or of something carried by the air [a *gust* of wind; *gusts* of smoke]. **2** a sudden outburst of laughter, rage, etc. ◆*v.* to blow in gusts. —**gust′y** *adj.*

Hh

hab·i·tat (hab′i tat′) *n.* the place where an animal or plant is normally found [Woodland streams are the *habitat* of beavers.]

hair·cut (her′kut) *n.* the act or a style of cutting the hair of the head.

half (haf) *n.* **1** either of the two equal parts of something [Five is *half* of ten.] **2** a half hour [It is *half* past two.] **3** either of the two parts of an inning in baseball, or of the two main time periods of a game of football, basketball, etc. —*pl.* **halves**

☆**hall·way** (hôl′wā) *n.* a passageway, as between rooms; corridor.

ham·burg·er (ham′burg ər) *n.* **1** ground beef **2** a small patty of ground beef, fried or broiled.

ham·mock (ham′ək) *n.* a long piece of netting or canvas that is hung with ropes at each end and is used as a bed or couch.

harsh (härsh) *adj.* **1** not pleasing to the senses [*harsh* music] **2** cruel or severe [*harsh* punishment]. —**harsh′er, harsh′est**

har·vest (här′vəst) *n.* **1** the act of gathering a crop of grain, fruit, etc. when it becomes ripe. **2** the time of the year when a crop is gathered. **3** all the grain, fruit, etc. gathered in one season; crop [a large *harvest*]. **4** the results of doing something [She reaped a *harvest* of love for all her good works.]

hast·y (hās′tē) *adj.* **1** done or made with haste; hurried [a *hasty* lunch]. **2** done or made too quickly, without enough thought; rash [a *hasty* decision]. —**hast′i·er, hast′i·est** —**hast′i·ly** *adv.* —**hast′i·ness** *n.*

haul (hôl) *v.* **1** to move by pulling; drag or tug [We *hauled* the boat up on the beach.] **2** to carry by wagon, truck, etc. [He *hauls* steel for a large company.] **3** to change the course of a ship by setting the sails.

hawk (hôk *or* häk) *n.* a large bird with a strong, hooked beak and claws, and keen sight. It captures and eats smaller birds and animals. ◆*v.* to hunt small game with the help of trained hawks.

heal (hēl) *v.* to make or become well, sound, or healthy; cure or be cured [The wound *healed* slowly.] —**healed, heal′ing**

health·y (hel′thē) *adj.* **1** having good health; well [a *healthy* child]. **2** showing good health [a *healthy* appetite]. **3** good for one's health; healthful [a *healthy* climate]. —**health′i·er, health′i·est** —**health′i·ness** *n.*

heav·y (hev′ē) *adj.* **1** hard to lift or move because of its weight; weighing very much [a *heavy* load]. **2** weighing more than is usual for its kind [Lead is a *heavy* metal.] **3** larger, deeper, greater, etc. than usual [a *heavy* vote; a *heavy* sleep; a *heavy* blow]. **4** full of sorrow; sad [a *heavy* heart]. **5** hard to do, bear, etc.; difficult [*heavy* work; *heavy* sorrow]. —**heav′i·er, heav′i·est** —**heav′i·ly** *adv.* —**heav′i·ness** *n.*

He·brew (hē′brōō) *n.* **1** a member of the ancient people of the Bible who settled in Canaan; Israelite. The Hebrews were the ancestors of the Jews. **2** the ancient language of the Israelites or the modern form of this language, used in Israel today. It is written in a different alphabet from English. ◆*adj.* of the Hebrews or of the Hebrew language.

hel·met (hel′mət) *n.* a hard covering to protect the head, worn by soldiers, certain athletes, motorcycle riders, etc.

hem·i·sphere (hem′i sfir′) *n.* **1** half of a sphere or globe [The dome of the church was in the shape of a *hemisphere*.] **2** any of the halves into which the earth's surface is divided in geography.

his·to·ry (his′tər ē) *n.* **1** what has happened in the life of a people, country, science, art, etc.; also, an account of this [the *history* of medicine; a *history* of England]. **2** the record of everything that has happened in the past [Nero was one of the worst tyrants in *history*.] **3** the science or study that keeps a record of past events [How will *history* treat our times?] **4** a story or tale [This hat has a strange *history*.] —*pl.* **his′to·ries**

hoax (hōks) *n.* something that is meant to trick or fool others, especially a practical joke. ◆*v.* to play a trick on; fool. —**hoax′er** *n.*

hope (hōp) *n.* **1** a feeling that what one wants will happen [We gave up *hope* of being rescued.] **2** the thing that one wants [It is my *hope* to go to college.] **3** a person or thing on which one may base some hope [The 1500-meter run is our last *hope* for a victory.] ◆*v.* **1** to have hope; want and expect [I *hope* to see you soon.] **2** to want to believe [I *hope* I didn't overlook anybody.] —**hoped, hop′ing**

helmets

a	ask, fat
ā	ape, date
ä	car, lot
e	elf, ten
ē	even, meet
i	is, hit
ī	ice, fire
ō	open, go
ô	law, horn
oi	oil, point
ōō	look, pull
ōō	ooze, tool
ou	out, crowd
u	up, cut
u	fur, fern
ə	a in ago
	e in agent
	e in father
	i in unity
	o in collect
	u in focus
ch	chin, arch
ŋ	ring, singer
sh	she, dash
th	thin, truth
th	then, father
zh	s in pleasure

iceberg

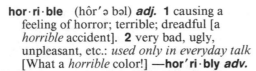

igloo

hor·ri·ble (hôr′ə bəl) *adj.* **1** causing a feeling of horror; terrible; dreadful [a *horrible* accident]. **2** very bad, ugly, unpleasant, etc.: *used only in everyday talk* [What a *horrible* color!] —**hor′ri·bly** *adv.*

hu·man·i·ty (hyōō man′ə tē) *n.* **1** all human beings; the human race [Could *humanity* survive an atomic war?] **2** kindness or sympathy [She showed her *humanity* by caring for the sick.] **3** the special qualities of all human beings; human nature [It is our common *humanity* to be selfish at one time and unselfish at another.] —*pl.* **hu·man′i·ties** —**the humanities,** studies that deal with human relations and human thought, as literature, philosophy, the fine arts, etc., but not the sciences.

hu·mid·i·ty (hyōō mid′ə tē) *n.* dampness; especially, the amount of moisture in the air.

hu·mor·ous (hyōō′mər əs) *adj.* funny or amusing; comical. —**hu′mor·ous·ly** *adv.*

Hun·ga·ry (huŋ′gər ē) a country in central Europe. —**Hun·gar′i·an** (huŋ ger′ē ən) *adj., n.*

hun·gry (huŋ′grē) *adj.* **1** wanting or needing food [Cold weather makes me *hungry.*] **2** having a strong desire; eager [*hungry* for praise]. —**hun′gri·er, hun′gri·est** —**hun′gri·ly** *adv.* —**hun′gri·ness** *n.*

hy·phen (hī′fən) *n.* the mark (-), used between the parts of a compound word (as *court-martial*), or between the parts of a word divided at the end of a line. ◆*v.* to hyphenate.

Ii

ice·berg (īs′bʉrg) *n.* a mass of ice broken off from a glacier and floating in the sea. The larger part of an iceberg is under water.

i·ci·cle (ī′sik əl) *n.* a hanging stick of ice formed by water freezing as it drips down.

i·den·ti·fi·ca·tion (ī den′tə fi kā′shən) *n.* **1** anything that identifies a person or thing [Fingerprints are used as *identification.*] **2** an identifying or being identified.

ig·loo (ig′lōō) *n.* a hut built by Eskimos using blocks of packed snow. —*pl.* **ig′loos**

il·lus·trate (il′ə strāt *or* i lus′trāt) *v.* **1** to make clear or explain by giving examples, making comparisons, etc. [Census figures *illustrate* how the city has grown.] **2** to put drawings or pictures in that explain or decorate [an *illustrated* book]. —**il′lus·trat·ed, il′lus·trat·ing**

i·mag·i·na·tion (i maj′i nā′shən) *n.* **1** the act or power of making up pictures or ideas in the mind of what is not present or of how things might be [The flying saucer you thought you saw is just in your *imagination.* It takes great *imagination* to write a play.] **2** the ability to understand and appreciate what others imagine, especially in art and literature [She hasn't enough *imagination* to know what that short story is about.]

im·i·ta·tion (im′i tā′shən) *n.* **1** the act of imitating or copying [The children danced in *imitation* of swaying trees.] **2** a copy or likeness [These jewels are clever *imitations* of precious gems.] ◆*adj.* made to look like something better; not real [a belt of *imitation* leather].

im·mense (im mens′) *adj.* very large; huge; vast [an *immense* territory]. —**im·mense′ly** *adv.*

im·merse (im mʉrs′) *v.* **1** to plunge or dip into a liquid. **2** to baptize a person by dipping under water. **3** to get or be deeply in; absorb [*immersed* in study; *immersed* in sadness]. —**im·mersed′, im·mers′ing** —**im·mer·sion** (im mʉr′shən) *n.*

im·mo·bile (im mō′bəl) *adj.* not moving or changing; without motion [The frightened deer stood *immobile.*] —**im′mo·bil′i·ty** *n.*

im·po·lite (im pə līt′) *adj.* not polite; rude. —**im·po·lite′ly** *adv.* —**im·po·lite′ness** *n.*

im·por·tance (im pôrt′ns) *n.* the fact of being important [news of little *importance*].

im·por·tant (im pôrt′nt) *adj.* **1** having much meaning or value [Our wedding anniversary is an *important* date in our lives.] **2** having power or authority, or acting as if one had power [an *important* official]. —**im·por′tant·ly** *adv.*

im·pose (im pōz′) *v.* to put on as a duty, burden, or penalty [to *impose* a tax on furs]. —**im·posed′, im·pos′ing**

im·pos·si·ble (im päs′ə bəl) *adj.* **1** that cannot be done, or happen; not possible [He found it *impossible* to lift the crate.] **2** very unpleasant or hard to put up with [You're always asking *impossible* questions!] —**im·pos′si·bil′i·ty** *n.* —**im·pos′si·bly** *adv.*

im·pres·sion (im presh′ən) *n.* **1** the act of impressing. **2** a mark or imprint made by pressing [The police took an *impression* of his fingerprints.] **3** an effect produced on the mind [The play made a great *impression* on us.] **4** the effect produced by some action [Cleaning made no *impression* on the stain.] **5** a vague feeling [I have the *impression* that someone was here.]

im·prop·er (im präp′ər) *adj.* **1** not proper or suitable; unfit [Sandals are *improper* shoes for tennis.] **2** not true; wrong; incorrect [an *improper* street address]. **3** not decent; in bad taste [*improper* jokes]. —**im·prop′er·ly** *adv.*

im·prove (im prōōv′) **v. 1** to make or become better [Business has *improved*.] **2** to make good use of [She *improved* her spare time by reading.] —**im·proved′, im·prov′ing**

im·pure (im pyoor′) **adj. 1** not clean; dirty [Smoke made the air *impure*.] **2** mixed with things that do not belong [*impure* gold] **3** not decent or proper [*impure* thoughts].

in·clude (in klōōd′) **v.** to have or take in as part of a whole; contain [Prices *include* taxes.] —**in·clud′ed, in·clud′ing**

in·come (in′kum) **n.** the money that one gets as wages, salary, rent, interest, profit, etc.

in·com·plete (in kəm plēt′) **adj.** not complete; without all its parts; not whole or finished. —**in·com·plete′ly adv.**

in·crease (in krēs′) **v.** to make or become greater, larger, etc.; add to or grow [When she *increased* her wealth, her power *increased*.] —**in·creased′, in·creas′ing** ◆**n.** (in′krēs) **1** an increasing; addition; growth [an *increase* in population]. **2** the amount by which something increases [a population *increase* of 10%].

in·de·pend·ence (in′dē pen′dəns) **n.** the state of being independent; freedom from the control of another or others.

in·ex·pen·sive (in′ek spen′siv) **adj.** not expensive; low-priced. —**in′ex·pen′sive·ly adv.**

in·fant (in′fənt) **n.** a very young child; baby. ◆**adj. 1** of or for infants [a book on *infant* care. **2** in a very early stage [an *infant* nation].

in·field (in′fēld) **n.** ☆**1** the part of a baseball field enclosed by the four base lines. ☆**2** all the infielders.

in·for·ma·tion (in′fər mā′shən) **n. 1** an informing or being informed [This is for your *information* only.] **2** something told or facts learned; news or knowledge; data [An encyclopedia gives *information* about many things.] **3** a person or service that answers certain questions [Ask *information* for the location of the shoe department.]

in·hale (in hāl′) **v.** to breathe in; draw into the lungs, as air or tobacco smoke. —**in·haled′, in·hal′ing** —**in·ha·la·tion** (in′hə lā′shən) **n.** —**in·hal′er n.**

in·ju·ry (in′jər ē) **n.** harm or damage done to a person or thing [*injuries* received in a fall; *injury* to one's good name]. —**pl. in′ju·ries**

in·quire (in kwīr′) **v.** to ask a question; ask about in order to learn [The students *inquired* about their grades. We *inquired* the way home.] —**in·quired′, in·quir′ing** —**in·quir′er n.**

in·se·cure (in′si kyoor′) **adj. 1** not secure or safe; dangerous; not dependable [an *insecure* mountain ledge; an *insecure* partnership]. **2** not feeling safe or confident [A person can feel *insecure* in a new job.] —**in′se·cure′ly adv.** —**in·se·cu·ri·ty** (in′si kyoor′ə tē) **n.**

in·spec·tor (in spek′tər) **n. 1** a person who inspects, as in a factory. **2** a police officer who ranks next below a superintendent.

in·spire (in spīr′) **v. 1** to cause, urge, or influence to do something [The sunset *inspired* her to write a poem.] **2** to cause to have a certain feeling or thought [Praise *inspires* us with confidence.] **3** to arouse or bring about [Your kindness *inspired* his love.] **4** to do or make as if guided by some higher power [The Bible is an *inspired* book.] —**in·spired′, in·spir′ing**

in·stant (in′stənt) **n. 1** a very short time; moment [Wait just an *instant*.] **2** a particular moment [At that *instant* I fell.] ◆**adj. 1** with no delay; immediate [an *instant* response]. **2** that can be prepared quickly; as by adding water [*instant* coffee].

in·sti·tu·tion (in′stə tōō′shən *or* in′stə tyōō′shən) **n. 1** an instituting or being instituted. **2** an established law, custom, practice, etc. [the *institution* of marriage]. **3** a school, church, prison, or other organization with a special purpose. —**in′sti·tu′tion·al adj.**

in·ter·pret·er (in tur′prə tər) **n.** a person who interprets, especially one whose work is translating things said in one language into another language.

in·ter·view (in′tər vyōō) **n. 1** a meeting of one person with another to talk about something [an *interview* with an employer about a job.] ☆**2** a meeting in which a person is asked about his or her opinions, activities, etc., as by a reporter. —**in′ter·view·er n.**

in·tes·tine (in tes′tin) **n.** *usually* **intestines**, *pl.* the tube through which food passes from the stomach. The long, narrow part with many coils is called the **small intestine**, and the shorter and thicker part is called the **large intestine**. Food is digested in the intestines as well as in the stomach.

in·tro·duce (in trə dōōs′ *or* in trə dyōōs′) **v. 1** to make known; make acquainted; present [Please *introduce* me to them.] **2** to bring into use; make popular or common [Science has *introduced* many new words.] **3** to make familiar with something [They *introduced* me to the music of Bach.] **4** to bring to the attention of others in a formal way [to *introduce* a bill into Congress]. —**in·tro·duced′, in·tro·duc′ing**

in·ven·to·ry (in′vən tôr′ē) **n. 1** a complete list of goods or property [The store makes an *inventory* of its stock every year.] **2** the stock of goods on hand [Because of fewer sales this year, dealers have large *inventories*.] —**pl. in′ven·to′ries** ◆**v.** to make an inventory or list of [to *inventory* our books]. —**in′ven·to′ried, in′ven·to′ry·ing**

in·ves·ti·gate (in ves′tə gāt′) **v.** to search into so as to learn the facts; examine in detail [to *investigate* an accident]. —**in·ves′ti·gat·ed, in·ves′ti·gat·ing** —**in·ves′ti·ga′tion n.** —**in·ves′ti·ga′tor n.**

infant

a	ask, fat
ā	ape, date
ä	car, lot
e	elf, ten
ē	even, meet
i	is, hit
ī	ice, fire
ō	open, go
ô	law, horn
oi	oil, point
oo	look, pull
ōō	ooze, tool
ou	out, crowd
u	up, cut
ʉ	fur, fern
ə	a in ago
	e in agent
	e in father
	i in unity
	o in collect
	u in focus
ch	chin, arch
ŋ	ring, singer
sh	she, dash
th	thin, truth
th	then, father
zh	s in pleasure

Jefferson

in·vis·i·ble (in viz′ə bəl) *adj.* not able to be seen [The moon was *invisible* behind the clouds.] —**in·vis′i·bly** *adv.*

i·ron (ī′ərn) *n.* **1** a strong metal that is a chemical element. It can be molded or stretched into various shapes after being heated, and is much used in the form of steel. **2** a device made of iron or other metal and having a flat, smooth bottom. It is heated and used for pressing clothes, etc. **3 irons,** *pl.* iron shackles or chains.

is·land (ī′lənd) *n.* **1** a piece of land smaller than a continent and surrounded by water. **2** any place set apart from what surrounds it [The oasis was an *island* of green in the desert.]

I·tal·ian (i tal′yən) *adj.* of Italy, its people, etc. ◆*n.* **1** a person born or living in Italy. **2** the language of Italy.

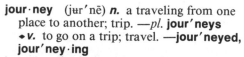

jack·et (jak′ət) *n.* **1** a short coat. **2** an outer covering, as the skin of a potato, or the paper wrapper for a book. ☆**3** a cardboard holder for a phonograph record.

Ja·pan (jə pan′) a country east of Korea, made up of many islands.

Jap·a·nese (jap ə nēz′) *n.* **1** a member of a people whose native country is Japan. —*pl.* **Jap·a·nese′ 2** the language of Japan. ◆*adj.* of Japan, its people, language, or culture.

Jef·fer·son (jef′ər sən), **Thomas** (täm′əs) 1743–1826; the third president of the United States, from 1801 to 1809.

jel·ly·fish (jel′ē fish′) *n.* a sea animal with a body that feels like jelly.

jellyfish

jin·gle (jiŋ′gəl) *v.* **1** to make ringing, tinkling sounds, as bits of metal striking together [The pennies *jingled* in my pocket.] **2** to make jingle [She *jingled* her keys.] **3** to have simple rhymes and a regular rhythm, as some poetry and music. —**jin′gled, jin′gling** ◆*n.* a ringing, tinkling sound.

join (join) *v.* **1** to bring together; connect; fasten [We *joined* hands and stood in a circle.] **2** to come together; meet [Where do the Ohio and Mississippi rivers *join*?] **3** to become a part or member of [Paula has *joined* our club.] **4** to go along with; accompany [*Join* us in a walk.] **5** to take part along with others [*Join* in the game.]

joint (joint) *n.* **1** a place where two things or parts are joined [Water leaked from the *joint* in the pipe.] **2** a place or part where two bones are joined, usually so that they can move [the elbow *joint*]. **3** a large cut of meat with the bone still in it. ◆*v.* **1** to connect by a joint or joints [Bamboo is *jointed*.] **2** to cut at the joints [The butcher *jointed* the chicken.]

jour·ney (jur′nē) *n.* a traveling from one place to another; trip. —*pl.* **jour′neys** ◆*v.* to go on a trip; travel. —**jour′neyed, jour′ney·ing**

jun·gle (juŋ′gəl) *n.* land thickly covered with trees, vines, etc., as in the tropics. Jungles are usually filled with animals that prey on one another.

ju·ry (joor′ē *or* jur′ē) *n.* **1** a group of people chosen to listen to the evidence in a law trial, and then to reach a decision, or verdict. **2** a group of people chosen to decide the winners in a contest. —*pl.* **ju′ries**

jus·tice (jus′tis) *n.* **1** the condition of being just or fair [There is *justice* in their demand.] **2** reward or punishment as deserved [The prisoner asked only for *justice*.] **3** the upholding of what is just or lawful [a court of *justice*]. **4** a judge [a *justice* of the Supreme Court].

Kan·sas (kan′zəs) a state in the central part of the U.S.: abbreviated **Kans., KS** —**Kan′san** *adj., n.*

kar·at (ker′ət) *n.* one 24th part of pure gold [14 *karat* gold is 14 parts pure gold and 10 parts other metal.]

keep·ing (kēp′iŋ) *n.* **1** care or protection [He left his money in her *keeping*.] **2** the observing of a rule, holiday, etc.

kid·ney (kid′nē) *n.* **1** either of a pair of organs in the central part of the body that take water and waste products out of the blood and pass them through the bladder as urine. **2** the kidney of an animal, used as food. —*pl.* **kid′neys**

kind·ness (kīnd′nəs) *n.* the condition or habit of being kind.

knead (nēd) *v.* **1** to keep pressing and squeezing dough, clay, etc. to make it ready for use. **2** to rub or press with the hands; massage [to *knead* a muscle].

knee·cap (nē′kap) *n.* the flat, movable bone that forms the front of a person's knee.

kneel (nēl) *v.* to rest on a knee or knees [Some people *kneel* when they pray.] —**knelt** or **kneeled, kneel′ing**

knob (näb) *n.* a handle that is more or less round on a door or drawer.

knock (näk) *v.* **1** to hit as with the fist; especially, to rap on a door [Who is *knocking*?] **2** to hit and cause to fall [The dog *knocked* down the papergirl.] **3** to make by hitting [to *knock* a hole in the wall]. **4** to make a pounding or tapping noise [An engine *knocks* when the combustion is faulty.]

knot (nät) *n.* **1** a lump, as in a string or ribbon, formed by a loop or a tangle drawn tight. **2** a fastening made by tying together parts or pieces of string, rope, etc. [Sailors make a variety of *knots*.] **3** a small group [a *knot* of people]. **4** something that joins closely, as the bond of marriage. **5** a unit of speed of one nautical mile (1,852 meters, or 6,076.12 feet) an hour [The ship averaged 20 *knots*.] —**knot′ted, knot′ting** *v.*

knot·hole (nät′hōl) *n.* a hole in a board or tree trunk where a knot has fallen out.

know (nō) *v.* **1** to be sure of or have the facts about [Do you *know* why grass is green? She *knows* the law.] **2** to be aware of; realize [He suddenly *knew* he would be late.] **3** to have in one's mind or memory [The actress *knows* her lines.] **4** to be acquainted with [I *know* your brother well.] **5** to recognize [I'd *know* that face anywhere.] **6** to be able to tell the difference in [It's not always easy to *know* right from wrong.] —**knew, known, know′ing**

knowl·edge (nä′lij) *n.* **1** the fact or condition of knowing [*Knowledge* of the crime spread through the town.] **2** what is known or learned through study, experience, etc. [a great *knowledge* of history].

known (nōn) *past participle of* **know.**

knuck·le (nuk′əl) *n.* **1** a joint of the finger; especially, a joint connecting a finger to the rest of the hand. **2** the knee or hock joint of a pig, calf, etc., used as food. —**knuck′led, knuck′ling**

la·bor (lā′bər) *n.* **1** work; toil. **2** a piece of work; task [We rested from our *labors*.] **3** workers as a group [an agreement between *labor* and management on wages.] **4** the act of giving birth to a child.

lab·o·ra·to·ry (lab′rə tôr′ē) *n.* a room or building where scientific work or tests are carried on, or where chemicals, drugs, etc. are prepared. —*pl.* **lab′o·ra·to′ries**

la·dies (lā′dēs) *n.* a polite form of address for women in a group ["*Ladies* and gentlemen," the speaker began.]

laugh (laf) *v.* **1** to make a series of quick sounds with the voice that show one is amused or happy or, sometimes, that show scorn. One usually smiles or grins when laughing. **2** to bring about, get rid of, etc. by means of laughter [*Laugh* your fears away.] ◆*n.* the act or sound of laughing.

laugh·ter (laf′tər) *n.* the act or sound of laughing [He shook with *laughter*.]

law·yer (lô′yər *or* lä′yər) *n.* a person whose profession is giving advice on law or acting for others in lawsuits.

lead·er (lēd′ər) *n.* a person or thing that leads, or guides. —**lead′er·ship** *n.*

leath·er (le*th*′ər) *n.* a material made from the skin of cows, horses, goats, etc. by cleaning and tanning it. ◆*adj.* made of leather.

leg·i·ble (lej′ə bəl) *adj.* clear enough to be read easily [*legible* handwriting].

lei·sure (lē′zhər *or* lezh′ər) *n.* free time not taken up with work or duty, that a person may use for rest or recreation ◆*adj.* free and not busy; spare [*leisure* time].

lep·re·chaun (lep′rə kôn *or* lep′rə kän) *n.* an elf in Irish folklore who can show a buried crock of gold to anyone who catches him.

lev·y (lev′ē) *v.* **1** to order the payment of [to *levy* a tax] **2** to wage; carry on [to *levy* war]. —**lev′ied, lev′y·ing**

li·brar·y (lī′brer′ē) *n.* **1** a place where a collection of books is kept for reading or borrowing. **2** a collection of books. —*pl.* **li′brar′ies**

li·cense (lī′səns) *n.* **1** a paper, card, etc. showing that one is permitted by law to do something [a marriage *license*; driver's *license*]. **2** freedom to ignore the usual rules [To take poetic *license* is to ignore, as in a poem, the usual rules of style, logic, etc. in order to gain a special effect.] **3** freedom of action or speech that goes beyond what is right or proper [Booing in a courtroom isn't free speech—it's *license*.] ◆*v.* to give a license to; permit by law [Are they *licensed* to fish?] —**li′censed, li′cens·ing**

like·li·hood (līk′lē hood′) *n.* the fact of being likely to happen; probability [There is a strong *likelihood* he will win.]

Lin·coln (liŋ′kən), **Abraham** (ā′brə ham) 1809–1865; 16th president of the United States, from 1861 to 1865. He was assassinated.

lit·er·a·ture (lit′ər ə chər) *n.* **1** all the writings of a certain time, country, etc.; especially, those that have lasting value because of their beauty, imagination, etc., as fine novels, plays, and poems. **2** the work or profession of writing such things; also, the study of such writings. **3** all the writings on some subject [medical *literature*].

liv·er (liv′ər) *n.* **1** a large organ of the body, near the stomach. It makes bile and helps break down food into substances that the body can absorb. **2** the liver of some animals, used as food.

loaf (lōf) *n.* a portion of bread baked in one piece, usually oblong in shape. —*pl.* **loaves**

loud (loud) *adj.* **1** strong in sound; not soft or quiet [a *loud* noise; a *loud* bell]. **2** noisy [a *loud* party]. **3** so strong as to force attention; forceful [*loud* demands]. ◆*adv.* in a loud way. —**loud′er, loud′est** —**loud′ly** *adv.* —**loud′ness** *n.*

Lincoln

a	ask, fat
ā	ape, date
ä	car, lot
e	elf, ten
ē	even, meet
i	is, hit
ī	ice, fire
ō	open, go
ô	law, horn
oi	oil, point
oo	look, pull
ōō	ooze, tool
ou	out, crowd
u	up, cut
ʉ	fur, fern
ə	a in ago
	e in agent
	e in father
	i in unity
	o in collect
	u in focus
ch	chin, arch
ŋ	ring, singer
sh	she, dash
th	thin, truth
th	then, father
zh	s in pleasure

loy·al (loi′əl) *adj.* **1** faithful to one's country [a *loyal* citizen]. **2** faithful to one's family, duty, beliefs, etc. [a *loyal* friend; a *loyal* member]. —**loy′al·ly** *adv.*

loy·al·ty (loi′əl tē) *n.* the condition of being loyal; faithfulness. —*pl.* **loy′al·ties**

lyr·ic (lir′ik) *adj.* **1** of or having to do with poetry that describes the poet's feelings and thoughts [Sonnets and odes are *lyric* poems.] **2** like a song or suitable for singing. **3** of or having a high voice that moves lightly and easily from note to note [a *lyric* soprano]. ◆*n.* **1** a lyric poem. **2** *usually* **lyrics,** *pl.* the words of a song.

Mm

mag·a·zine (mag ə zēn′ *or* mag′ə zēn) *n.* **1** a publication that comes out regularly, as weekly or monthly, and contains articles, stories, pictures, etc. **2** a place for storing things, as military supplies. **3** a space, as in a warship, for storing explosives.

mag·ni·fy (mag′nə fī) *v.* to make look or seem larger or greater than is really so [This lens *magnifies* an object to ten times its size. He *magnified* the seriousness of his illness.] —**mag′ni·fied, mag′ni·fy·ing**

ma·jor (mā′jər) *adj.* **1** greater in size, importance, amount, etc. [the *major* part of his wealth; a *major* poet]. **2** in music, that is separated from the next tone by a full step instead of a half step [a *major* interval]. ◆*n.* **1** a military officer ranking just above a captain. ☆**2** the main subject that a student is studying [History is my *major.*]

mam·mal (mam′əl) *n.* any animal with glands in the female that produce milk for feeding its young. —**mam·ma·li·an** (mə mā′lē ən) *adj., n.*

mam·moth (mam′əth) *n.* a large, extinct elephant with hairy skin and long tusks that curved upward ◆*adj.* very big; huge [a *mammoth* arena].

man·ag·er (man′ij ər) *n.* a person who manages a business.

man·ner (man′ər) *n.* **1** a way in which something happens or is done; style [the *manner* in which an artist sketches a scene]. **2** a way of acting; behavior [an angry *manner*]. **3 manners,** *pl.* ways of behaving or living, especially polite ways of behaving [It is good *manners* to say "Thank you."] **4** kind; sort [What *manner* of man is he?]

man·tle (man′təl) *n.* a loose cloak without sleeves; cape.

mas·sive (mas′iv) *adj.* large, solid, heavy, etc. [a *massive* statue]. —**mas′sive·ly** *adv.* —**mas′sive·ness** *n.*

may·or (mā′ər) *n.* the head of the government of a city or town.

mead·ow (med′ō) *n.* **1** a piece of land where grass is grown for hay. **2** low, level grassland near a stream or lake.

meas·ure (mezh′ər) *v.* to find out the size, amount, or extent of something, often by comparing with something else [*Measure* the child's height with a yardstick.] —**meas′ured, meas′ur·ing** ◆*n.* the size, amount, or extent of something, found out by measuring [The *measure* of the bucket is 15 liters.]

me·chan·ic (mə kan′ik) *n.* a worker skilled in using tools or in making, repairing, and using machinery.

me·di·a (mē′dē ə) *n.* a plural of **medium.**

med·i·cal (med′i kəl) *adj.* having to do with the practice or study of medicine [*medical* care].

me·di·um (mē′dē əm) any way by which something is done; especially, a way of communicating with the general public, as TV or newspapers: *in this meaning the plural* **media** *is sometimes used as a singular noun* [The *media* is covering the president's inauguration.]

mem·ber·ship (mem′bər ship) *n.* **1** the condition of being a member. **2** all the members of a group. **3** the number of members.

mem·o·rize (mem′ə rīz) *v.* ☆to fix in one's memory exactly or word for word; learn by heart. —**mem′o·rized, mem′o·riz·ing** —**mem′o·ri·za′tion** *n.*

men·tal (ment′l) *adj.* **1** of, for, by, or in the mind [*mental* ability; *mental* arithmetic]. **2** sick in mind [a *mental* patient]. **3** for the sick in mind [a *mental* hospital].

mer·ry (mer′ē) *adj.* filled with fun and laughter; lively and cheerful [a *merry* party]. —**mer′ri·er, mer′ri·est** —**make merry,** to have fun. —**mer′ri·ly** *adv.* —**mer′ri·ness** *n.*

Mex·i·co (mek′si kō) a country in North America, south of the U.S.

mid·air (mid er′) *n.* any point in space, not touching the ground or other surface.

mid·day (mid′dā) *n., adj. another word for* **noon.**

mid·dle (mid′əl) *n.* the point or part that is halfway between the ends or that is in the center [the *middle* of the morning; an island in the *middle* of the lake]. ◆*adj.* being in the middle or center [the *middle* toe].

mid·night (mid′nīt) *n.* twelve o'clock at night; the middle of the night. ◆*adj.* **1** of or at midnight [a *midnight* ride]. **2** like midnight; very dark [*midnight* blue].

mid·stream (mid′strēm) *n.* the middle of a stream.

mid·way (mid′wā *or* mid wā′) *adj., adv.* in the middle; halfway ◆*n.* (mid′wā) the part of a fair, circus, or amusement park where sideshows or rides are located.

mid·win·ter (mid′win′tər) *n.* **1** the middle of the winter. **2** the period around December 22.

min·i·mize (min′ə mīz) *v.* to make as small as possible; reduce to a minimum [Safe storage of gas will *minimize* the danger of fire.] —**min′i·mized, min′i·miz·ing**

mir·ror (mir′ər) *n.* **1** a smooth surface that reflects light; especially, a piece of glass coated with silver on the back; looking glass. **2** anything that gives a true description [A good novel is a *mirror* of life.] ◆*v.* to reflect as in a mirror [The moon was *mirrored* in the lake.]

mis·be·have (mis′bē hāv′) *v.* to behave in a bad way; do what one is not supposed to do. —**mis′be·haved′, mis′be·hav′ing** —**mis·be·hav·ior** (mis′bi hāv′yər) *n.*

mis·for·tune (mis fôr′chən) *n.* bad luck; trouble.

mis·judge (mis juj′) *v.* to judge unfairly or wrongly. —**mis·judged′, mis·judg′ing**

mis·lead (mis lēd′) *v.* **1** to lead in a wrong direction [That old road map will *mislead* you.] **2** to cause to believe what is not true; deceive [She *misled* us into thinking she would help.] —**mis·led′, mis·lead′ing**

mis·place (mis plās′) *v.* **1** to put in a wrong place [He *misplaced* the book of poems in the art section.] **2** to give trust, love, etc. to one who does not deserve it [I *misplaced* my confidence in you.] —**mis·placed′, mis·plac′ing**

mis·pro·nounce (mis prə nouns′) *v.* to pronounce in a wrong way [Some people *mispronounce* "cavalry" as "calvary".] —**mis·pro·nounced′, mis·pro·nounc′ing** —**mis·pro·nun·ci·a·tion** (mis′prə nun′sē ā′shən) *n.*

mis·sion (mish′ən) *n.* **1** the special duty or errand that a person or group is sent out to do, as by a church, government, air force, etc. [a *mission* to gain converts; a *mission* to increase trade; a *mission* to bomb a factory]. **2** a group of missionaries, or the place where they live, work, etc. [the foreign *missions* of a church]. **3** a group of persons sent to a foreign government to carry on dealings, as for trade, a treaty, etc.

mis·sion·ar·y (mish′ən er′ē) *n.* a person sent out by a church to spread its religion in a foreign country. —*pl.* **mis′sion·ar′ies**

mis·spell (mis spel′) *v.* to spell incorrectly. —**mis·spelled′** or **mis·spelt′, mis·spell′ing**

mis·take (mi stāk′) *n.* an idea, answer, act, etc. that is wrong; error or blunder. ◆*v.* **1** to get a wrong idea of; misunderstand [You *mistake* his real purpose.] **2** to think that someone or something is some other person or thing [to *mistake* one twin for the other]. —**mis·took′, mis·tak′en, mis·tak′ing**

mis·trust (mis trust′) *n.* a lack of trust or confidence; suspicion; doubt [He felt *mistrust* of the stranger.] ◆*v.* to have no trust or confidence in; doubt. —**mis·trust′ful** *adj.*

mis·un·der·stand (mis′un dər stand′) *v.* to understand in a way that is wrong; give a wrong meaning to. —**mis·un·der·stood** (mis′un dər stood′), —**mis′un·der·stand′ing**

mod·ern (mäd′ərn) *adj.* **1** of or having to do with the present time or the period we live in [a *modern* poet]. **2** of the period after about 1450 [the *modern* history of Europe]. **3** of or having to do with the latest styles, methods, or ideas; up-to-date [He travels the *modern* way, by jet airplane.] ◆*n.* a person who lives in modern times or has up-to-date ideas.

mod·i·fy (mäd′ə fī) *v.* **1** to make a small or partial change in [Exploration has *modified* our maps of Antarctica.] **2** in grammar, to limit the meaning of; describe or qualify [In the phrase "old man" the adjective "old" *modifies* the noun "man."] —**mod′i·fied, mod′i·fy·ing**

mois·ture (mois′chər) *n.* liquid causing a dampness, such as fine drops of water in the air.

mois·tur·ize (mois′chər īz) *v.* to add, supply, or restore moisture to the skin, the air, etc. —**mois′tur·ized, mois′tur·iz·ing** —**mois′tur·iz·er** *n.*

Mont·re·al (män′trē ôl′) a city in southern Quebec, Canada, on an island in the St. Lawrence River.

mon·u·ment (män′yōō mənt) *n.* **1** something put up in memory of a person or happening, as a statue, building, etc. **2** something great or famous, especially from long ago [Shakespeare's plays are *monuments* of English culture.]

☆**moose** (mōōs) *n.* a large animal related to the deer, of the northern U.S. and Canada. The male has broad antlers with many points. —*pl.* **moose**

mort·gage (môr′gij) *n.* **1** an agreement in which a person borrowing money gives the lender a claim to property as a pledge that the debt will be paid [The bank holds a *mortgage* of $15,000 on our house.] **2** the legal paper by which such a claim is given. ◆*v.* to pledge by a mortgage in order to borrow money [to *mortgage* a home]. —**mort′gaged, mort′gag·ing**

moth·er (muth′ər) *n.* **1** a woman as she is related to her child or children; a female parent. **2** the origin, source, or cause of something [Virginia is the State known as the *mother* of Presidents.] **3** a nun who is the head of a convent, school, etc.: *the full name is* **mother superior.** ◆*adj.* of, like, or as if from a mother [*mother* love; one's *mother* tongue]. ◆*v.* to care for as a mother does. —**moth′er·hood** *n.* —**moth′er·less** *adj.*

mo·ti·vate (mōt′ə vāt) *v.* to give a motive to or be a motive for [Love *motivated* my actions.] —**mo′ti·vat·ed, mo′ti·vat·ing** —**mo′ti·va′tion** *n.*

moose

a	ask, fat
ā	ape, date
ä	car, lot
e	elf, ten
ē	even, meet
i	is, hit
ī	ice, fire
ō	open, go
ô	law, horn
oi	oil, point
͝oo	look, pull
͞oo	ooze, tool
ou	out, crowd
u	up, cut
ʉ	fur, fern
ə	a in ago
	e in agent
	e in father
	i in unity
	o in collect
	u in focus
ch	chin, arch
ŋ	ring, singer
sh	she, dash
th	thin, truth
th	then, father
zh	s in pleasure

moun·tain·eer (mount'n ir´) *n.* **1** a person who lives in a region of mountains. **2** a person who climbs mountains. ◆*v.* to climb mountains, as for sport.

moun·tain·ous (mount'n əs) *adj.* **1** full of mountains. **2** very large [a *mountainous* debt].

move·ment (mo͞ov´mənt) *n.* **1** the act of moving or a way of moving [a *movement* of the branches; the regular *movement* of the stars]. **2** a working together to bring about some result [the *movement* for world peace].

mus·cle (mus´əl) *n.* the tissue in the body that is made up of bundles of long cells or fibers that can be stretched or squeezed together to move parts of the body [Eating protein helps build *muscle.*]

mys·ter·y (mis´tər ē *or* mis´trē) *n.* **1** something that is not known or explained, or that is kept secret [the *mystery* of life]. **2** anything that remains unexplained or is so secret that it makes people curious [That murder is still a *mystery.*] **3** a story or play about such a happening. **4** mysteries, *pl.* secret rites, especially religious rites, that are known only to a small group of people. —*pl.* **mys´ter·ies**

nar·row (ner´ō) *adj.* **1** small in width; less wide than usual [a *narrow* road]. **2** small or limited in size, amount, or degree [I was the winner by a *narrow* majority.] **3** with barely enough space, time, means, etc.; close [a *narrow* escape]. —**nar´row·ly** *adv.* —**nar´row·ness** *n.*

nat·u·ral (nach´ər əl) *adj.* **1** produced by nature; not made by man [*natural* resources; *natural* curls]. **2** of or dealing with nature [Biology and chemistry are *natural* sciences.] **3** that is part of one from birth; native [He has a *natural* ability in music.] **4** free and easy; not forced or artificial [a *natural* laugh]. —**nat´u·ral·ness** *n.*

naugh·ty (nôt´ē *or* nät´ē) *adj.* **1** not behaving; bad, disobedient, mischievous, etc. [*naughty* children]. **2** not nice or proper [*naughty* words]. —**naugh´ti·er, naugh´ti·est**—**naugh´ti·ly** *adv.* —**naugh´ti·ness** *n.*

nec·tar (nek´tər) *n.* **1** the sweet liquid in many flowers, made into honey by bees. **2** the drink of the gods in Greek myths.

nec·tar·ine (nek tə rēn´) *n.* a kind of peach that has a smooth skin.

nee·dle (nēd´əl) *n.* **1** a small, slender piece of steel with a sharp point and a hole for thread, used for sewing. **2** a slender rod of steel, bone, plastic, etc., used in knitting or crocheting. **3** a short, slender piece of metal, often tipped with diamond, that moves in the grooves of a phonograph record to pick up the vibrations. **4** the pointer of a compass, gauge, meter, etc. —**nee´dled, nee´dling** *v.*

neg·a·tive (neg´ə tiv) *adj.* **1** saying that something is not so or refusing; answering "no" [a *negative* reply]. **2** that does not help, improve, etc. [*negative* criticism]. **3** opposite to or lacking something that is positive [He always takes a *negative* attitude and expects the worst.] **4** showing that a certain disease, condition, etc. is not present [The reaction to her allergy test was *negative.*] —**neg´a·tive·ly** *adv.*

neigh·bor·hood (nā´bər ho͝od) *n.* **1** a small part or district of a city, town, etc. [an old *neighborhood*]. **2** the people in such a district [The whole *neighborhood* helped.]

nei·ther (nē´thər *or* nī´thər) *adj., pron.* not one or the other of two; not either [*Neither* boy went. *Neither* of them was invited.] ◆*conj.* not either; nor yet.

news·pa·per (no͞oz´pā pər *or* nyo͞oz´pā pər) *n.* a daily or weekly publication printed on large, folded sheets of paper and containing news, opinions, advertisements, etc.

niece (nēs) *n.* **1** the daughter of one's brother or sister. **2** the daughter of one's brother-in-law or sister-in-law.

no·ble (nō´bəl) *adj.* **1** having or showing a very good character or high morals; lofty [*noble* ideals] **2** of or having a high rank or title; aristocratic [a *noble* family].

nois·y (noi´zē) *adj.* **1** making noise [a *noisy* bell]. **2** full of noise [a *noisy* theater]. —**nois´i·er, nois´i·est** —**nois´i·ly** *adv.* —**nois´i·ness** *n.*

noon (no͞on) *n.* twelve o'clock in the daytime: also **noon´day, noon´tide, noon´time.**

nor·mal (nôr´məl) *adj.* **1** agreeing with a standard or norm; natural; usual; regular; average [It is *normal* to make a mistake sometimes.] **2** in good health; not ill or diseased.

north·east (nôrth ēst´ *or* nôr ēst´) *n.* **1** the direction halfway between north and east. **2** a place or region in or toward this direction.

nov·el (näv´əl) *adj.* new and unusual [In the year 1920, flying was still a *novel* way of travel.] ◆*n.* a long story, usually a complete book about imaginary people and happenings.

nov·el·ist (näv´əl ist) *n.* a person who writes novels.

☆**ny·lon** (nī´län) *n.* **1** a very strong, elastic material made from chemicals and used for thread, bristles, etc. **2** nylons, *pl.* stockings made of nylon yarn.

Oo

o·bey (ō bā') **v. 1** to carry out the orders of [Soldiers must *obey* their officers.] **2** to do as one is told [My dog always *obeys*.] —**o·beyed', o·bey'ing, o·beys' —o·bey'er** *n.*

ob·jec·tion (äb jek'shən) *n.* **1** a feeling of dislike or disapproval; protest [I have no *objection* to that plan.] **2** a reason for disliking or disapproving [My main *objection* to this climate is its dampness.]

ob·ser·va·tion (äb zər vā'shən) *n.* the act or power of seeing or noticing [It's a good night for *observation* of the stars.] ◆*adj.* for observing [an *observation* tower].

oc·cu·pant (äk'yoo pənt) *n.* a person who occupies land, a house, or a position [a former *occupant* of the White House].

oc·cu·py (äk'yoo pī') **v. 1** to take possession of a place by capturing it or settling in it [The Germans *occupied* much of France during World War II. Pioneers *occupied* the wilderness.] **2** to have or hold [She *occupies* an important post in the government.] **3** to live in [to *occupy* a house]. **4** to keep busy; employ [Many activities *occupy* his time.] —**oc'cu·pied, oc'cu·py·ing**

o·pin·ion (ə pin'yən) *n.* **1** a belief that is not based on what is certain, but on what one thinks to be true or likely [In my *opinion*, it will rain before dark.] **2** what one thinks about how good or valuable something is [What is your *opinion* of that painting?] **3** a judgment made by an expert [It would be better to get several medical *opinions*.]

op·por·tu·ni·ty (äp'ər too'nə tē *or* äp'ər tyoo'nə tē) *n.* a time or occasion that is right for doing something; good chance [You will have an *opportunity* to ask questions after the talk.] —*pl.* **op'por·tu'ni·ties**

op·po·site (äp'ə zit) *adj.* **1** different in every way; exactly reverse or in contrast [Up is *opposite* to down.] **2** at the other end or side; directly facing or back to back [the *opposite* end of a table; the *opposite* side of a coin]. ◆*n.* anything opposite or opposed [Love is the *opposite* of hate.] ◆*prep.* across from; facing [We sat *opposite* each other.] —**op'po·site·ly** *adv.*

op·ti·cal (äp'ti kəl) *adj.* **1** of the sense of sight; visual [an *optical* illusion]. **2** made to give help in seeing [Lenses are *optical* instruments.] —**op'ti·cal·ly** *adv.*

o·rang·u·tan (ô raŋ'ə tan') *n.* a large ape with very long arms and shaggy, reddish hair, found in Borneo and Sumatra. *Also* **o·rang·ou·tang** (ô raŋ'ə taŋ').

or·ches·tra (ôr'kəs trə) *n.* **1** a group of musicians playing together, especially with some stringed instruments. **2** the instruments of such a group. —**or·ches·tral** (ôr kəs'trəl) *adj.*

or·chid (ôr'kid) *n.* a plant with flowers having three petals: the middle petal is larger than the others and has the shape of a lip.

Or·e·gon (ôr'ə gən *or* ôr'ə gän) a State in the northwestern part of the U.S.

o·rig·i·nal (ə rij'ə nəl) *adj.* **1** having to do with an origin; first or earliest [the *original* settlers of North America]. **2** that has never been before; not copied; fresh; new [an *original* idea; *original* music]. **3** able to think of new things; inventive [Edison had an *original* mind.] **4** being the one of which there are copies [the *original* letter and three carbon copies]. —**o·rig·i·nal·i·ty** (ə rij'ə nal'ə tē) *n.*

out·ra·geous (out rā'jəs) *adj.* doing great injury or wrong [*outrageous* crimes]. —**out·ra'geous·ly** *adv.*

o·val (ō'vəl) *adj.* shaped like an egg or like an ellipse. ◆*n.* anything with such a shape.

o·ver·board (ō'vər bôrd) *adv.* from a ship into the water [He fell *overboard*.]

o·ver·come (ō vər kum') **v. 1** to get the better of; defeat; master [to *overcome* an enemy; to *overcome* a problem]. **2** to make weak or helpless [We were *overcome* by laughter.] **3** to be victorious; win. —**o·ver·came', o·ver·come', o·ver·com'ing**

o·ver·due (ō vər doo' *or* ō vər dyoo') *adj.* **1** not paid by the time set for payment [an *overdue* bill] **2** delayed past the arrival time; late [Her bus was long *overdue*.]

o·ver·look (ō vər look') **v. 1** to give a view of from above; look down on [Your room *overlooks* the sea.] **2** to fail to notice [I *overlooked* no detail.] **3** to pay no attention to; excuse [I can *overlook* her rudeness.]

o·ver·re·act (ō'vər rē akt') **v.** to respond to something with greater feeling or force than seems necessary.

own·er·ship (ōn'ər ship) *n.* the condition of being an owner; possession.

ox·y·gen (äks'i jən) *n.* a gas that has no color, taste, or odor and is a chemical element. It makes up almost one fifth of the air and combines with nearly all other elements. All living things need oxygen.

oys·ter (ois'tər) *n.* a shellfish with a soft body enclosed in two rough shells hinged together. Some are used as food, and pearls are formed inside others.

o·zone (ō'zōn) *n.* a pale-blue gas that is a form of oxygen with a sharp smell. It is formed by an electrical discharge in the air and is used as a bleach, water purifier, etc.

oyster

a	ask, fat
ā	ape, date
ä	car, lot
e	elf, ten
ē	even, meet
i	is, hit
ī	ice, fire
ō	open, go
ô	law, horn
oi	oil, point
oo	look, pull
oo	ooze, tool
ou	out, crowd
u	up, cut
ʉ	fur, fern
ə	a in ago
	e in agent
	e in father
	i in unity
	o in collect
	u in focus
ch	chin, arch
ŋ	ring, singer
sh	she, dash
th	thin, truth
th	then, father
zh	s in pleasure

Pp

pack·age (pak′ij) *n.* **1** a thing or things wrapped or tied up, as in a box or in wrapping paper; parcel. ☆**2** a number of things offered together as one [a retirement *package*]. ◆☆*v.* to put into a package. —**pack′aged, pack′ag·ing**

pain (pān) *n.* **1** a feeling of hurting in some part of the body [a sharp *pain* in a tooth]. **2** suffering of the mind; sorrow [The memory of that loss brought us *pain*.] ◆*v.* to give pain to; cause to suffer; hurt [The wound *pains* me.   Their insults *pained* us.]

pain·ful (pān′fəl) *adj.* causing pain; hurting; unpleasant [a *painful* wound; *painful* embarrassment]. —**pain′ful·ly** *adv.* —**pain′ful·ness** *n.*

pan·cake (pan′kāk) *n.* a thin, flat cake made by pouring batter onto a griddle or into a pan and frying it; flapjack.

pan·cre·as (pan′krē əs) *n.* a large gland behind the stomach that sends a juice into the small intestine to help digestion. —**pan·cre·at·ic** (pan′krē at′ik) *adj.*

pan·el (pan′əl) *n.* **1** a flat section or part of a wall, door, etc., either raised above or sunk below the surfaces around it. **2** a board or section containing dials, controls, etc. as for an airplane or a system of electric wiring. **3** a picture or painting that is long and narrow. **4** a strip of different material sewn lengthwise into a skirt or dress. —**pan′eled** or **pan′elled, pan′el·ing** or **pan′el·ling** *v.*

pa·pa·ya (pə pī′ə) *n.* **1** a tree of tropical America, a little like the palm, with a yellowish-orange fruit like a small melon. **2** this fruit, used as food.

pa·per·back (pā′pər bak) *n.* a book bound in paper, instead of cloth, leather, etc.

par·a·graph (per′ə graf) *n.* **1** a separate section of a piece of writing, that deals with a particular point and is made up of one or more sentences.   Each paragraph begins on a new line that is usually moved in from the margin. **2** a short note or item in a newspaper or magazine.

par·al·lel (per′ə lel) *adj.* **1** moving out in the same direction and always the same distance apart so as to never meet, as the tracks of a sled in the snow. **2** similar or alike [Their lives followed *parallel* courses.] ◆*n.* **1** a parallel line, plane, etc. **2** something similar to or like something else [Your experience is a *parallel* to mine.] —**par′al·leled** or **par′al·lelled, par′al·lel·ing** or **par′al·lel·ling** *v.*

par·ent (per′ənt) *n.* **1** a father or mother. **2** any animal or plant as it is related to its offspring. **3** anything from which other things come; source; origin [Latin is the *parent* of various languages.] —**par′ent·hood** *n.*

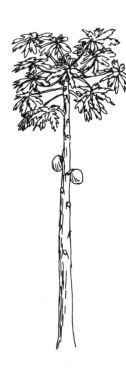

papaya

par·tic·i·pant (pär tis′ə pənt) *n.* a person who takes part in something.

part·ner (pärt′nər) *n.* **1** a person who takes part in something with another or others; especially, one of the owners of a business who shares in its profits and risks. **2** either of two players on the same side or team [my tennis *partner*]. **3** either of two persons dancing together. **4** a husband or wife.

part·ner·ship (pärt′nər ship) *n.* **1** the condition or relationship of being a partner. **2** a business firm made up of two or more partners.

pas·sage (pas′ij) *n.* the act of passing [the *passage* of a bill into law].

pat·tern (pat′ərn) *n.* **1** a plan or model used as a guide for making things [a dress *pattern*]. **2** a person or thing taken as a model or example [Sir Galahad was the *pattern* of the pure knight.] **3** the arrangement of parts; design [wallpaper *patterns*]. **4** a habit or way of acting that does not change [the migration *pattern* of the swallow].

pause (pôz *or* päz) *n.* **1** a short stop, as in speaking or working. **2** a musical sign (⌢ or ⌣) placed below or above a note or rest that is to be held longer. ◆*v.* to make a pause; stop for a short time [He *paused* to catch his breath.] —**paused, paus′ing**

pay·ee (pā ē′) *n.* the person to whom a check, money, etc. is to be paid.

pay·ment (pā′mənt) *n.* **1** a paying or being paid [the *payment* of taxes]. **2** something paid [a monthly rent *payment* of $168].

peace·ful (pēs′fəl) *adj.* **1** free from noise or disorder; quiet; calm [the *peaceful* countryside]. **2** fond of peace; not fighting [a *peaceful* people]. **3** of or fit for a time of peace [*peaceful* trade between nations]. —**peace′ful·ly** *adv.* —**peace′ful·ness** *n.*

peas·ant (pez′ənt) *n.* mainly in Europe and Asia, a member of the class of farm workers and farmers with small farms.

peck (pēk) *n.* **1** a measure of volume for grain, fruit, vegetables, etc. It is equal to 1/4 bushel or eight quarts. **2** a basket, etc. that holds a peck.

pent·a·gon (pen′tə gän) *n.* **1** a flat figure having five sides and five angles. ☆**2 Pentagon**, the five-sided office building of the Defense Department, near Washington, D.C. —**pen·tag·o·nal** (pen tag′ə n'l) *adj.*

per·form (pər fôrm′) *v.* **1** to do or carry out [to *perform* a task; to *perform* a promise]. **2** to do something to entertain an audience; act, play music, sing, etc. —**per·form′er** *n.*

pe·ri·od·i·cal (pir′ē äd′i kəl) *n.* a magazine published every week, month, etc. ◆*adj.* **1** published every week, month, etc. **2** of periodicals [a *periodical* index]. —**pe·ri·od′i·cal·ly** *adv.*

per·sist·ent (pər sis′tənt) *adj.* refusing to give up; steady and determined [a *persistent* job seeker]. —**per·sist′ent·ly** *adv.*

per·son·al·ly (pur′sə nəl ē) *adv.* **1** by oneself, without the help of others [I'll ask them *personally*.] **2** as a person [I dislike the artist *personally,* but I admire her paintings.] **3** speaking for oneself [*Personally,* I think you're right.] **4** as though aimed at oneself [You should not take my remarks *personally*.]

per·suade (pər swād′) *v.* to get someone to do or believe something, as by making it seem like a good idea; convince. —**per·suad′ed, per·suad′ing**

pes·ti·cide (pes′tə sīd) *n.* any poison used to kill insects, weeds, etc.

pet·al (pet′l) *n.* any of the brightly colored leaves that make up the flower of a plant.

pho·no·graph (fō′nə graf) *n.* an instrument for playing records with a spiral groove on them in which sounds of music or speech have been recorded.

pho·tog·ra·phy (fə täg′rə fē) *n.* the art or method of making pictures by means of a camera.

phys·i·cal (fiz′i kəl) *adj.* **1** of nature or matter; material; natural [the *physical* universe]. **2** of the body rather than the mind [Swimming is good *physical* exercise.] **3** of or having to do with the natural sciences or the laws of nature [the *physical* force that makes an object move]. ◆*n.* ☆a medical examination of the whole body.

pic·co·lo (pik′ə lō) *n.* a small flute that sounds notes an octave higher than an ordinary flute does. —*pl.* **pic′co·los**

pick·le (pik′əl) *n.* **1** a cucumber or other vegetable preserved in salt water, vinegar, or spicy liquid. **2** a liquid of this kind used to preserve food. ◆*v.* to preserve in a pickle liquid [*pickled* beets]. —**pick′led, pick′ling**

piece (pēs) *n.* **1** a part broken or separated from a whole thing [The glass shattered and I swept up the *pieces*.] **2** a part or section of a whole, thought of as complete by itself [a *piece* of meat; a *piece* of land]. **3** any one of a set or group of things [a dinner set of 52 *pieces*; a chess *piece*]. **4** a work of music, writing, or art [a *piece* for the piano]. —**pieced, piec′ing** *v.*

pis·til (pis′təl) *n.* the part of a flower in which the seeds grow. A single pistil is made up of a stigma, style, and ovary.

plan (plan) *n.* **1** a method or way of doing something, that has been thought out ahead of time [vacation *plans*]. **2** a drawing that shows how the parts of a building or piece of ground are arranged [floor *plans* of a house; a *plan* of the battlefield]. ◆*v.* **1** to think out a way of making or doing something [They *planned* their escape carefully.] **2** to make a drawing or diagram of beforehand [An architect is *planning* our new school.] —**planned, plan′ning**

plas·tic (plas′tik) *adj.* **1** that can be shaped or molded [Clay is a *plastic* material.] **2** that gives form or shape to matter [Sculpture is a *plastic* art.] **3** made of plastic [a *plastic* comb]. ◆*n.* a substance, made from various chemicals, that can be molded and hardened into many useful products. —**plas·tic·i·ty** (plas tis′ə tē) *n.*

Platte (plat) a river in central Nebraska.

pleas·ant (plez′ənt) *adj.* **1** giving pleasure; bringing happiness; enjoyable [a *pleasant* day in the park] **2** having a look or manner that gives pleasure; likable [a *pleasant* person].

pleas·ing (plēz′iŋ) *adj.* giving pleasure; enjoyable [a *pleasing* smile].

pleas·ure (plezh′ər) *n.* **1** a feeling of delight or satisfaction; enjoyment [I get *pleasure* from taking long walks.] **2** a thing that gives pleasure [Her voice is a *pleasure* to hear.] **3** one's wish or choice [For dessert, what is your *pleasure*?]

pledge (plej) *n.* **1** a promise or agreement [the *pledge* of allegiance to the flag]. **2** something promised, especially money to be given as to a charity. **3** a thing given as a guarantee or token of something [They gave each other rings as a *pledge* of their love.] ◆*v.* to promise to give [to *pledge* $100 to a building fund]. —**pledged, pledg′ing**

plen·ti·ful (plen′ti fəl) *adj.* great in amount or number; more than enough [a *plentiful* food supply]. —**plen′ti·ful·ly** *adv.*

pli·ers (plī′ərz) *pl.n.* a tool like small pincers, used for gripping small objects or bending wire.

plu·ral (ploor′əl) *adj.* showing that more than one is meant [The *plural* form of "box" is "boxes."] ◆*n.* the form of a word which shows that more than one is meant.

poach (pōch) *v.* to cook an egg without its shell, in boiling water or in a small cup put over boiling water.

poise (poiz) *n.* **1** balance, as in the way one carries oneself [the perfect *poise* of a tiger that is ready to spring]. **2** calmness and easiness of manner; self-control [I lost my *poise* when they laughed at me.] ◆*v.* to balance or be held balanced [The stork *poised* itself on one leg. The earth is *poised* in space.] —**poised, pois′ing**

poi·son·ous (poi′zə nəs) *adj.* that is a poison; harming or killing by poison [a *poisonous* berry].

po·lar (pō′lər) *adj.* **1** of or near the North or South Pole. **2** of a pole or poles.

Pol·ish (pōl′ish) *adj.* of Poland, its people, language, etc. ◆*n.* the language of Poland.

po·lite (pə līt′) *adj.* **1** having or showing good manners; thoughtful of others; courteous [a *polite* note of thanks]. **2** behaving in a way that is considered refined or elegant [Such things aren't done in *polite* society.] —**po·lite′ly** *adv.* —**po·lite′ness** *n.*

pistil

a	ask, fat
ā	ape, date
ä	car, lot
e	elf, ten
ē	even, meet
i	is, hit
ī	ice, fire
ō	open, go
ô	law, horn
oi	oil, point
͝oo	look, pull
͞oo	ooze, tool
ou	out, crowd
u	up, cut
ʉ	fur, fern
ə	a in ago
	e in agent
	e in father
	i in unity
	o in collect
	u in focus
ch	chin, arch
ŋ	ring, singer
sh	she, dash
th	thin, truth
th	then, father
zh	s in pleasure

pol·li·nate (päl′ə nāt) **v.** to place pollen on the pistil of a flower; fertilize. —**pol′li·nat·ed, pol′li·nat·ing** —**pol′li·na′tion** **n.**

pol·y·es·ter (päl′ē es′tər) **n.** an artificial resin used in making plastics, fibers for fabrics, etc.

pop·u·lar (päp′yōō lər) **adj.** **1** having many friends; very well liked. **2** liked by many people. **3** of, for, or by all the people or most people. —**pop·u·lar·i·ty** (päp′yə lar′ə tē) **n.** —**pop′u·lar·ly** **adv.**

pop·u·la·tion (päp′yōō lā′shən) **n.** **1** the people living in a country, city, etc.; especially, the total number of these. **2** the act of populating or the fact of being populated.

pos·si·ble (päs′ə bəl) **adj.** **1** that can be [The highest *possible* score in bowling is 300.] **2** that may or may not happen [colder tomorrow, with *possible* showers]. **3** that can be done, known, got, used, etc. [two *possible* routes to Denver].

post·game (pōst′gām′) **adj.** having to do with activities after a game.

post·pone (pōst pōn′) **v.** to put off until later; delay [I *postponed* my trip because of illness.] —**post·poned′, post·pon′ing** —**post·pone′ment** **n.**

pos·ture (päs′chər) **n.** **1** the way one holds the body in sitting or standing; carriage [good *posture* with the back held straight]. **2** a special way of holding the body or of acting, as in posing [Doubling up a fist is a *posture* of defiance.] ◆**v.** to take on a posture; pose. —**pos′tured, pos′tur·ing**

post·war (pōst′wôr′) **adj.** after the war.

po·ta·to (pə tāt′ō) **n.** **1** a plant whose tuber, or thick, starchy underground stem, is used as a vegetable. **2** this tuber. —*pl.* **po·ta′toes**

pow·der (pou′dər) **n.** a dry substance in the form of fine particles like dust, made by crushing or grinding [talcum *powder;* baking *powder;* gun*powder*]. ◆**v.** to sprinkle, dust, or cover as with powder [Snow *powdered* the rooftops.]

pow·er·ful (pou′ər fəl) **adj.** having much power; strong or influential [a *powerful* leader]. —**pow′er·ful·ly** **adv.**

☆**prai·rie** (prer′ē) **n.** a large area of level or rolling grassy land without many trees.

preach·er (prēch′ər) **n.** a person who preaches; especially, a clergyman.

pre·pare (prē per′) **v.** **1** to make or get ready [to *prepare* for a test; to *prepare* ground for planting]. **2** to furnish with what is needed; equip [to *prepare* an expedition]. **3** to make or put together out of parts or materials [to *prepare* a medicine]. —**pre·pared′, pre·par′ing**

pre·serv·a·tive (prē zurv′ə tiv) **n.** anything that preserves; especially, a substance added to food to keep it from spoiling.

pre·serve (prē zurv′) **v.** **1** to protect from harm or damage; save [to *preserve* our national forests]. **2** to keep from spoiling or rotting. **3** to prepare food for later use by canning, pickling, or salting it. —**pre·served′, pre·serv′ing** ◆**n.** *usually* **preserves,** *pl.* fruit preserved by cooking it with sugar and canning it.

pres·i·dent (prez′i dənt) **n.** ☆**1** the highest officer of a company, club, college, etc. **2** *often* **President,** the head of government in a republic.

pres·sure (presh′ər) **n.** **1** a pressing or being pressed; force of pushing or of weight [the *pressure* of the foot on the brake]. **2** a condition of trouble, strain, etc. that is hard to bear [She never gave in to the *pressure* of her grief.] **3** influence or force to make someone do something [His friends put *pressure* on him to resign as president.] **4** urgent demands; urgency [She neglected her homework and now has to work under *pressure* of time.] —**pres′sured, pres′sur·ing** **v.**

pre·tend (prē tend′) **v.** **1** to make believe, as in play [Let's *pretend* we're cowboys.] **2** to claim or act in a false way [She *pretended* to be angry, but she wasn't.] —**pre·tend′ed** **adj.**

pre·vail (prē vāl′) **v.** **1** to be successful or win out [to *prevail* over an enemy]. **2** to be or become more common or widespread, as a custom or practice.

pre·vent (prē vent′) **v.** **1** to stop or hinder [A storm *prevented* us from going.] **2** to keep from happening [Careful driving *prevents* accidents.] —**pre·vent′ed, pre·vent′ing**

pris·on·er (priz′ən ər *or* priz′nər) **n.** a person who is kept shut up, as in a prison, or held as a captive, as in war.

prob·lem (präb′ləm) **n.** **1** a condition, person, etc. that is difficult to deal with or hard to understand [Getting the table through that narrow door will be a *problem*.] **2** a question to be solved or worked out [an arithmetic *problem*; the *problem* of reckless drivers].

pro·ceed (prō sēd′) **v.** to go on, especially after stopping for a while [After eating, we *proceeded* to the next town.] —**pro·ceed′ed, pro·ceed′ing**

pro·ces·sion (prə sesh′ən) **n.** **1** a number of persons or things moving forward in an orderly way. **2** the act of moving in this way.

pro·duce (prə dōōs′ *or* prə dyōōs′) **v.** **1** to bring forth; bear; yield [trees *producing* apples; a well that *produces* oil]. **2** to make or manufacture [a company that *produces* bicycles]. **3** to bring out into view; show [*Produce* your fishing license.] **4** to get ready and bring to the public, as a play, movie, etc. —**pro·duced′, pro·duc′ing** ◆**n.** (prō′dōōs) —**pro·duc′er** **n.**

potatoes

pro·fes·sion·al (prə fesh′ən əl) *adj.* **1** of or in a profession [the *professional* ethics of a lawyer]. **2** earning one's living from a sport or other activity not usually thought of as an occupation [a *professional* golfer]. **3** engaged in by professional players [*professional* football]. —**pro·fes′sion·al·ism** *n.* —**pro·fes′sion·al·ly** *adv.*

prof·it·a·ble (präf′it ə bəl) *adj.* that brings profit or benefit [a *profitable* sale; a *profitable* idea]. —**prof′it·a·bly** *adv.*

pro·mote (prə mōt′) *v.* **1** to raise to a higher rank, grade, or position [She was *promoted* to manager.] **2** to help to grow, succeed, etc. [New laws were passed to *promote* the general welfare.] ☆**3** to make more popular, increase the sales of, etc. by advertising or giving publicity [to *promote* a product]. ☆**4** to move a student forward a grade in school. —**pro·mot′ed, pro·mot′ing** —**pro·mot′er** *n.* —**pro·mo′tion** *n.*

pro·pose (prə pōz′) *v.* **1** to suggest for others to think about, approve, etc. [We *propose* that the city build a zoo. I *propose* Robin for treasurer.] **2** to plan or intend [Do you *propose* to leave us?] **3** to make an offer of marriage. —**pro·posed′, pro·pos′ing**

pro·tec·tion (prō tek′shən) *n.* **1** a protecting or being protected [The guard carried a club for *protection*.] **2** a person or thing that protects [Being careful is your best *protection* against accidents.]

pro·test (prō test′ *or* prō′test) *v.* **1** to speak out against; object [They joined the march to *protest* against injustice.] **2** to say in a positive way; insist [Bill *protested* that he would be glad to help.] ◆*n.* (prō′test) the act of protesting; objection [They ignored my *protest* and continued hammering.] —**pro·test′er** *or* **pro·tes′tor** *n.*

pro·trac·tor (prō trak′tər *or* prō′trak tər) *n.* an instrument used for drawing and measuring angles. It is in the form of a half circle marked with degrees.

pro·vide (prō vīd′) *v.* **1** to give what is needed; supply; furnish [The school *provides* free books.] **2** to furnish the means of support [How large a family do you *provide* for?] **3** to get ready ahead of time; prepare [You'd better *provide* for rain by taking umbrellas.] **4** to set forth as a condition, as in a contract [Our lease *provides* that rent will be paid monthly.] —**pro·vid′ed, pro·vid′ing**

prune (prōōn) *v.* **1** to cut off or trim branches, twigs, etc. from [to *prune* hedges]. **2** to make shorter by cutting out parts [to *prune* a novel]. —**pruned, prun′ing**

psy·chol·o·gy (sī käl′ə jē) *n.* **1** the science that studies the mind and the reasons for the ways that people think and act. **2** the ways of thinking and acting of a person or group [the *psychology* of the child; mob *psychology*]. —*pl.* **psy·chol′o·gies** —**psy·chol′o·gist** *n.*

pub·lic (pub′lik) *adj.* **1** of or having to do with the people as a whole [*public* affairs; *public* opinion]. **2** for the use or the good of everyone [a *public* park]. **3** acting for the people as a whole [a *public* official]. **4** known by all or most people; open [a *public* figure; a *public* scandal].

pump·kin (pum′kin *or* pump′kin) *n.* a large, round, orange fruit that grows on a vine and has many seeds.   The pulp is much used as a filling for pies.

punc·tu·a·tion (puŋk′chōō ā′shən) *n.* **1** the use of commas, periods, etc. in writing [rules of *punctuation*]. **2** punctuation marks [What *punctuation* is used to end sentences?]

pup·pet·eer (pup ə tir′) *n.* a person who works the strings that make puppets move or one who puts on puppet shows.

pyr·a·mid (pir′ə mid) *n.* **1** a solid figure whose sloping sides are triangles that come together in a point at the top. **2** anything having this shape; especially, any of the huge structures with a square base and four sides in which ancient Egyptian rulers were buried. ◆*v.* to build up or heap up in the form of a pyramid.

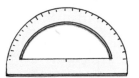

protractor

pyramid

qual·i·fi·ca·tion (kwôl′ə fi kā′shən *or* kwä′lə fi kā′shən) *n.* **1** a qualifying or being qualified. **2** a thing that changes, limits, or holds back [I can recommend the book without any *qualification*.] **3** any skill, experience, special training, etc. that fits a person for some work, office, etc.

qual·i·fy (kwôl′ə fī *or* kwä′lə fī) *v.* to make or be fit or suitable for a particular role, job, or activity [Your training and education *qualify* you for the job.] —**qual′i·fied, qual′i·fy·ing**

quar·rel (kwôr′əl) *n.* **1** an argument or disagreement, especially an angry one; dispute. **2** a reason for arguing [I have no *quarrel* with the way things are being done.] ◆*v.* **1** to argue or disagree in an angry way. **2** to find fault; complain [She *quarrels* with his methods, not with his results.] —**quar′reled** *or* **quar′relled, quar′rel·ing** *or* **quar′rel·ling**

quar·ter (kwôrt′ər) *n.* **1** any of the four equal parts of something; fourth [a *quarter* of a mile; the third *quarter* of a football game]. **2** one fourth of a year; three months. **3** the point fifteen minutes before or after any given hour [It's a *quarter* after five.] **4** a coin of the U.S. or Canada, worth 25 cents; one fourth of a dollar.

a	ask, fat
ā	ape, date
ä	car, lot
e	elf, ten
ē	even, meet
i	is, hit
ī	ice, fire
ō	open, go
ô	law, horn
oi	oil, point
oo	look, pull
ōō	ooze, tool
ou	out, crowd
u	up, cut
u	fur, fern
ə	a in ago
	e in agent
	e in father
	i in unity
	o in collect
	u in focus
ch	chin, arch
ŋ	ring, singer
sh	she, dash
th	thin, truth
th	then, father
zh	s in pleasure

ques·tion (kwes′chən) *n.* **1** something that is asked in order to learn or know [The athlete refused to answer the reporter's *questions*.] **2** doubt [There is no *question* about his honesty.] **3** a matter to be considered; problem [It's not a *question* of money.] ◆*v.* to ask questions of [The lawyer started to *question* the witness.] —**ques′·tion·er** *n.*

quick (kwik) *adj.* **1** done with speed; rapid; swift [We took a *quick* trip.] **2** done or happening at once; prompt [I was grateful for her *quick* reply.] **3** able to learn or understand easily [You have a *quick* mind.] **4** easily stirred up; touchy [Lynn has a *quick* temper.] —**quick′ly** *adv.* —**quick′ness** *n.*

qui·et (kwī′ət) *adj.* **1** not noisy; hushed [a *quiet* motor]. **2** not talking; silent [She was *quiet* during dinner.] **3** not moving; still; calm [a *quiet* pond]. **4** peaceful and relaxing [We spent a *quiet* evening at home.] —**qui′et·ly** *adv.* —**qui′et·ness** *n.*

ra·dar (rā′där) *n.* a device or system that sends out radio waves and picks them up after they strike some object and bounce back.

☆**ra·di·o** (rā′dē ō′) *n.* **1** a way of sending sounds through space by changing them into electric waves which are sent and picked up, without wires, by a receiver that changes them back to sounds. **2** the act or business of broadcasting news, music, talks, etc. by radio. —*pl.* **ra′di·os′** —**ra′di·oed′, ra′di·o′ing** *v.*

ra·di·us (rā′dē əs) *n.* **1** any straight line that goes from the center to the outside of a circle or sphere. **2** a round area as measured by its radius [no houses within a *radius* of five miles]. **3** the thicker of the two bones in the forearm. —*pl.* **ra·di·i** (rā′dē ī′) or **ra′di·us·es**

rail·way (rāl′wā) *n.* a track made up of parallel steel rails along which trains run.

rain·bow (rān′bō) *n.* a curved band across the sky with all the colors of the spectrum in it. It is seen when the sun's rays pass through falling rain or mist.

rai·sin (rā′zən) *n.* a sweet grape dried for eating.

rasp·ber·ry (raz′ber′ē) *n.* **1** a small, juicy, red or black fruit with many tiny seeds. **2** the shrub it grows on. —*pl.* **rasp′ber′ries**

☆**ray·on** (rā′än) *n.* a fiber made from cellulose, or a fabric woven from such fibers.

read·i·ly (red′əl ē) *adv.* **1** without hesitation; willingly **2** without difficulty; easily.

re·al·ist (rē′ə list) *n.* a person who sees things as they really are; practical person.

re·ap·pear (rē ə pir′) *v.* to appear again. —**re′ap·pear′ance** *n.*

re·ar·range (rē ə rānj′) *v.* to arrange again or in a different way. —**re·ar·ranged′, re·ar·rang′ing** —**re′ar·range′ment** *n.*

re·ceive (rē sēv′) *v.* **1** to take or get what has been given or sent to one [to *receive* a letter]. **2** to meet with; be given; undergo [to *receive* punishment; to *receive* applause]. **3** to find out about; learn [He *received* the news calmly.] **4** to greet guests and let them come in [Our hostess *received* us at the door.] —**re·ceived′, re·ceiv′ing**

re·cent (rē′sənt) *adj.* of a time just before now; made or happening a short time ago [*recent* news; a *recent* storm]. —**re′cent·ly** *adv.*

rec·og·nize (rek′əg nīz) *v.* **1** to be aware of as something or someone seen, heard, etc. before; know again [to *recognize* a street; to *recognize* a tune]. **2** to know by a certain feature; identify [to *recognize* a giraffe by its long neck]. **3** to take notice of; show approval of [a ceremony to *recognize* those employees with ten years or more of service]. **4** to admit as true; accept [to *recognize* defeat]. —**rec′og·nized, rec′og·niz·ing**

rec·om·mend (rek ə mend′) *v.* **1** to speak of as being good for a certain use, job, etc.; praise [to *recommend* a good plumber; to *recommend* a book]. **2** to make pleasing or worth having [That summer camp has much to *recommend* it.] **3** to give advice; advise [I *recommend* that you study harder.]

rec·re·a·tion (rek′rē ā′shən) *n.* **1** the act of refreshing one's body or mind, as after work [He plays chess for *recreation*.] **2** any sport, exercise, hobby, amusement, etc. by which one does this. —**rec′re·a′tion·al** *adj.*

rec·tan·gle (rek′taŋ′gəl) *n.* any flat figure with four right angles and four sides.

re·cy·cle (rē sī′kəl) *v.* to use again and again, as a single supply of water in a fountain or for cooling, metal to be melted down and recast, or paper processed for use again. —**re·cy′cled, re·cy′cling**

re·duce (rē dōōs′ *or* rē dyōōs′) *v.* **1** to make smaller, less, fewer, etc.; decrease [to *reduce* speed; to *reduce* taxes]. **2** to lose weight, as by dieting. **3** to make lower, as in rank or condition; bring down [to *reduce* a major to the rank of captain; a family *reduced* to poverty]. **4** to change into a different form or condition [to *reduce* peanuts to a paste by grinding]. —**re·duced′, re·duc′ing** —**re·duc′er** *n.* —**re·duc′i·ble** *adj.*

ref·er·ence ′ (ref′ər əns *or* ref′rəns) *n.* **1** the act or fact of referring; mention [They made no *reference* to the accident.] **2** the fact of having to do with; relation; connection [I am writing in *reference* to your letter.] **3** a mention, as in a book, of some other work where information can be found; also, the work so mentioned [Most of the author's *references* are useful.] **4** something that gives information [Look in the encyclopedia and other *references*.]

re·flect (rē flekt′) *v.* **1** to throw back or be thrown back, as light, heat, or sound [A polished metal surface *reflects* both light and heat.] **2** to give back an image of [The calm lake *reflected* the trees on the shore.] **3** to bring as a result [Your success *reflects* credit on your teachers.] **4** to bring blame, doubt, etc.

reg·u·lar (reg′yə lər) *adj.* **1** formed or arranged in an orderly way; balanced [a *regular* pattern; a face with *regular* features]. **2** according to some rule or habit; usual; customary [Sit in your *regular* place.] **3** steady and even; not changing [a *regular* rhythm]. **4** in grammar, changing form in the usual way in showing tense, number, etc. ["Walk" is a *regular* verb, but "swim" is not.] —**reg·u·lar·i·ty** (reg′yə lar′ə tē) *n.* —**reg′u·lar·ly** *adv.*

rel·a·tive (rel′ə tiv) *n.* a person of the same family by blood or by marriage.

re·lax (rē laks′) *v.* **1** to make or become less firm, tense, or strict; loosen up [The body *relaxes* in sleep. The parents never *relaxed* their watch over their child.] **2** to rest from work or effort [He *relaxes* by going fishing.] —**re′lax·a′tion** *n.*

re·lay (rē′lā) *n.* **1** a fresh group that takes over some work from another group; shift [The carpenters worked in *relays* to finish the project on time.] **2** a race in which each member of a team runs only a certain part of the whole distance: *the full name is* **relay race.** ◆*v.* to get and pass on [to *relay* a message]. —**re′layed, re′lay·ing**

re·li·ant (rē lī′ənt) *adj.* having or showing trust or confidence; depending [The needy are *reliant* on our help.]

re·lieve (rē lēv′) *v.* **1** to reduce or ease pain or worry [Cold water *relieves* a swelling.] **2** to free from pain or worry [We were *relieved* of our fear when the danger passed.] —**re·lieved′, re·liev′ing**

re·li·gion (rē lij′ən) *n.* **1** belief in, or the worship of, God or a group of gods. **2** a particular system of belief or worship built around God, moral ideals, a philosophy of life, etc.

re·mem·ber (rē mem′bər) *v.* **1** to think of again [I suddenly *remembered* I was supposed to mow the lawn.] **2** to bring back to mind by trying; recall [I just can't *remember* your name.] **3** to be careful not to forget [*Remember* to look both ways before crossing.] **4** to mention as sending greetings [*Remember* me to your family.]

re·mote (rē mōt′) *adj.* **1** far off or far away in space or time; distant. **2** not closely related. **3** slight or faint. —**re·mot′er, re·mot′est** —**re·mote′ly** *adv.* —**re·mote′ness** *n.*

re·pel·lent (rē pel′ənt) *adj.* that repels in any of various ways [a *repellent* smell; a water-*repellent* jacket]. ◆*n.* something that repels, as a spray that keeps insects away.

re·print (rē print′) *v.* to print again [The book was *reprinted*.] —**re·print′ed, re·print′ing**

re·quire (rē kwīr′) *v.* **1** to be in need of [Most plants *require* sunlight.] **2** to order, command, or insist upon [He *required* us to leave.] —**re·quired′, re·quir′ing**

res·cue (res′kyōō) *v.* to free or save from danger, evil, etc. [to *rescue* people from a burning building]. ◆*n.* the act of rescuing. —**res′cued, res′cu·ing** —**res′cu·er** *n.*

res·i·dent (rez′i dənt) *n.* a person who lives in a place, not just a visitor. ◆*adj.* living or staying in a place, as while working.

re·sign (rē zīn′) *v.* to give up one's office, position, membership, etc. [We *resigned* from the club.]

re·source·ful (rē sôrs′fəl) *adj.* skillful at solving problems or getting out of trouble. —**re·source′ful·ly** *adv.* —**re·source′ful·ness** *n.*

re·spon·si·ble (rē spän′sə bəl) *adj.* **1** supposed or expected to take care of something or do something [Harry is *responsible* for mowing the lawn.] **2** that must get the credit or blame [All of us are *responsible* for our own actions.] **3** having to do with important duties [a *responsible* job]. **4** that can be trusted or depended upon; reliable [a *responsible* person].

re·turn (rē turn′) *v.* **1** to go or come back [When did you *return* from your trip?] **2** to bring, send, carry, or put back [Our neighbor *returned* the ladder.] **3** to pay back by doing the same [to *return* a visit; to *return* a favor]. **4** to throw, hit, or run back a ball. —**re·turned′, re·turn′ing, re·turns′**

re·view (rē vyōō′) *v.* **1** to go over or study again [to *review* a subject for a test]. **2** to think back on [She *reviewed* the events that led to their quarrel.] **3** to inspect or examine in an official way [to *review* troops]. **4** to tell what a book, play, etc. is about and give one's opinion of it.

rev·o·lu·tion (rev′ə lōō′shən) *n.* **1** overthrow of a government or a social system, with another taking its place [the American *Revolution*; the Industrial *Revolution*]. **2** a complete change of any kind [The telephone caused a *revolution* in communication.] **3** the act of revolving; movement in an orbit [the *revolution* of the moon around the earth]. **4** a turning motion of a wheel, etc. around a center or axis; rotation.

a	ask, fat
ā	ape, date
ä	car, lot
e	elf, ten
ē	even, meet
i	is, hit
ī	ice, fire
ō	open, go
ô	law, horn
oi	oil, point
ōō	look, pull
o͞o	ooze, tool
ou	out, crowd
u	up, cut
u	fur, fern
ə	a in ago
	e in agent
	e in father
	i in unity
	o in collect
	u in focus
ch	chin, arch
ŋ	ring, singer
sh	she, dash
th	thin, truth
th	then, father
zh	s in pleasure

ridge

re·ward (rē wôrd´) *n.* **1** something given in return, especially for good work or a good deed [a *reward* for bravery]. **2** money offered, as for returning something lost.

ridge (rij) *n.* **1** a top or high part that is long and narrow; crest [the *ridge* of a roof]. **2** a range of hills or mountains. **3** any narrow, raised strip [Waves made tiny *ridges* in the sand.]

roast (rōst) *v.* **1** to cook with little or no liquid, as in an oven or over an open fire [to *roast* a chicken or a whole ox]. **2** to dry or brown with great heat [to *roast* coffee]. **3** to make or become very hot. —**roast´ed, roast´ing**

rot (rät) *v.* to fall apart or spoil by the action of bacteria or dampness; to decay [A dead tree will *rot*.] —**rot´ted, rot´ting**

rub·ble (rub´əl) *n.* **1** rough, broken pieces of stone, brick, etc. **2** masonry made up of such pieces. **3** broken pieces from buildings, etc. damaged or destroyed by an earthquake, bombing, etc.

Rus·sian (rush´ən) *n.* **1** a person born or living in Russia. **2** the chief language of Russia and the U.S.S.R. ◆*adj.* of Russia, its people, their language, etc.

salmon

sa·li·va (sə lī´və) *n.* the watery liquid produced in the mouth by certain glands; spit. It helps to digest food.

salm·on (sam´ən) *n.* a large food fish with silver scales and flesh that is orange pink when cooked. Salmon live in the ocean but swim up rivers to lay their eggs. —*pl.* **salm´on** or **salm´ons**

sat·in (sat´n) *n.* a cloth of silk, nylon or rayon having a smooth finish, glossy on the front side and dull on the back.

sat·u·rate (sach´ər āt) *v.* **1** to soak through and through [The baby's bib was *saturated* with milk.] **2** to fill so completely or dissolve so much of something that no more can be taken up [to *saturate* water with salt]. —**sat´u·rat·ed, sat´u·rat·ing** —**sat´u·ra´tion** *n.*

sau·cer (sô´sər *or* sä´sər) *n.* **1** a small, shallow dish, especially one for a cup to rest on. **2** anything round and shallow like this dish.

sau·sage (sô´sij *or* sä´sij) *n.* pork or other meat, chopped up and seasoned and, usually, stuffed into a tube made of thin skin.

scan (skan) *v.* **1** to look at very carefully; examine [Columbus *scanned* the horizon for land.] ☆**2** to glance at or look over quickly [I *scanned* the list of names to find yours.] **3** to show the pattern of rhythm in the lines of a poem [We can *scan* a line this way: Má rў Má rў quíte cŏn trár ў.] —**scanned, scan´ning** —**scan´ner** *n.*

scare·crow (sker´krō) *n.* a figure of a man made with sticks, old clothes, etc. and set up in a field to scare birds away from crops.

scarf (skärf) *n.* **1** a long or broad piece of cloth worn about the head, neck, or shoulders for warmth or decoration. **2** a long, narrow piece of cloth used as a covering on top of a table, bureau, etc. —*pl.* **scarfs** or **scarves** (skärvz)

scar·y (sker´ē) *adj.* causing fear; frightening. —**scar´i·er, scar´i·est** —**scar´i·ness** *n.*

schol·ar·ship (skä´lər ship) *n.* **1** the knowledge of a learned person; great learning **2** the kind of knowledge that a student shows [Her paper shows good *scholarship*.]

sci·ence (sī´əns) *n.* knowledge made up of an orderly system of facts that have been learned from study, observation, and experiments [*Science* helps us to understand how things happen.]

sci·en·tist (sī´ən tist) *n.* an expert in science, such as a chemist, biologist, etc.

scram·ble (skram´bəl) *v.* **1** to climb or crawl in a quick, rough way [The children *scrambled* up the steep hill.] **2** to struggle or scuffle for something [The puppies *scrambled* for the meat.] ☆**3** to cook eggs while stirring the mixed whites and yolks. **4** to mix up electronic signals, as those containing a secret message, so that the message cannot be understood without special equipment. —**scram´bled, scram´bling**

scrape (skrāp) *v.* **1** to make smooth or clean by rubbing with a tool or with something rough [to *scrape* the bottom of a ship]. **2** to remove in this way [*Scrape* off the old paint.] **3** to scratch or rub the skin from [He fell and *scraped* his knee.] **4** to rub with a harsh or grating sound [The shovel *scraped* across the sidewalk.] —**scraped, scrap´ing**

☆**screen·play** (skrēn´plā) *n.* the written script from which a movie is made.

sec·re·tar·y (sek´rə ter´ē) *n.* **1** a person whose work is keeping records, writing letters, etc. for a person, organization, etc. **2** the head of a department of government [the *Secretary* of State]. **3** a writing desk, especially one with a bookcase built at the top. —*pl.* **sec´re·tar·ies** —**sec·re·tar·i·al** (sek´rə ter´ē əl) *adj.*

seek (sēk) *v.* to try to find; search for [to *seek* gold]. —**sought, seek´ing**

seize (sēz) **v.** to take hold of in a sudden, strong, or eager way; grasp [to *seize* a weapon and fight]. **—seized, seiz′ing**

se·lec·tive (sə lek′tiv) **adj. 1** of or set apart by selection. **2** tending to select. **3** having the power to select [A *selective* radio set brings in each station clearly.] **—se·lec′tive·ly adv. —se·lec·tiv·i·ty** (sə lek′tiv′ə tē) **n.**

self-con·trol (self′kən trōl′) **n.** control of oneself or of one's feelings and actions.

self-pres·er·va·tion (self′prez ər vā′shən) **n.** the act or instinct of keeping oneself safe and alive.

sen·ate (sen′ət) **n. 1** an assembly or council. **2 Senate**, the upper and smaller branch of Congress or of a State legislature.

sen·a·tor (sen′ə tər) **n.** a member of a senate. **—sen·a·to·ri·al** (sen′ə tôr′ē əl) **adj.**

sen·si·ble (sen′sə bəl) **adj. 1** having or showing good sense; reasonable; wise [*sensible* advice]. **2** having understanding; aware [She was *sensible* of his unhappiness.] **3** that can be felt or noticed by the senses [a *sensible* change in temperature]. **4** that can receive sensation [The eye is *sensible* to light rays.] **—sen′si·ble·ness n. —sen′si·bly adv.**

se·pal (sē′pəl) **n.** any of the leaves that form the calyx at the base of a flower.

sep·a·rate (sep′ər āt) **v. 1** to set apart; divide into parts or groups [*Separate* the good apples from the bad ones.] **2** to keep apart or divide by being or putting between [A hedge *separates* his yard from ours.] **3** to go apart; stop being together or joined [The friends *separated* at the crossroads.] **—sep′a·rat·ed, sep′a·rat·ing ◆adj.** (sep′ər ət *or* sep′rət) single or individual [the body's *separate* parts]. **—sep′a·rate·ly adv. —sep′a·ra·tion n.**

se·quence (sē′kwens) **n. 1** the following of one thing after another; succession [The *sequence* of events in their lives led to marriage.] **2** the order in which things follow one another [Line them up in *sequence* from shortest to tallest.] **3** a series of things that are related [a *sequence* of misfortunes].

se·ri·ous (sir′ē əs) **adj. 1** having or showing deep thought; not frivolous; solemn; earnest [a *serious* student]. **2** not joking or fooling; sincere [Is she *serious* about wanting to help?] **3** needing careful thought; important [a *serious* problem]. **4** that can cause worry; dangerous [a *serious* illness]. **—se′ri·ous·ly adv. —se′ri·ous·ness n.**

set·tle·ment (set′l mənt) **n.** a place where people have gone to settle; colony [early English *settlements* in Virginia].

shake (shāk) **v. 1** to move quickly up and down, back and forth, or from side to side [to *shake* one's head in approval]. **2** to clasp another's hand, as in greeting. **3** to bring, force, throw, stir up, etc. by short, quick movements [I'll *shake* salt on the popcorn. *Shake* the medicine well before taking it.] **4** to tremble or make tremble [His voice *shook* with fear. Chills *shook* his body.] **—shook, shak·en** (shāk′'n), **shak′ing**

shal·low (shal′ō) **adj. 1** not deep [a *shallow* lake]. **2** not serious in thinking or strong in feeling [a *shallow* mind]. **◆n.** a shallow place, as in a river.

shame·ful (shām′fəl) **adj. 1** bringing shame or disgrace. **2** not moral or decent. **—shame′ful·ly adv.**

sharp·en (shärp′ən) **v.** to make or become sharp or sharper. **—sharp′en·er n.**

she'll (shēl) **1** she will **2** she shall.

sher·bet (shur′bət) **n.** a frozen dessert of fruit juice, sugar, and water or milk.

sher·iff (sher′if) **n.** ☆the chief officer of the law in a county.

shield (shēld) **n. 1** a piece of armor carried on the arm to ward off blows in battle. **2** something that guards or protects, as a safety guard over machinery. **3** anything shaped like a shield, as a coat of arms. **◆v.** to guard or protect [Trees *shield* our house from the sun.]

ship (ship) **n. 1** any vessel, larger than a boat, for traveling on deep water. **2** the crew of a ship. **3** an aircraft or spaceship. **◆v.** to put, take, go, or send in a ship or boat [The cargo was *shipped* from New York.] **—shipped, ship′ping**

ship·wreck (ship′rek) **n. 1** the remains of a wrecked ship. **2** the loss or ruin of a ship, as in a storm or crash. **◆v.** to wreck or destroy a ship.

shoe·lace (shoo′lās) **n.** a lace of cord, leather, etc. used for fastening a shoe.

shore·ward (shôr′wərd) **adj., adv.** toward the shore [Two boats were headed *shoreward*.]

☆**short·age** (shôrt′ij) **n.** a lack in the amount that is needed or expected [a *shortage* of help].

shred (shred) **n. 1** a long, narrow strip or piece cut or torn off [My shirt was torn to *shreds*.] **2** a tiny piece or amount; fragment [a story without a *shred* of truth]. **◆v.** to cut or tear into shreds [*shredded* coconut]. **—shred′ded** or **shred, shred′ding**

shy (shī) **adj. 1** easily frightened; timid [a *shy* animal]. **2** not at ease with other people; bashful [a *shy* child]. **—shi′er** or **shy′er, shi′est** or **shy′est —shied, shy′ing v. —shy′ly adv. —shy′ness n.**

sepal

a	ask, fat
ā	ape, date
ä	car, lot
e	elf, ten
ē	even, meet
i	is, hit
ī	ice, fire
ō	open, go
ô	law, horn
oi	oil, point
oo	look, pull
o͞o	ooze, tool
ou	out, crowd
u	up, cut
ʉ	fur, fern
ə	a in ago
	e in agent
	e in father
	i in unity
	o in collect
	u in focus
ch	chin, arch
ŋ	ring, singer
sh	she, dash
th	thin, truth
th	then, father
zh	s in pleasure

sig·nal (sig'nəl) *n.* **1** something that tells when some action is to start or end, or is used as a warning or direction [A loud bell is the *signal* for a fire drill. The traffic *signal* is green, telling us to go.] **2** the electrical waves sent out or received as sounds or pictures in radio and television. —**sig'naled** or **sig'nalled, sig'nal·ing** or **sig'nal·ling** *v.*

si·lence (sī'ləns) *n.* **1** a keeping still and not speaking, making noise, etc. [His *silence* meant he agreed.] **2** absence of any sound or noise; stillness [There was complete *silence* in the deep forest.] **3** failure to keep in touch, write letters, etc. —**si'lenced, si'lenc·ing** *v.* —**si'lenc·er** *n.*

sin·cere (sin sir') *adj.* not pretending or fooling; honest; truthful [Are you *sincere* in wanting to help?] —**sin·cer'er, sin·cer'est**

sin·cer·i·ty (sin ser'ə tē) *n.* the condition of being sincere; honesty; good faith.

six (siks) *n. adj.* one more than five; the number 6.

six·ty-four (siks'tē fôr') *n., adj.* the cardinal number that is equal to six times ten plus four; 64.

skid (skid) *n.* ☆**1** a plank, log, etc. used as a support or as a track on which to slide something heavy. **2** a sliding wedge used as a brake on a wheel. ◆*v.* to slide without turning, as a wheel does on ice when it is held by a brake. —**skid'ded, skid'ding**

slaugh·ter (slôt'ər *or* slät'ər) *n.* the act of killing people or animals in a cruel way or in large numbers ◆*v.* to kill for food; butcher [to *slaughter* a hog]. —**slaugh'tered, slaugh'ter·ing**

sleep·y (slē'pē) *adj.* **1** ready or likely to fall asleep; drowsy. **2** not very active; dull; quiet [a *sleepy* little town]. —**sleep'i·er, sleep'i·est** —**sleep'i·ly** *adv.* —**sleep'i·ness** *n.*

slight (slīt) *adj.* **1** small in amount or degree; not great, strong, important, etc. [a *slight* change in temperature; a *slight* advantage; a *slight* bruise]. **2** light in build; slender [Most jockeys are short and *slight*.]◆*v.* to pay little or no attention to; neglect, snub, etc. [to *slight* one's homework; to *slight* a neighbor]. —**slight'ly** *adv.* —**slight'er, slight'est**

snout (snout) *n.* the part, including the nose and jaws, that sticks out from the face of pigs, dogs, and certain other animals.

snow·drift (snō'drift) *n.* a bank or pile of snow heaped up by the wind.

soil (soil) *v.* **1** to make or become dirty; stain; spot. **2** to disgrace [to *soil* one's honor]. ◆*n.* the act of soiling or a soiled spot; stain.

sor·row (sär'ō) *n.* a sad or troubled feeling; sadness; grief.

so·vi·et (sō'vē ət) *n.* any of the councils, or groups of people, chosen to govern a certain area in the U.S.S.R., ranging from the small soviets of villages and towns to the **Supreme Soviet**, the national congress. ◆*adj.* **Soviet**, of or having to do with the U.S.S.R.

spa·ghet·ti (spə get'ē) *n.* long, thin strings of dried flour paste, cooked by boiling or steaming and served with a sauce.

Span·ish (span'ish) *adj.* of Spain, its people, etc. ◆*n.* the language of Spain and Spanish America. —**the Spanish,** the people of Spain.

Spanish America Mexico and those countries in Central and South America and the West Indies in which Spanish is the chief language.

spar·kle (spär'kəl) *v.* **1** to give off sparks or flashes of light; glitter; glisten [A lake *sparkles* in sunlight.] **2** to be lively and witty [There was much *sparkling* talk at the party.] **3** to bubble as ginger ale does. —**spar'kled, spar'kling**

spar·row (sper'ō) *n.* a small, often brown or gray songbird with a short beak.

speak·er (spē'kər) *n.* **1** a person who speaks or makes speeches. **2** the person who serves as chairman of a group of lawmakers, especially ☆**Speaker,** the chairman of the U.S. House of Representatives: *the full name is* **Speaker of the House. 3** a device that changes electric current into sound waves, used as part of a hi-fi system, radio, etc.

spe·cies (spē'shēz *or* spē'sēz) *n.* **1** a group of plants or animals that are alike in certain ways [The lion and tiger are two different *species* of cat.] **2** a kind or sort [a *species* of bravery]. —*pl.* **spe'cies** —**the species,** the human race.

speech (spēch) *n.* **1** the act or way of speaking [We knew from their *speech* that they were from the South.] **2** the power to speak [She lost her *speech* from a stroke.] **3** something spoken; remark, utterance, etc. **4** a talk given in public [political *speeches* on TV].

spell·bound (spel'bound) *adj.* held fast as if by a spell; fascinated; enchanted.

spin (spin) *v.* **1** to draw out the fibers of and twist into thread [to *spin* cotton, wool, flax, etc.]. **2** to make from a thread given out by the body [Spiders *spin* webs.] **3** to tell slowly, with many details [to *spin* out a story]. **4** to whirl around swiftly [The earth *spins* in space. *Spin* the wheel.] —**spun, spin'ning** —**spin'ner** *n.*

spi·ral (spī'rəl) *adj.* circling around a center in a flat or rising curve that keeps growing larger or smaller, as the thread of a screw, or that stays the same, as the thread of a bolt. ◆*n.* a spiral curve or coil [The mainspring of a watch is a *spiral*.] ◆*v.* to move in or form into a spiral. —**spi'raled** or **spi'ralled, spi'ral·ing** or **spi'ral·ling** —**spi'ral·ly** *adv.*

splen·did (splen'did) *adj.* **1** very bright, brilliant, showy, magnificent, etc. [a *splendid* display; a *splendid* gown]. **2** deserving high praise; glorious; grand [your *splendid* courage]. **3** very good; excellent; fine: *used only in everyday talk* [a *splendid* trip]. —**splen'did·ly** *adv.*

spoil (spoil) *v.* to make or become useless, worthless or rotten; to damage; to ruin [Meat *spoils* fast in warm weather.] —**spoiled** or **spoilt, spoil'ing**

spo·ken (spō'kən) *v.* past participle of **speak** ◆*adj.* said aloud; oral [a *spoken* order].

sprawl (sprôl) *v* to sit or lie with the arms and legs spread out in a relaxed or awkward way [He *sprawled* on the grass.] —**sprawled, sprawl'ing**

squawk (skwôk *or* skwäk) *n.* a loud, harsh cry such as a chicken or parrot makes. *v.* ☆to complain loudly: *used only in everyday talk.* —**squawk'er** *n.*

sta·di·um (stā'dē əm) *n.* a place for outdoor games, meetings, etc., with rising rows of seats around the open field.

stain (stān) *v.* to spoil with dirt or a patch of color; to soil or spot [The rug was *stained* with ink.] —**stained, stain'ing** ◆*n.* a dirty or colored spot [grass *stain*].

sta·men (stā'mən) *n.* the part of a flower in which the pollen grows, including the anther and its stem.

state·ment (stāt'mənt) *n.* 1 the act of stating. 2 something stated or said [May we quote your *statement*?] 3 a report or record, as of money owed [The customers receive monthly *statements*.]

sta·tion·ar·y (stā'shə ner'ē) *adj.* 1 not to be moved; fixed [*stationary* seats]. 2 not changing in condition, value, etc. [*stationary* prices].

stat·ue (stach'ōō) *n.* the form or likeness of a person or animal carved in wood, stone, etc., modeled in clay, or cast in plaster or a metal.

stead·y (sted'ē) *adj.* 1 firm; not shaky [a *steady* chair]. 2 not changing or letting up; regular [a *steady* gaze; a *steady* worker]. 3 not easily excited; calm [*steady* nerves]. 4 serious and sensible; reliable [a *steady* young person]. —**stead'i·er, stead'i·est** —**stead'ied, stead'y·ing** *v.* —**stead'i·ly** *adv.* —**stead'i·ness** *n.*

stick·y (stik'ē) *adj.* 1 that sticks; gluey; clinging [His fingers were *sticky* with candy.] 2 hot and damp; humid: *used only in everyday talk* [a *sticky* August day]. —**stick'i·er, stick'i·est** —**stick'i·ness** *n.*

stiff·ness (stif'nəs) *n.* the condition of being hard to bend or stretch.

stom·ach (stum'ək) *n.* 1 the large, hollow organ into which food goes after it is swallowed.   Food is partly digested in the stomach. 2 the belly, or abdomen [The fighter was hit in the *stomach*.]

strange (strānj) *adj.* 1 not known, seen, or heard before; not familiar [I saw a *strange* person at the door.] 2 different from what is usual; peculiar; odd [wearing a *strange* costume]. 3 not familiar; without experience [She is *strange* to this job.] —**strang'er, strang'est** —**strange'ly** *adv.*

straw·ber·ry (strô'ber'ē *or* strä'ber'ē) *n.* 1 the small, red, juicy fruit of a low plant of the rose family. 2 this plant. —*pl.* **straw'ber'ries**

strut (strut) *v.* to walk in a self-confident way, usually as if to attract attention [The famous singer *strutted* across the stage.] —**strut'ted, strut'ting**

stur·dy (stur'dē) *adj.* 1 strong and hardy [a *sturdy* oak]. 2 not giving in; firm [*sturdy* defiance]. —**stur'di·er, stur'di·est** —**stur'di·ly** *adv.* —**stur'di·ness** *n.*

sub·due (səb dōō' *or* səb dyōō') *v.* 1 to conquer or overcome; get control over [to *subdue* an invading army; to *subdue* a bad habit]. 2 to make less strong or harsh; soften [*subdued* anger; *subdued* light; *subdued* colors]. —**sub·dued', sub·du'ing**

sub·ject (sub'jekt) *adj.* 1 under the power or control of another [The *subject* peoples in colonies often revolt.] 2 likely to have; liable [He is *subject* to fits of anger.] ◆*n.* 1 a person under the power or control of a ruler, government, etc. 2 a course of study, as in a school [What is your favorite *subject*?] —**sub·jec'tion** *n.*

sub·ma·rine (sub'mə rēn) *n.* a kind of ship that can travel underwater.

sub·merge (sub murj') *v.* to put, go, or stay underwater [Whales can *submerge* for as long as half an hour.] —**sub·merged', sub·merg'ing**

sub·mit (sub mit') *v.* 1 to give or offer to others for them to look over, decide about, etc.; refer [A new tax law was *submitted* to the voters.] 2 to give in to the power or control of another; surrender [We will never *submit* to the enemy.] —**sub·mit'ted, sub·mit'ting**

sub·scribe (səb skrīb') *v.* 1 to agree to take and pay for [We *subscribed* to the magazine for a year.] 2 to promise to give [She *subscribed* $100 to the campaign for a new museum.] 3 to agree with or approve of [I *subscribe* to the principles in the Constitution.] —**sub·scribed', sub·scrib'ing** —**sub·scrib'er** *n.*

sub·side (səb sīd') *v.* 1 to sink to a lower level; go down [In June the river began to *subside*.] 2 to become quiet or less active [The angry waves *subsided*. The teacher's temper *subsided*.] —**sub·sid'ed, sub·sid'ing**

sub·sti·tute (sub'stə tōōt *or* sub'stə tyōōt) *n.* a person or thing that takes the place of another [He is a *substitute* for the regular teacher.] ◆*v.* to use as or be a substitute [to *substitute* vinegar for lemon juice; to *substitute* for an injured player]. —**sub'sti·tut·ed, sub'sti·tut·ing** —**sub'sti·tu'tion** *n.*

sub·tract (səb trakt') *v.* to take away, as a part from a whole or one number from another [If 3 is *subtracted* from 5, the remainder is 2.]

stamen

a	ask, fat
ā	ape, date
ä	car, lot
e	elf, ten
ē	even, meet
i	is, hit
ī	ice, fire
ō	open, go
ô	law, horn
oi	oil, point
͝o͝o	look, pull
o͞o	ooze, tool
ou	out, crowd
u	up, cut
u	fur, fern
ə	a in ago
	e in agent
	e in father
	i in unity
	o in collect
	u in focus
ch	chin, arch
ŋ	ring, singer
sh	she, dash
th	thin, truth
th	then, father
zh	s in pleasure

suc·ceed (sək sēd′) *v.* **1** to manage to do or be what was planned; do or go well [I *succeeded* in convincing them to come with us.] **2** to come next after; follow [Carter *succeeded* Ford as President.]

suc·cess (sək ses′) *n.* **1** the result that was hoped for; satisfactory outcome [Did you have *success* in training your dog?] **2** the fact of becoming rich, famous, etc. [Her *success* did not change her.] **3** a successful person or thing [Our play was a *success*.]

suf·fer (suf′ər) *v.* **1** to feel or have pain, discomfort, etc. [to *suffer* from a headache]. **2** to experience or undergo [The team *suffered* a loss when Sal was hurt.] **3** to become worse or go from good to bad [Her grades *suffered* when she didn't study.] **4** to put up with; bear [He won't *suffer* criticism.]

sug·gest (səg jest′) *v.* **1** to mention as something to think over, act on, etc. [I *suggest* we meet again.] **2** to bring to mind as something similar or in some way connected [The white dunes *suggested* snow-covered hills.   Clouds *suggest* rain.]

sun·ny (sun′ē) *adj.* **1** bright with sunlight [Today is a *sunny* day.] **2** like or from the sun [A *sunny* beam shone through.] **3** cheerful; bright [Lynn has a *sunny* smile.] —**sun′ni·er, sun′ni·est**

sun·shine (sun′shīn) *n.* **1** the shining of the sun. **2** the light and heat from the sun. **3** cheerfulness, happiness, etc. —**sun′shin·y** *adj.*

sup·ply (sə plī′) *v.* **1** to give what is needed; furnish [The camp *supplies* sheets and towels.   The book *supplied* us with the facts.] **2** to take care of the needs of [to *supply* workers with tools]. **3** to make up for; fill [These pills *supply* a deficiency of iron.] —**sup·plied′, sup·ply′ing**

sup·port (sə pôrt′) *v.* **1** to carry the weight or burden of; hold up [Will that old ladder *support* you?] **2** to take the side of; uphold or help [She worked to *support* our cause.] **3** to earn a living for; provide for [He *supports* a large family.] **4** to help prove [Use examples to *support* your argument.] —**sup·port′er** *n.*

sur·prise (sər prīz′) *v.* **1** to cause to feel wonder by being unexpected [Her sudden anger *surprised* us.] **2** to come upon suddenly or unexpectedly [I *surprised* him in the act of stealing the watch.] **3** to attack or capture suddenly. —**sur·prised′, sur·pris′ing**

sur·round (sər round′) *v.* to form or arrange around on all or nearly all sides; enclose [The police *surrounded* the criminals.   The house is *surrounded* with trees.]

sur·vey (sər vā′) *v.* to look over in a careful way; examine; inspect [The lookout *surveyed* the horizon.] —**sur·veyed′, sur·vey′ing**

sur·vive (sər vīv′) *v.* **1** to continue to live or exist [Thanksgiving is a Pilgrim custom that *survives* today.] **2** to live or last longer than; outlive [Most people *survive* their parents.] **3** to continue to live or exist in spite of [We *survived* the fire.] —**sur·vived′, sur·viv′ing**

swal·low (swä′lō) *v.* **1** to let food, drink, etc. go through the throat into the stomach. **2** to move the muscles of the throat as in swallowing something [I *swallowed* hard to keep from crying.] **3** to take in; engulf [The waters of the lake *swallowed* him up.] **4** to put up with; bear with patience [We refused to *swallow* their insults.]

sweat·er (swet′ər) *n.* a knitted outer garment for the upper part of the body.

Swed·ish (swēd′ish) *adj.* of Sweden or the Swedes. ◆*n.* the language of the Swedes.

sweep (swēp) *v.* **1** to clean as by brushing with a broom [to *sweep* a floor]. **2** to clear away as with a broom [*Sweep* the dirt from the porch.] **3** to carry away or destroy with a quick, strong motion [The tornado *swept* the shed away.] —**swept, sweep′ing** ◆*n.* the act of sweeping, as with a broom.

sweep·er (swēp′ər) *n.* **1** a person or thing that sweeps **2** a device for cleaning carpets.

sweet (swēt) *adj.* **1** having the taste of sugar; having sugar in it [a *sweet* apple]. **2** pleasant in taste, smell, sound, manner, etc. [*sweet* perfume; *sweet* music; a *sweet* child]. ◆*adv.* in a sweet manner. —**sweet′er, sweet′est** —**sweet′ish** *adj.* —**sweet′ly** *adv.* —**sweet′ness** *n.*

sym·bol (sim′bəl) *n.* an object, mark, sign, etc. that stands for another object, or for an idea, quality, etc. [The dove is a *symbol* of peace. · The mark $ is the *symbol* for dollar or dollars.]

sym·pho·ny (sim′fə nē) *n.* **1** a long piece of music for a full orchestra, usually divided into four movements with different rhythms and themes. **2** a large orchestra for playing such works: *its full name is* **symphony orchestra**. **3** harmony, as of sounds, color, etc. [The dance was a *symphony* in motion.] —*pl.* **sym′pho·nies** —**sym·phon·ic** (sim fän′ik) *adj.* —**sym·phon′i·cal·ly** *adv.*

tar·dy (tär′dē) *adj.* not on time; late; delayed [to be *tardy* for class]. —**tar′di·er, tar′di·est**

tel·e·graph (tel′ə graf) *n.* a device or system for sending messages by a code of electrical signals that are sent over a wire, by radio or by microwave.

tel·e·phone (tel′ə fōn) *n.* ☆**1** a way of sending sounds over distances by changing them into electric signals which are sent through a wire and then changed back into sounds. ☆**2** a device for sending and receiving sounds in this way. —**tel′e·phoned, tel′e·phon·ing** *v.* —**tel·e·phon·ic** (tel′ə făn′ik) *adj.*

tem·per·a·ture (tem′prə chər *or* tem′pər ə chər) *n.* **1** the degree of hotness or coldness, as of air, liquids, the body, etc., usually as measured by a thermometer. **2** a body heat above the normal, which is about 37°C or 98.6°F; fever.

ter·ri·ble (ter′ə bəl) *adj.* **1** causing great fear or terror; dreadful [a *terrible* flood]. **2** very great; severe [*terrible* suffering]. **3** very bad or unpleasant: *used only in everyday talk* [Our guest had *terrible* manners.] —**ter′ri·bly** *adv.*

Tex·as (teks′əs) a State in the south central part of the U.S.: abbreviated **Tex., TX** —**Tex′an** *adj., n.*

thaw (thô *or* thä) *v.* to melt [The snow *thawed.*] —**thawed, thaw′ing**

the·o·ry (thē′ə rē *or* thir′ē) *n.* an explanation of how or why something happens, especially one based on scientific study and reasoning [Charles Darwin's *theory* of evolution]. —*pl.* **the′o·ries**

they've (thāv) they have.

thick·en (thik′ən) *v.* to make or become thick or thicker [Adding flour will *thicken* the gravy.] —**thick′ened, thick′en·ing**

thief (thēf) *n.* a person who steals, especially one who steals secretly. —*pl.* **thieves** (thēvz)

throb (thräb) *v.* to beat or vibrate hard or fast, as the heart does when one is excited. —**throbbed, throb′bing** ◆*n.* the act of throbbing; a strong beat.

throw (thrō) *v.* **1** to send through the air by a fast motion of the arm; hurl, toss, etc. [to *throw* a ball]. **2** to make fall down; upset [to *throw* someone in wrestling]. **3** to send or cast in a certain direction, as a glance, light, shadow, etc. **4** to put suddenly into some condition or place [to *throw* into confusion; to *throw* into prison]. —**threw, thrown, throw′ing**

tick·le (tik′əl) *v.* **1** to touch or stroke lightly, as with a finger or feather, so as to cause twitching, laughter, etc. **2** to have such a scratching or twitching feeling [The dust makes my nose *tickle*.] **3** to give pleasure to; amuse; delight [The joke really *tickled* her.] —**tick′led, tick′ling** —**tick′ler** *n.*

tight (tīt) *adj.* **1** made so that water, air, etc. cannot pass through [a *tight* boat]. **2** put together firmly or closely [a *tight* knot]. **3** fitting too closely [a *tight* shirt]. **4** stretched and strained; taut [a *tight* wire; *tight* nerves]. —**tight′ly** *adv.* —**tight′ness** *n.*

tight·en (tīt′n) *v.* to make or become tight or tighter.

toad·stool (tōd′stool) *n.* a mushroom, especially one that is poisonous.

toast (tōst) *v.* **1** to brown the surface of by heating, as bread. **2** to warm [*Toast* yourself by the fire.] ◆*n.* toasted bread. —**toast′er** *n.*

toil (toil) *v.* **1** to work hard; labor. **2** to go slowly with pain or effort [to *toil* up a hill]. ◆*n.* hard work. —**toil′er** *n.*

to·ma·to (tə māt′ō *or* tə mät′ō) *n.* **1** a red or yellow, round fruit, with a juicy pulp, used as a vegetable. **2** the plant it grows on. —*pl.* **to·ma′toes**

to·mor·row (tə mär′ō) *adv.* on the day after today. ◆*n.* **1** the day after today. **2** some future time.

tor·na·do (tôr nā′dō) *n.* a high, narrow column of air that is whirling very fast. It is often seen as a slender cloud shaped like a funnel, that usually destroys everything in its narrow path. —*pl.* **tor·na′does** *or* **tor·na′dos**

tor·pe·do (tôr pē′dō) *n.* a large, exploding missile shaped like a cigar: it moves under water under its own power to blow up enemy ships. —*pl.* **tor·pe′does**

tor·rent (tôr′ənt) *n.* **1** a swift, rushing stream of water. **2** any wild, rushing flow [a *torrent* of insults]. **3** a heavy fall of rain.

tough (tuf) *adj.* **1** that will bend or twist without tearing or breaking [*tough* rubber]. **2** that cannot be cut or chewed easily [*tough* meat]. **3** strong and healthy; robust [a *tough* pioneer]. **4** very difficult or hard [a *tough* job]. —**tough′ness** *n.*

tour·ist (toor′ist) *n.* a person who tours or travels for pleasure. ◆*adj.* of or for tourists.

tow·el (tou′əl *or* toul) *n.* a piece of soft paper or cloth for drying things by wiping.

trans·fer (trans fur′ *or* trans′fər) *v.* **1** to move, carry, send, or change from one person or place to another [He *transferred* his notes to another notebook. Jill has *transferred* to a new school.] **2** to move a picture, design, etc. from one surface to another, as by making wet and pressing. ☆**3** to change from one bus, train, etc. to another. —**trans·ferred′, trans·fer′ring**

trans·late (trans lāt′ *or* tranz lāt′) *v.* **1** to put into words of a different language [to *translate* a Latin poem into English]. **2** to change into another form [to *translate* ideas into action]. **3** to change from one place or condition to another; especially, to carry up to heaven. —**trans·lat′ed, trans·lat′ing**

trans·mit (trans mit′ *or* tranz mit′) *v.* to send from one person, place, or thing to another; pass on; transfer [to *transmit* a disease]. —**trans·mit′ted, trans·mit′ting**

trans·par·ent (trans per′ənt) *adj.* so clear or so fine that objects on the other side can be easily seen [*transparent* glass].

tornado

a	ask, fat
ā	ape, date
ä	car, lot
e	elf, ten
ē	even, meet
i	is, hit
ī	ice, fire
ō	open, go
ô	law, horn
oi	oil, point
oo	look, pull
ōō	ooze, tool
ou	out, crowd
u	up, cut
ʉ	fur, fern
ə	a in ago
	e in agent
	e in father
	i in unity
	o in collect
	u in focus
ch	chin, arch
ŋ	ring, singer
sh	she, dash
th	thin, truth
th	then, father
zh	s in pleasure

187

trans·plant (trans plant′) *v.* **1** to dig up from one place and plant in another. **2** to move tissue or an organ by surgery from one person or part of the body to another; graft. ◆*n.* (trans′plant) something transplanted, as a body organ or seedling.

trans·port (trans pôrt′) *v.* **1** to carry from one place to another [to *transport* goods by train or truck]. **2** to cause strong feelings in [*transported* with delight]. **3** to send to a place far away as a punishment.

treas·ure (trezh′ər) *n.* **1** money, jewels, etc. collected and stored up. **2** a person or thing that is loved or held dear. ◆*v.* **1** to love or hold dear; cherish [I *treasure* their friendship.] **2** to store away or save up, as money; hoard. —**treas′ured, treas′ur·ing**

tri·an·gle (trī′aŋ′gəl) *n.* **1** a flat figure with three sides and three angles. **2** anything shaped like this. **3** a musical instrument that is a steel rod bent in a triangle. It makes a high, tinkling sound when struck with a metal rod.

tri·o (trē′ō) *n.* **1** a piece of music for three voices or three instruments. **2** the three people who sing or play it. **3** any group of three. —*pl.* **tri′os**

tri·ple (trip′əl) *adj.* **1** made up of three [A *triple* cone has three dips of ice cream.] **2** three times as much or as many. ◆*n.* **1** an amount three times as much or as many. ☆**2** a hit in baseball on which the batter gets to third base. —**tri′pled, tri′pling** *v.*

tri·plet (trip′lət) *n.* **1** any one of three children born at the same time to the same mother **2** any group of three.

tri·pod (trī′päd) *n.* a stand, frame, etc. with three legs. Cameras and small telescopes are often held up by tripods.

tri·umph (trī′əmf) *n.* **1** a victory, as in a battle; success [His *triumph* over illness inspired us.] **2** great joy over a victory or success [She grinned in *triumph* when she won the race.] ◆*v.* to be the winner; win victory or success [to *triumph* over an enemy]. —**tri·um·phal** (trī um′f′l) *adj.*

trout (trout) *n.* a small food fish of the salmon family, found mainly in fresh water.

trudge (truj) *v.* to walk, especially in a tired way or with effort. —**trudged, trudg′ing** ◆*n.* a long or tiring walk.

☆**type·writ·er** (tīp′rīt′ər) *n.* a machine with a keyboard for making printed letters or figures on paper.

ty·phoid (tī′foid) *n.* a serious disease that is spread as by infected food or drinking water, and causing fever, sores in the intestines, etc. *The full name is* **typhoid fever.**

ty·phoon (tī foon′) *n.* any violent tropical cyclone that starts in the western Pacific.

tripod

un- **1** *a prefix meaning* not *or* the opposite of [An *unhappy* person is one who is not happy, but sad.] **2** *a prefix meaning* to reverse or undo the action of [To *untie* a shoelace is to reverse the action of tying it.]

un·a·vail·a·ble (un ə vēl′ə bəl) *adj.* not able to be gotten, used, or reached [This book is now *unavailable.*]

un·cooked (un kookt′) *adj.* not cooked; raw.

un·cov·er (un kuv′ər) *v.* **1** to remove the cover or covering from. **2** to make known; disclose, as a hidden fact. **3** to take off one's hat, as in showing respect.

un·der·neath (un dər nēth′) *adv., prep.* under; below; beneath.

un·der·sea (un dər sē′) *adj., adv.* beneath the surface of the sea.

un·der·wa·ter (un′dər wôt′ər *or* un′dər wät′ər) *adj., adv.* under the surface of the water.

un·for·giv·a·ble (un fər giv′ə bəl) *adj.* not deserving to be pardoned; inexcusable.

u·nit (yoon′it) *n.* **1** a single person or group, especially as a part of a whole [an army *unit*]. **2** a single part with some special use [the lens *unit* of a camera]. **3** a fixed amount or measure used as a standard [The ounce is a *unit* of weight.] **4** the smallest whole number; one.

un·just (un just′) *adj.* not just or right; unfair [an *unjust* rule]. —**un·just′ly** *adv.*

un·law·ful (un lô′fəl *or* un lä′fəl) *adj.* against the law; illegal. —**un·law′ful·ly** *adv.* —**un·law′ful·ness** *n.*

un·like·ly (un līk′lē) *adj.* **1** not likely to happen or be true [an *unlikely* story]. **2** not likely to be right or successful [an *unlikely* place to dig for gold].

un·sel·fish (un sel′fish) *adj.* not selfish; putting the good of others above one's own interests. —**un·self′ish·ly** *adv.* —**un·self′ish·ness** *n.*

un·u·su·al (un yoo′zhoo əl) *adj.* not usual or common; rare; remarkable. —**un·u′su·al·ly** *adv.*

us·a·ble or **use·a·ble** (yoo′zə bəl) *adj.* that can be used; fit or ready for use.

va·ca·tion (vā kā′shən) *n.* ☆a period of time when one stops working, going to school, etc. in order to rest and have recreation. ◆*v.* to take one's vacation.

val·u·a·ble (val'yoo ə bəl *or* val'yə bəl) *adj.*
1 having value or worth; especially, worth much money. **2** thought of as precious, useful, worthy, etc. ◆*n.* something of value, as a piece of jewelry.

valve (valv) *n.* **1** a device, as in a pipe, that controls the flow of a gas or liquid by means of a flap, lid, or plug that closes off the pipe. **2** a membrane in the body that acts in this way [The *valves* of the heart let the blood flow in one direction only.] **3** a device, as in a trumpet, that opens a branch to the main tube so as to change the pitch. **4** one of the parts making up the shell of a clam, oyster, etc.

va·por (vā'pər) *n.* **1** a thick mist or mass of tiny drops of water floating in the air, as steam or fog. **2** the gas formed when a substance that is usually liquid or solid is heated [Mercury *vapor* is used in some lamps.]

vault (vôlt) *n.* **1** an arched ceiling or roof. **2** a room with such a ceiling, or a space that seems to have an arch [the *vault* of the sky]. ☆**3** a room for keeping money, valuable papers, etc. safe, as in a bank.

ve·hi·cle (vē'i kəl *or* vē'hi kəl) *n.* **1** a means of carrying persons or things, especially over land or in space, as an automobile, bicycle, spacecraft, etc. **2** a means by which something is expressed, passed along, etc. [TV is a *vehicle* for advertising.] **3** a liquid, as oil or water, with which pigments are mixed to make paint.

vein (vān) *n.* **1** any blood vessel that carries blood back to the heart from some part of the body. **2** any of the fine lines, or ribs, in a leaf or in an insect's wing. **3** a layer of mineral, rock, etc. formed in a crack in different rock [a *vein* of silver or of coal].

ver·dict (vur'dikt) *n.* **1** the decision reached by a jury in a law case [a *verdict* of "not guilty"]. **2** any decision or opinion.

vet·er·an (vet'ər ən *or* ve'trən) *n.* **1** a person who has served in the armed forces. **2** a person with much experience in some kind of work.
◆*adj.* having had long experience in some work or service [*veteran* troops; a *veteran* diplomat].

vic·tim (vik'tim) *n.* **1** someone or something killed, hurt, sacrificed, etc. [a *victim* of the storm; the *victims* of prejudice]. **2** a person who is cheated or tricked [a *victim* of swindlers].

vic·to·ry (vik'tər ē) *n.* the winning of a battle, struggle, or contest; success in defeating an enemy or rival. —*pl.* **vic'to·ries**

vil·lage (vil'ij) *n.* **1** a group of houses in the country, smaller than a town. **2** the people of a village. —**vil'lag·er** *n.*

vi·o·lence (vī'ə ləns) *n.* great strength or force [the *violence* of a tornado].

vi·o·lent (vī'ə lənt) *adj.* showing or acting with great force that causes damage or injury [*violent* winds]. —**vi'o·lent·ly** *adv.*

vis·i·ble (viz'ə bəl) *adj.* that can be seen or noticed; evident [a barely *visible* scar; a *visible* increase in crime]. —**vis'i·bly** *adv.*

vo·cal·ist (vō'kəl ist) *n.* a person who sings; singer.

vol·ca·no (vôl kā nō *or* väl kā'nō) *n.* **1** an opening in the earth's surface through which molten rock from inside the earth is thrown up. **2** a hill or mountain of ash and molten rock built up around such an opening. —*pl.* **vol·ca'noes** *or* **vol·ca'nos**

vol·ume (väl'yoom) *n.* **1** a book [You may borrow four *volumes* at a time.] **2** one of the books of a set [*Volume* III of the encyclopedia]. **3** the amount of space inside something, measured in cubic inches, feet, etc. [The *volume* of this box is 27 cubic feet, or .756 cubic meter.]

vol·un·teer (väl ən tir') *n.* a person who offers to do something of his or her own free will, as one who enlists in the armed forces by choice. ◆*adj.* of or done by volunteers [a *volunteer* regiment; *volunteer* help].

vot·er (vōt'ər) *n.* a person who votes or has the right to vote.

voy·age (voi'ij) *n.* **1** a journey by water [an ocean *voyage*]. **2** a journey through the air or through outer space [a *voyage* by rocket]. ◆*v.* to make a voyage. —**voy'aged, voy'ag·ing** —**voy'ag·er** *n.*

volcano

waf·fle (wäf'əl) *n.* a crisp cake with small, square hollows, cooked in a waffle iron.

walk·way (wôk'wā) *n.* a passage for walking.

war·ri·or (wôr'ē ər) *n.* a soldier: *not often used today.*

wash·a·ble (wôsh'ə bəl *or* wäsh'ə bəl) *adj.* able to be washed without being damaged.

wa·ter·mel·on (wôt'ər mel ən *or* wät'ər mel ən) *n.* a large melon with a green rind and juicy, red pulp with many seeds.

wealth (welth) *n.* **1** much money or property; riches. **2** a large amount [a *wealth* of ideas]. **3** any valuable thing or things [the *wealth* of the oceans].

weath·er (weth'ər) *n.* the conditions outside at any particular time with regard to temperature, sunshine, rainfall, etc. [We have good *weather* today for a picnic.] ◆*v.* to pass through safely [to *weather* a storm].

weird (wird) *adj.* **1** strange or mysterious in a ghostly way [*Weird* sounds came from the cave.] **2** very odd, strange, etc. [What a *weird* hat! What *weird* behavior!] —**weird'ly** *adv.* —**weird'ness** *n.*

wheel·bar·row (hwēl'bar ō *or* wēl'ber ō) *n.* a small kind of cart pushed or pulled by hand and having a single wheel.

a	ask, fat
ā	ape, date
ä	car, lot
e	elf, ten
ē	even, meet
i	is, hit
ī	ice, fire
ō	open, go
ô	law, horn
oi	oil, point
oo	look, pull
ōō	ooze, tool
ou	out, crowd
u	up, cut
u	fur, fern
ə	a in ago
	e in agent
	e in father
	i in unity
	o in collect
	u in focus
ch	chin, arch
ŋ	ring, singer
sh	she, dash
th	thin, truth
th	then, father
zh	s in pleasure

wolf

whis·tle (hwis′əl *or* wis′əl) *v.* **1** to make a high, shrill sound as by forcing breath through puckered lips or by sending steam through a small opening. **2** to move with a high, shrill sound [The arrow *whistled* past her ear.] **3** to blow a whistle. **4** to produce by whistling [to *whistle* a tune].
—**whis′tled, whis′tling** ◆*n.* a device for making whistling sounds. —**whis′tler** *n.*

whole·sale (hōl′sāl) *n.* the sale of goods in large amounts, especially to retail stores that resell them to actual users. ◆*adj.* **1** of or having to do with such sale of goods [a *wholesale* dealer; a *wholesale* price]. **2** widespread or general [*wholesale* destruction by the volcano]. ◆*adv.* **1** in wholesale amounts or at wholesale prices [We are buying the clothes *wholesale*.] **2** in a widespread or general way [The members refused to obey the new rules *wholesale*.] ◆*v.* to sell or be sold in large amounts, usually at lower prices. —**whole′saled, whole′sal·ing** —**whole′sal·er** *n.*

who'll (hōōl) **1** who shall. **2** who will.

wil·der·ness (wil′dər nəs) *n.* a wild region; wasteland or overgrown land with no settlers.

wis·dom (wiz′dəm) *n.* **1** the quality of being wise; good judgment, that comes from knowledge and experience in life [She had the *wisdom* to save money for her old age.] **2** learning; knowledge [a book filled with the *wisdom* of India].

with·draw (with drô′ *or* with drô′) *v.* **1** to take or pull out; remove [to *withdraw* one's hand from a pocket]. **2** to move back; go away; retreat [She *withdrew* behind the curtain.] **3** to leave; retire or resign [to *withdraw* from school]. **4** to take back; recall [I *withdraw* my statement.] —**with·drew′, with·drawn′, with·draw′ing**

wolf (woolf) *n.* **1** a wild animal that looks like a dog. It kills other animals for food. **2** a person who is fierce, cruel, greedy, etc. —*pl.* **wolves**

wolves (woolvz) *n. plural of* **wolf**.

wom·an (woom′ən) *n.* **1** an adult, female human being. **2** women as a group. **3** a female servant. —*pl.* **wom′en**

wom·en (wim′ən) *n. plural of* **woman**.

won·der·ful (wun′dər fəl) *adj.* **1** that causes wonder; marvelous; amazing. **2** very good; excellent: *used only in everyday talk.*
—**won′der·ful·ly** *adv.*

wor·ry (wur′ē) *v.* **1** to be or make troubled in mind; feel or make uneasy or anxious [Don't *worry*. Her absence *worried* us.] **2** to annoy, bother, etc. [Stop *worrying* me with such unimportant matters.] **3** to bite at and shake about with the teeth [The dog *worried* an old shoe.] —**wor′ried, wor′ry·ing** ◆*n.* a troubled feeling; anxiety; care. —*pl.* **wor′ries**

wreath

wrap·per (rap′ər) *n.* **1** a person or thing that wraps. **2** a covering or cover [a newspaper mailed in a paper *wrapper*]. **3** a woman's dressing gown.

wrath (rath) *n.* great anger; rage; fury.

wreath (rēth) *n.* **1** a ring of leaves, flowers, etc. twisted together. **2** something like this [*wreaths* of smoke]. —*pl.* **wreaths** (rēthz)

wres·tle (res′əl) *v.* **1** to struggle with, trying to throw or force to the ground without striking blows with the fists. **2** to struggle hard, as with a problem; contend.
—**wres′tled, wres′tling** ◆*n.* **1** the action or a bout of wrestling. **2** a struggle or contest. —**wres′tler** *n.*

wrin·kle (riŋ′kəl) *n.* a small or uneven crease or fold [*wrinkles* in a coat; *wrinkles* in skin]. ◆*v.* **1** to make wrinkles in [a brow *wrinkled* with care]. **2** to form wrinkles [This cloth *wrinkles* easily.]
—**wrin′kled, wrin′kling**

write (rīt) *v.* **1** to form words, letters, etc., as with a pen or pencil. **2** to form the words, letters, etc. of [*Write* your address here.] **3** to be the author or composer of [Dickens *wrote* novels. Mozart *wrote* symphonies.]
—**wrote, writ′ten, writ′ing**

writ·ten (rit′n) *past participle of* **write**.

yes·ter·day (yes′tər dā) *adv.* on the day before today. ◆*n.* **1** the day before today. **2** some time in the past.

yield (yēld) *v.* **1** to give up; surrender [to *yield* to a demand; to *yield* a city]. **2** to give or grant [to *yield* the right of way; to *yield* a point]. **3** to give way [The gate would not *yield* to our pushing.] **4** to bring forth or bring about; produce; give [The orchard *yielded* a good crop. The business *yielded* high profits.]

yolk (yōk) *n.* the yellow part of an egg.

you'd (yōōd) **1** you had. **2** you would.

you've (yōōv) you have.

zo·ol·o·gy (zō äl′ə jē) *n.* the science that studies animals and animal life. —**zo·ol′o·gist** *n.*